The Bowring Story
of the
VARSITY MATCH

The Bowring Story
of the
VARSITY MATCH

DAVID
FROST

Macdonald
Queen Anne Press

A *Queen Anne Press* BOOK

© David Frost 1988

First published in Great Britain in 1988 by
Queen Anne Press, a division of
Macdonald & Co (Publishers) Ltd
3rd Floor
Greater London House
Hampstead Road
London NW1 7QX

A member of Maxwell Pergamon Publishing Corporation plc

British Library Cataloguing in Publication Data

Frost, David, *1929–*
    The Bowring Story of the Varsity Match.
    1. University of Cambridge — Rugby football
    2. University of Oxford — Rugby football
    3. Rugby football — England — Cambridge
    (Cambridgeshire) — History   4. Rugby football
    — England — Oxford (Oxfordshire) — History
    I. Title
    796.33′372   GV945.9.G7

    ISBN 0-356-12006-6

Typeset by Leaper & Gard Ltd, Bristol
Printed and bound in Great Britain by Butler & Tanner Ltd, Frome

Contents

PICTURE CREDITS

Foreword
by Philip Wroughton
Chairman and Chief Executive of C.T. Bowring & Co. Ltd
– International Insurance & Reinsurance Brokers –

The story you will read in these pages – the story of the Annual Inter-Varsity Rugby Match between the two Blues, Oxford and Cambridge – is nearly as old as the story of international rugby itself. The first international match, between England and Scotland, took place in March 1871. The first Varsity Match followed close on its heels in February 1872. These two annual fixtures in the rugby calendar have remained compulsive, if not 'compulsory', for all true rugby enthusiasts. Dates in such a story as this are perhaps more significantly related than usual for it was not so many years before, in 1849 to be exact, that Bowring Brothers was founded as an insurance agency. As sponsors of the Varsity Match we at Bowring like to think that the Company developed, as did rugby, out of the same formative and dynamic spirit that marked the pioneering years of the mid-19th century.

You will read here, in great and fascinating detail, how Oxbridge rugby and the Varsity Match itself have, throughout a century and a quarter, contributed very greatly to the development and refinement of the game of rugby from its original mauling and brawling basis to the techniques of open play and flowing movement that make a good international or Varsity Match such a pleasure and a thrill to watch today. Not only that, the story lays equal emphasis on the organisational aspect of the game within the two Universities: the establishment and raising of its status alongside that of other sports for which the Universities were already famed; the training, coaching and development of potential in players; and very importantly, the careful and planned integration of approach to the game's demanding requirements, and of time available to meet them, with the primary needs of academic study.

Through our yearly sponsorship of the Varsity Match since 1976, symbolised by the Bowring Bowl which is fought for so fiercely, we at Bowring are proud to be associated with such revered names as Vassall, Marriott, Poulton, Wakefield and many others of the early days who laid the foundations of modern rugby and of the Varsity Match itself as we know it today. Sponsorship, like most worthwhile relationships, is essentially a two-way affair; it must benefit both donor and recipient. When Bowring were first approached by the Rugby Football Union, rising costs were making it difficult for the two University clubs to meet expenses, and gate takings at the Varsity Match were on the slide. It is gratifying to know that the annual sponsorship money, which at the time of publication of this book has already been trebled, has contributed through improved training and ground facilities of different but equally important forms at both Universities to a positive reversal of this situation.

On the 'donor' side Bowring has benefited and continues to benefit not only from the fairly obvious effect of publicity, through wide exposure of the Company name to a viewing, listening and watching public at home and overseas every year; but also from a steady and satisfying flow of recruits into the Company organisation of men of calibre with that balance of academic achievement, team spirit and individual thrust that the combination of University and top-class rugby can bestow. Overlaying this, however, the basic benefit must be to the game itself. To quote Clem Thomas, who won his Cambridge Blue in 1949, 'Cambridge and Oxford are tremendous breeding-grounds for great players ... the influence of the Varsity Match on rugby in this country is enormous. It is important that we have this breeding-ground for this type of man'.

These are sentiments which we at Bowring echo to the full. I feel confident that by translating them into practicality through sponsorship, we shall continue to make our contribution towards proving their truth for many years to come. The Universities, Bowring and rugby, must all be the richer thereby.

1
The Big Event

If a foreign power decided to invade England they could pick no better first target than Twickenham on the second Tuesday in December. If you want to know who runs the country then the RFU headquarters is the place to be. There are probably more important City people per square inch in the West Car Park than inhabit the square mile on Varsity Match day. The ground is thronged with politicians, the higher echelons of the legal professions and a fair sprinkling of military personnel, not to mention the cream of the country's young brains, both on and off the pitch.

But for the match to attract so much interest and crowds of over 40,000 its appeal must extend beyond the Oxbridge set. The game probably attracts one of the biggest cross-sections of society to be found at any sporting event. Merchant bankers rub shoulders with bank managers and bricklayers while crowds of schoolchildren mingle with boisterous students. Quite simply, the Varsity Match is an *event*, a unique sporting occasion which has become a vital part of the social calendar. It is hard to judge who enjoys themselves more, the Fortnum and Mason hamper brigade breaking open the bubbly in the West Car Park, or the lads queuing up for hot dogs with a pint in their hands.

As the major international matches have seen the growth of hospitality packages so the Varsity Match has become big business to the entrepreneur. Not only will you find marquees and buses dispensing food and drink but rooms in pubs, clubs and wine bars in the area are being taken over for pre- and post-match hospitality. Some people start planning for the Match more than a year in advance. Every November Oxford treasurer Alan Tayler's telephone starts to ring with enquiries about the following year's game. 'The calls are usually from company secretaries who are organising the Annual General Meeting and want to be sure that the meeting is arranged for the Monday before the Varsity Match so that everyone can assemble in London and have an excuse for being there,' he explains.

For the players the biggest hurdle comes ten days before the actual game. Both Oxford and Cambridge play their last matches that Saturday and afterwards the captains pick their Varsity Match teams, usually informing the lucky ones on the Sunday. In recent years the teams have been officially announced to the press at Bowring's pre-Varsity Match press luncheon a week before the game but, in the keeping with tradition, the Oxford list is pinned up in the window of Elmer

Cotton's shop in The Turl while the Cambridge team goes on display in the window of Ryder and Amies in King's Parade. The teams' build-up during the week before the Match very much depends on the captain. In the 1930s both teams used to go to the seaside for a few days to relax and play golf, but that doesn't happen today. The captains decide what the schedule will be and how much training should be done in that final week.

The pressure begins to build and everywhere the players go there are friends, students and tutors talking about the game and wishing them well. There are various get-togethers for the teams during this week, ranging from informal drinks parties to special dinners. On the Sunday the Cambridge team are invited to Christmas lunch at the home of their treasurer, John Dingle. But there's no avoiding the talk of rugby and the big match, and the players eat, sleep and breathe the game.

On Monday the teams assemble at their respective grounds, Cambridge at Grange Road and Oxford at Iffley Road, and load up the coach to London with suitcases and bags as well as their kit — for most the match will signal the end of term. Both teams spend the night in London, Oxford at the Lensbury Club which is by the river in Teddington, and Cambridge at the Petersham Hotel in Richmond. Around midday on Tuesday the two team coaches, fronted by outriders, make their way to Headquarters. By this time students, Old Blues, parties of schoolchildren and thousands of ordinary rugby supporters will be converging on Twickenham. Cars and coaches choke up the Chertsey Road while in the bars at Waterloo station the faithful swill their drinks while keeping an eye on the clock. On stumbling out of the station at the other end they will be confronted by the usual scene of happy chaos. Supporters spill out of pubs like the Cabbage Patch and the Rugby Tavern, hoping to meet up with some long lost friend in the frightful scrum that surrounds every pub entrance. And, as always, the souvenir-sellers and hot dog stands line the route to the ground.

Life in the West Car Park is a little more sedate. Little groups cluster round Rolls Royces, eating the very best in picnic fayre and sipping champagne. The Varsity Match must be the ultimate in school and college reunions as respectable members of society remember life as inky fourth-formers or debauched undergraduates. For many Old Blues the reunion is a little more dignified. Each gets one free ticket and where possible all are seated together in rows according to the year in which they played. The older and more venerable you become, the nearer the front you get.

As the two teams take to the field they are met by the noisiest crowd of the year at Twickenham. Players often talk about the incessant buzz that prevails during the game and, unlike in International games, they often find they can pick out friends and fellow students in the crowd.

After the Match the winners receive the Bowring Bowl, and all the players receive special tankards. The sponsor's Public Relations Officer, Carole Bowring, has a recurring nightmare in which the trophy goes missing, so the night before the game she sleeps with it under her bed. The chairman of Bowring and his deputy will take a dozen bottles of champagne into the dressing-rooms so that the players can either celebrate or drown their sorrows. When the players have washed and changed they make their way to the tea room under the West Stand for a chat with players, officials and friends. Half-an-hour later, as Twickenham still echoes to the sound of drunken revelry, they climb back on to the coach and make for the Oxford and Cambridge Club in the centre of London. After cocktails the two teams have separate dinners, and then it is time

A scene from the unique sporting event that has become part of the social calendar: Andrew Martin scores for Cambridge in 1984.

Memories of an Old Blue: the late Cyril Lowe, who scored a record 8 tries for England in the 1913–14 International Championship, relives the 1913 Varsity Match.

The Bowring Bowl

Oxford University R.F.C. versus Cambridge University R.U.F.C.

Left: The coveted Bowring Bowl awaits the Varsity Match winners.

Right: An early team picture from the days of rugby's infancy: the Cambridge XV, 1878.

for the Varsity Ball, where both teams get the chance to mingle and chat about the game. The following day there are a lot of tired and hung-over people waking up in various parts of London. But whereas the players can usually go straight home to begin their Christmas vacation, the spectators have to negotiate a day's work, often vowing never to do it again — well, perhaps not for a year anyway!

Today the Varsity Match is one of the great sporting and social occasions of Twickenham's season. It was not ever thus. The Match has during its history been played on various grounds, among them Blackheath, Kennington Oval and Queen's Club. In the early days each team comprised 20 players, sporting long knickerbockers down to their stockings. There was no referee, there were no touch-judges: the captains made decisions on points of Law. Oxford once turned up seven men short, borrowed a Cambridge man, and the two captains agreed to play 14-a-side instead of 20-a-side. No Blues were awarded for rugby in the early days. During the fixture's period at Blackheath the players arrived by train and had to carry their kit from the station to a pub on the Common called The Princess of Wales, where they changed. They then walked more than a mile to the ground and hung their coats and scarves on some poles beside the pitch. After the game they had the same long walk back to the pub, where they were provided with a dozen or so small tin hand-basins to wash in. Finally they had to walk to the station to catch a train back to the Metropolis.

One Varsity Match at Queen's Club in Kensington was almost brought to a halt when one of the Victorian chimneys in the pavilion caught fire and belched out thick smoke across the pitch. On another occasion there was a stampede as over-eager spectators rushed the Queen's turnstiles. Later, there was the story of the Russian Prince, Obolensky, who consumed a dozen oysters before playing.

The history of the Varsity Match reflects the development of the game of rugby, mirroring the social changes within the two Universities. It reflects the different attitudes to sport over a period of more than 100 years. It is probably true that without Oxford and Cambridge rugby would never have become the popular worldwide sport it is today. Certainly in the early days the two Universities led the way in the development of tactics, methods and drills. The names of innovators such as Vassall, Wakefield and Poulton are respected as much for what they achieved with their University sides as for the impetus and direction they gave the game as a whole. The history of the Varsity Match is only a few months shorter than the history of international rugby itself, which began when Scotland met England at Raeburn Place, Edinburgh on 27 March 1871. Since the start of the series the two Universities have provided more than 600 international players between them. Their contribution to the game of rugby is second to none.

There have been three distinct periods in the development of the Varsity Match as a social occasion. In the early days the match was a largely domestic battle which drew the attention of members of the two Universities but not many of the general public. Between the First and Second World Wars the general public, not necessarily those connected with rugby, grew increasingly interested in the annual warfare between Oxford and Cambridge. Then, after the Second World War, while the Varsity Match attracted some of its biggest crowds, the man in the street paid less attention to it.

As evidence of the enthusiasm of the general populace Jenny Greenwood, the Cambridge captain in 1912 and 1919, recalled what happened when he was dining in the middle of London on the night after one Varsity Match. 'Some of us had dinner at the old Café de l'Europe, next to The Empire, and a good deal of horseplay went on. Marie Lloyd, who was dining there, was not amused. Word got about that I was there, and I had to go to the steps at the entrance and address the crowd in Leicester Square.' Imagine a current Oxbridge captain being called out from his meal to harangue the multitude in a London street! Greenwood also recalled that the grand way to travel from your Cambridge college to play in a game at Grange Road was to hire a hansom cab. 'The cabby generally waited outside, if there was a good match on, as he was able to see over the fence from his seat on top of the cab.' It is difficult to imagine a present-day Cambridge taxi-driver doing anything remotely similar.

One reason why the Varsity Match had a more popular appeal between the two World Wars than it has today may be that Oxbridge rugby as a whole was given far greater coverage in the national newspapers than it receives now. Columns were wider and print smaller, but it was regular practice for newspapers to devote whole columns to the Universities' term-time matches against club sides. As the Varsity Match approached, the two sides and their methods and tactics would be analysed, not just on the morning of the match but in lengthy articles the previous week. In some of the newspapers the previews that appeared on the day of the Match and the Varsity Match reports were more than 2,000 words long. In 1912 *The Times* devoted considerably more than 2,000 words to the Match, and the authorship of all these words was attributed simply to 'our Special Correspondent', a credit which appeared between brackets.

A few years later the headlines read 'Varsity Rugby', 'Cambridge just win at Queen's', 'The King Present'. Rather more colourful was the headline to an article by E.H.D. Sewell, written in the late 1930s: 'Match that Thrills the Empire'. Sewell wrote: 'Probably 40,000 spectators will be looking on at the annual rugby football battle between Oxford and Cambridge at Twickenham on Tuesday, but many more thousands of Varsity men in British outposts will be eagerly listening in to every detail of the game, for this is one of the matches that gird the Empire. There are two annual matches, and two only, on the menu of Higher Rugby which no self-respecting rugby man who can afford the time and the money ever misses. One is England v Scotland and the other the Inter-Varsity.'

Many of the national magazines would devote columns of space to the Varsity Match. A report from *Country Life* from the days before the First World War began: 'Never was there better proof of the unquenchable enthusiasm aroused by the University Rugby Football Match than that furnished by the crowd assembled at Queen's Club on Tuesday. A murky, yellow haze hung like a pall over the ground while the rain drummed quite steadily and pitilessly down upon innumerable umbrellas, and yet hundreds of ladies came to the uncovered seats at least half-an-hour before play began and sat themselves courageously down upon copies of the illustrated papers. It was the most depressing of all recorded days. When Cambridge came out first from the pavilion amid

A cartoon from the Illustrated London News *of December 1919, depicting the notorious fog-bound matches at Queen's.*

A REAL OXFORD-V-CAMBRIDGE (RUGGER) DAY. NOT PERHAPS, SUCH A GOOD FOG AS USUAL BUT STILL SATISFACTORY.

TICKET PLEASE.

I WISH IT HAD BEEN A BRIGHT AFTERNOON IN MARCH

NONSENSE. THIS IS AN IDEAL DAY. POSITIVELY IDEAL.

THE VERY FIRST ITEM OF THE MATCH. HALF A DOZEN OR SO OF THE CAMBRIDGE XV TAKING A RUN ROUND. NAMES; READING FROM LEFT TO RIGHT, ?—?—?—?—?—?

A SHINING EXAMPLE OF DETERMINATION. K.R.J. SAXON THOUGHT THE BALL WOULD BE BETTER IN TOUCH. G.B. CROLE HAD THE BALL. SAXON CARRIED THEM BOTH OVER THE LINE.

CLEM LEWIS ABOUT TO SCORE FROM A PENALTY. OXFORD, THROUGH TAMPERING WITH THE RULES ON THEIR OWN DOORSTEP, GAVE THE MATCH AWAY WITH THIS KICK.

SMALLWOOD DROPPED A GOAL. SMALLWOOD. ESSES-EMMA-ACK-L-L W-O-O-DON. GOT THAT?

FIELD TELEPHONE WHICH MIGHT BE USED BY MR. R.C. POTTER-IRWIN FOR COMMUNICATING EVENTS TO SPECTATORS.

I WISH —

DON'T WISH SO MUCH. WE DIDN'T INVITE YOU HERE, DID WE?

NO, BUT I THOUGHT THE WAR WAS GOING TO MAKE US ALL DEMOCRATIC.

BUT THE WAR IS OVER!

J.E. GREENWOOD LED HIS MEN TRULY AND WELL.

(C)

(B)

THE BEST HAPPENING OF THE AFTERNOON. IT WENT SO:— CROLE AVOIDED SAXON (A) KICKED OVER THE FULL BACKS HEAD (B) SCORED HIS TRY. (C)

(A)

THE PEOPLE THAT WALKED IN DARKNESS HAVE SEEN (BITS OF) A GREAT GAME.

rousing cheers, the umbrellas all round the ground went down with one simultaneous snap, as if by magic.'

In those days magazines like *The Illustrated Sporting and Dramatic News* published full-page cartoon stories of the Varsity Match. In these the perennial fog at Queen's gave scope for drawings of one or other captain leading his side out of the pavilion carrying a lantern in his search for the pitch. It is no wonder that, with all the publicity, the Varsity Match became too big for Queen's and had to be moved to Twickenham in 1921.

In the last century rugby, as played by boys, was confined to the major independent schools, and this is reflected in the composition of the sides for the early Varsity Matches. Schools such as Rugby, Marlborough and Wellington predominated. Gradually, as the game spread, other schools took up rugby, especially the grammar schools. Oddly, with the recent demise of many of the old grammar schools, the game, in England at least, seems to be going back towards the days when the public schools were the chief nurseries of rugby.

Preparations for the Varsity Match have changed considerably over the years. Before the First World War the teams would travel down to London the day before the Match and stay the night in a hotel in London. This procedure was changed by Cambridge when Jenny Greenwood was captain in 1912, because he thought it better for his men to stay in their familiar beds and then travel to London on the day of the Match. In the relatively affluent 1920s, however, a tradition arose for both Varsity Match teams to spend the weekend before the Match in Eastbourne, though in different hotels. Wavell Wakefield recalled that a certain amount of horseplay used to take place, such as when the Cambridge team, late at night, decided to dress up a statue outside Oxford's hotel in exotic clothing, the idea being that the Oxford team would get the blame. The Cambridge efforts backfired, however, when the local constabulary arrived. Fortunately Wakefield and his men saw the police approaching and demonstrated their fitness and pace by eluding their pursuers. After the weekend in Eastbourne there would be a procession in bedecked Rolls Royces all the way to Twickenham. There's style for you.

There is a tendency nowadays to think that the present-day Oxbridge players, with their coaches, work much harder at their rugby than players did in, say, the 1920s and 1930s. This is not borne out by the accounts of some of the players of yesteryear. Certainly as far back as the early 1920s, and probably before that, the University captains persuaded eminent international players to travel to Oxford and Cambridge to advise them on their preparations.

Jenny Greenwood recalled that when not playing — his sides sometimes played three matches a week — they would be busy practising. He used to get his forwards to scrummage against an opposing pack made up of ten players. Furthermore, in those days the players had more time to devote to their rugby: academic work was given much less emphasis than has been the case since the Second World War. Greenwood, for example, remembered that he had no academic work to do at all in the period leading up to two of his five Varsity Matches. The players of the 1980s may be under greater pressure than their predecessors but it is doubtful that they actually spend more time on their rugby than their forebears.

Nevertheless the Varsity Match comes as a climax to an immense amount of practice and preparation throughout the preceding term. Planning begins almost a year in advance. Shortly after one Varsity Match the captain is elected for the following year. He finds out early in the next term which of his Blues are expected to be available again for the following December, and the matches in that term are used by the new captain for developing his side for the big match. Those seniors who have not yet won Blues are observed and incorporated, and the squad is then modified the following October when the form of promising freshmen has been studied.

2
The Oxbridge Factor

Alec Ramsay captained Oxford in 1953 and represented the University on the Rugby Football Union from 1962 until he became the RFU's president in 1979, achieving a unique family feat by following his father, who was president in 1954-55 and also in the RFU centenary season of 1970-71. Ramsay is reasonably optimistic about the future of Oxford rugby, suggesting that standards of fitness and playing ability have risen recently. The club gets strong support from the Old Blue network, and the fact that the club owns the Iffley Road ground gives it a welcome independence from the University authorities.

Another encouraging sign for the future, Ramsay believes, is the number of post-graduates at the University. He points to the great expansion of the medical school, for example, and to the increase in the amount of laboratory research. This has led to a larger number of mature students becoming available to the club. 'Some people have suggested that post-graduates should not play in the Varsity Match,' says Ramsay, 'but they are all students. The growth of the number of post-graduates is simply part of the evolution of the University. There is no reason why they should not play rugby for Oxford. We welcome the post-graduates: without them we would have to field a terribly young side against the clubs, and it would be difficult to compete against the leading teams.' If you took the post-graduates out of the University teams, the results against leading clubs would be dispiriting. More than that, some of the clubs might well decide to drop their fixtures against the Universities in favour of stronger opposition. This would leave the teams of undergraduates to play against lesser clubs from whom they would learn much less.

There have been suggestions that the number of post-graduates in a University side should be artificially limited. It is difficult to make a strong case for changing the system: there is a lot to be said for the present arrangement, because not only can the Universities maintain their fixtures against good clubs, but the young undergraduates can also profit from playing alongside the more experienced post-graduates. The latest figures show that roughly a third of the students at each University are now post-graduates. Oxford in 1987 had 3,290 post-graduates in their total of 12,915 students. At Cambridge the post-graduates numbered 2,413 out of 12,219.

There are two contrasting views about the participation of post-graduates in Oxbridge rugby teams. On the one hand it is true, as Ramsay says, that without the post-graduates the Universities would no longer be able to hold their own in matches against first-class club sides. On the other hand there is the valid point that the presence of post-graduates denies places in the University teams to undergraduates who need the experience of playing against top clubs if they are to fulfil their potential.

Ramsay recalls that Oxford have been fortunate, in the time he has been associated with them, to have had some fine captains, and at the same time he emphasises the valuable continuity provided in organising the club by the senior members of the University on the OURFC committee. As examples he points to the work now being done by Alan Tayler, the current hon. treasurer, and before him by men such as Greig Barr, Philip Landon and Sir George Mallaby. Landon, a fellow and tutor in law at Trinity from 1920 until 1956, first became hon. treasurer and subsequently a senior member of the committee from 1948 until his death in 1960. Mallaby, who later produced a famous report on the state of the game in England for the Rugby Football Union, was hon. treasurer for only a short time in the mid-1930s, but he played for the Greyhounds regularly between 1924 and 1934 while teaching at St Edward's School, and was closely involved in Oxford rugby for longer than that.

Ramsay also points out that you cannot measure the contribution the Universities have made, and are still making, to rugby in general simply by looking at the number of famous players they have produced. 'There have been an astonishing number of Oxbridge men who have continued to take a close interest in the game long after their playing days were over', he says. 'You will find them as administrators of clubs and counties and also serving on the RFU committee.' A quick look at the RFU Handbook for 1985-86 showed ten Oxbridge men on the committee. 'They all want to keep in touch and to help. And we mustn't forget the contribution University tours, especially Oxford's first tour to Japan in 1952, have made to helping rugby in countries overseas. As far as help given to us is concerned, the sponsorship of Bowring has been of immense value. They have funded the renovation of facilities at Iffley Road; they have encouraged us; they have given the Varsity Match great support with the right kind of publicity and by taking a large number of tickets for their own use. And, of course, the players now have the Bowring Bowl to play for each year at Twickenham.'

Alan Tayler has been associated with Oxford rugby for many years and became honorary treasurer of OURFC in the mid-1970s. During that time he has seen Varsity rugby go through some trying times. Not only did the Varsity Match decline in popularity, but there was the problem of administering the club and the Iffley Road ground in a fast-changing world. In the late 1960s the club was run by the team captain and a student secretary, but in recent years Oxford have introduced a new structure which will alleviate much of the workload and put the club on a sound administrative and financial footing.

'We own our ground so we have to attend to all the problems which arise from running such an enterprise and, of course, because we have a public name there's a lot of public interaction. The administration of the rugby club is quite complicated; I get an average of four letters a day from Twickenham alone. We are obliged to take a more professional approach to the game in terms of organisation, coaching and recruitment. If you are going to stay in the big league you are really forced to do this. There's a lot of tension in the club because of it — many Old Blues don't like the way modern rugby is going and we've resisted change for a long time.

'We were in a state of decline. Gates had fallen and we had no money, and there seemed to be no way out. Money was raised by selling land and through the Bowring sponsorship. If we hadn't

Oxford's Nigel Roberts wins a line-out in the 1980 Varsity Match.

had land to sell and sponsorship I don't see how we could have pulled ourselves out of that downward spiral. From a treasurer's point of view, I determined that we needed to sort out the ground first, so I spent the first ten years getting us out of the financial mess caused by the cost of the upkeep of the ground.'

Apart from the Bowring sponsorship, which has helped to keep the club in the black over the years, the ground has recently benefited from a sponsorship deal with the Ricoh company, which has already paid for a mini gym at Iffley Road and is due to contribute to a new scoreboard and entrance area. As a result of these developments, the club is now considering employing a part-time manager. 'Once the ground was settled and the situation stable we were able to turn our attention to the playing side. It isn't a question only of money but of people, and how to find the right ones. External events, like the advent of the League system, have made life difficult for University clubs, and have destroyed our fixture lists. We have had to respond to these pressures and, by and large, the response has been rather slow. I would say that the 15-year trough has been caused by Oxford and Cambridge dealing with a change in the game, and that perhaps Cambridge have responded a bit quicker.' Oxford is now on a sound financial footing and the signs are that the club has come to grips with the challenges of rugby in the modern era.

Ian Beer has been closely associated with Cambridge rugby for more than 30 years. He played in the Varsity Matches of 1952, 1953 and 1954, captaining the side in his last year, and since 1971 he has been the University's representative on the Rugby Football Union committee. He has a clear picture of how the relative maturity of Cambridge players has varied over the years and as a schoolmaster — he is now Head Master of Harrow — he knows how changing admissions policies at the Universities have influenced the calibre of the rugby intake.

Beer points out that, although by the early 1950s most of the mature men who had fought in the Second World War had finished their time at Oxbridge, there was still compulsory National Service which meant that the men arriving at the Universities had, in most cases, been out of

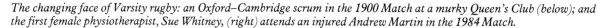

The changing face of Varsity rugby: an Oxford–Cambridge scrum in the 1900 Match at a murky Queen's Club (below); and the first female physiotherapist, Sue Whitney, (right) attends an injured Andrew Martin in the 1984 Match.

school for two years. By the mid-1950s, however, this supply of relatively mature men had begun to dry up. How was it, then, that Cambridge continued to do well in their matches against the leading clubs?

'The University in those days still had one big advantage over the clubs', Beer says. 'We were very much better organised. Unlike the clubs, we could train many days per week. We did not have better players than the clubs, but we sat down and thought about the game with magnetic counters on a board and that sort of thing. When we played for clubs in the vacation we were amazed at what a shambles existed. There were no line-out signals, for instance.' Ironically, Beer himself had much to do with the bringing of proper organisation to club rugby preparation in England. He was chairman of the Rugby Football Union's advisory panel — which consisted of such men as Jeff Butterfield, the England centre; Ray Williams, now secretary of the Welsh Rugby Union, and Mark Sugden, the Ireland scrum-half — who produced the RFU's historic *A Guide for Coaches*, the manual which went out to clubs and hastened the advent of the coaching network.

'Clubs in England now realised that by working out signals and so forth they could improve their game a great deal', says Beer. 'In doing this they removed the one advantage University players had had over them. Cambridge were faced not just with older and heavier men but also by players who were now well organised. Since those days rugby has evolved into a more physical game, one in which tall men and heavy men have an even greater advantage. This puts the Universities at an even greater disadvantage. The forwards, especially, get worn out physically, which has prompted the question of whether or not they should be expected to play more than once a week, as they do. There is also now pressure on them to play in Divisional, County Championship and club league games. The trouble is that the term is very short as regards preparing for the Varsity Match.'

It is often said, no doubt with a certain amount of exaggeration, that up to the Second World War Oxford and Cambridge would give places to outstanding games-players just as long as they could read and write. After the War, however, there was a dramatic change in the admissions policy. 'I think it probably started before the War', says Beer. 'Certainly the old system finished with the return of servicemen to the Universities after the War. Under Labour Governments from 1945 onwards it became, rightly in my view, progressively more important to be scholastic and less important to be a games-player. Cambridge had to make sure it got its share of bright pupils, and this eventually led to a total disregard for the other side of a man's ability.

'A new generation of young dons was appointed who were not so interested in what the under-graduate did in his spare time. Those who were responsible for admissions did not give weight to qualities other than the academic. There was also greater competition from other universities: the school all-rounder was no longer considered bright enough to be accepted by Cambridge, so he went to Loughborough or Exeter or Durham, and these establishments started to produce many of the best players. Then came the demise of the grammar schools. They became comprehensives whose P.E. teachers tended not to be versed in rugby but keen to encourage the playing of such sports as volleyball, basketball, golf and swimming. These schools were not nurseries of rugby as the old grammar schools had been. So one important source of young players more or less dried up.'

In spite of the problems, Beer draws encouragement from the number of present-day dons who work to help the rugby club and from the effects of the Bowring sponsorship. Before the advent of Bowring, he says, there had been a tremendous drop in the Varsity Match gate at Twickenham, partly as a result of several boring games and partly because the atmosphere in the country in the late 1960s and early 1970s discouraged attendance at sporting events. 'It got to the stage where the income from the Varsity Match was not going to be enough to sustain the club. We needed a sponsor, and Bowring have been the saviour.' One of the most crucial improvements achieved with the Bowring money was the building of a club-room and bar at Grange Road. 'Imagine a rugby club without a bar for something like 100 years', says Beer. The building of the bar led naturally to bar takings, which generated enough money to build a house for the groundsman and to finance improvements and safety precautions for the stand. 'Bowring have been to the Varsity Match everything anyone could have wished — they have never interfered, they have shown utter integrity and, as a result of their sponsorship, players have been able to go on tour more often, thus improving the standard of their game.'

Nevertheless, Beer is anxious about the future. 'If the image of the game does not improve, we shall get fewer boys playing, and this will mean fewer rugby-playing recruits at Cambridge', he says. 'The University is the nursery for all that is best in the game, and it should be the breeding ground not just for future international players but also for schoolmasters, coaches and administrators. A huge number of graduates from Oxbridge have become club secretaries, presidents of the RFU and county administrators. I hope this will continue. I am very pleased that Oxbridge have joined forces to play for the Combined Students. Will Oxbridge ever play in the UAU Championship? I wonder.'

3
The Early Days

The first rugby football match between the Universities of Oxford and Cambridge was played in The Parks at Oxford on 10 February 1872. The initiative behind that historic encounter came from Cambridge, who despatched a Trinity man, H.A. Hamilton, to meet a Trinity Oxford man, C.W.L. Bulpett, at Oxford to discuss the idea. The fact that 16 of this first Oxford team were from Rugby School and the other four from Marlborough gives two clues to the nature of the game at this time. First, it was played 20-a-side and, second, it was largely confined to former pupils of some leading public schools.

Rugby in 1872 had scarcely been refined from the kind of mob sport it had been in its earliest days, when 40 or more people on each side struggled for all they were worth to force the ball through their opponents to the other end of the field. It was a game of brawn and had very little use for the brain. Oxford and Cambridge were to give the lead in bringing refinement and skills to rugby and in guiding its development. In the middle of the 19th century there was no clear-cut distinction between rugby and soccer as exists today, and rules varied dramatically from school to school. When young men wanted to let off steam on the field, they would first have to decide which set of rules they would play to. There were no referees, the captains having the authority to settle any arguments. Such games had taken place at Oxford and Cambridge long before 1872, but it was not until November 1869 that the adherents to the rugby rules at Oxford were sufficiently organised to form themselves into a club. Cambridge formed their club early in 1872, deciding to abide by the rules of the Rugby Football Union, which had been founded in January 1871. So the stage was set for the first Varsity Match.

The arrangements did not work out entirely according to plan. Cambridge, who made the awkward cross-country journey to Oxford by train, were forced to leave behind their captain, E. Winnington Ingram, who was detained by important studies. I.C. Lambert was hastily elected captain in his stead. The earliest team photographs show Oxford in white jerseys, but it is generally accepted that they wore Dark Blue for the Match. Cambridge, however, wore pink rather than the Light Blue that later became traditional. Cambridge assembled their 20 players in a slightly different formation to Oxford. While Oxford used 14 forwards, three half-backs and three backs, their opponents had 15 forwards, three half-backs and two backs. It was one of the outnumbered Oxford forwards who gained the distinction of scoring the first points in a Varsity

Match: R.W. Isherwood ran over the Cambridge line after the ball had been thrown in from touch and proceeded to kick the conversion from close to the touch-line. This goal came shortly before the interval and, since there was no scoring in the second half, the first Varsity Match victory went to Oxford.

For the second Varsity Match, played on Parker's Piece, Cambridge, on 27 February 1873, Oxford experienced even more difficulty in raising a full side than had Cambridge the previous year. The game was again scheduled to be played 20-a-side, but the Oxford team arrived at Cambridge seven men short. This gave the 1873 Varsity Match two unique features: Oxford borrowed a player from Cambridge, Duncan Pearce, who thus became the only man ever to play for one University while in residence at the other; and the match was played 14-a-side. Hardly surprisingly Cambridge had their revenge, achieving a goal and two tries while Oxford failed to score. Nevertheless, six Oxford men from those first two Varsity Matches were capped for England.

Two significant changes were made in time for the third meeting between the Varsity sides in 1873. It was felt that the staging of the game at one of the two Universities gave too much advantage to the home side, which could more or less guarantee to put its full team on to the field, in contrast to the opponents. So a neutral ground was found: Kennington Oval in London was to be the home of the Varsity Match until 1880. It was also thought that the spring term was not a suitable time of the year to stage the match because of the conflicting demands of exams. The third Varsity Match was thus the first to be played on the nowadays traditional early December date. This meant, incidentally, that there were in fact two Varsity Matches played in 1873 though not, of course, in the same season. However, this change of venue and date did not mean that everything now proceeded smoothly. One of the Cambridge forwards, Temple Gurdon, arrived too late

Temple Gurdon, of Cambridge, who missed the start of the 1873 Match because of a delayed train. He later became president of the RFU.

The Varsity Match at The Oval, 1880.

at The Oval, and F.M. Hull had to deputise for him. In this instance, however, exams could not be blamed: the culprit was a delayed train. That the incident was not held against Temple Gurdon for long is borne out by the fact that he subsequently won 16 caps for England and went on to become president of the Rugby Football Union.

It was during the seven-match period at The Oval that three important changes were made. The first was that the number of players in each team was reduced from 20 to 15. Early in the 1874-75 season Oxford had experimented with 15-a-side, and found that this number provided more fluent and open rugby. They tried to persuade Cambridge to play 15-a-side in the 1874 Varsity Match but Cambridge, who had a particularly big and heavy pack, and who were not as well equipped behind the scrum, not unreasonably declined.

For the 1875 match, though, Cambridge agreed to the change, and lined up with ten forwards, two half-backs, one threequarter and two backs. This formation was altered in 1877, when the forwards were reduced to nine and a second threequarter was introduced. There were no further changes until 1882, when three threequarters were fielded, the additional player being necessitated by the reduction in the number of backs from two to one. It was not until 1893 that the forwards were reduced to eight and the threequarters increased to four. The Universities' decision to play 15-a-side for the 1875 match came two years before international sides were reduced from 20. Thus, for by no means the only time, the Universities were in the vanguard of rugby theory and practice.

The second important innovation made in this period was the alteration to the scoring values. Until 1875 a try was merely the means by which a kicker obtained the opportunity to try to kick a goal; this is why the act of touching the ball down behind the opponents' line is termed a 'try'. Two months before the 1875 Varsity Match it was agreed that a try should count in its own right. This was just as well for Oxford, for they won the Match by a try to nothing. The third major change was the appointment of umpires for the first time. Before 1875 the control of a game was entirely in the hands of the two captains, but it was now agreed that there should be two umpires, one appointed by each side. Even then the umpires did not run about the field blowing whistles; they merely watched from the touch-lines, waiting for the captains to appeal in the event of a disagreement. It was not until 1885 that a referee was added to the two umpires and only in 1892 that the referee took sole charge.

The Oval period is also interesting for the fact that two consecutive Varsity Matches, those of 1878-79 and 1879-80, had to be postponed from December until February because of frost. Curiously, in the second of these two seasons the Oxford captain, A.H. Evans, resigned at Christmas and gave up rugby in favour of soccer. He was invited to play for the University at this sport but declined, not wishing to hurt the feelings of his old rugby friends. He did, however, captain Oxford at cricket. Other notable figures in these early years included H.G. Fuller, who gained the distinction of playing for Cambridge in six consecutive Varsity Matches between 1878 and 1883 (the rule that 'a man may play for his University for four years from matriculation' was not brought in until 1885). Oxford's captain in 1875-76, W.H. Bolton, was the first Scot to play for Oxford and the first Oxford man to play for Scotland, and J. Allen, a Cambridge forward in 1875 and 1876, was the first Australian to play for either University.

By 1877 the number of spectators at The Oval had risen to more than a thousand, a clear sign of the fixture's rising prestige.

4
From Strength to Strength

Although the Varsity Match had acquired increasing status at The Oval, the Universities decided to move to Blackheath in the 1880-81 season. The turf on the high ground there was considered less soggy in wet weather than that of the low-lying Kennington, and Blackheath was already a rugby-playing area where a larger crowd could be expected for the game. Accordingly, the next three Varsity Matches were staged on the Blackheath club's pitches at Richardson's Field. There might have been more games played there, but in the winter of 1882-83 the land was bought by a building society for development. The Blackheath club then moved to the Rectory Field, which remains their home, and which was the venue for the next four Varsity Matches.

In 1886, however, the Queen's Club, the first purpose-built multi-sports centre in the world, was opened, and this became the natural home for the Varsity Match from December 1887. Nowadays Queen's is primarily associated with lawn tennis, real tennis and rackets, but when it was opened just over 100 years ago it catered for rugby, soccer, athletics and other sports as well. The sight of the winter men tearing up the turf with their scrummaging cannot have been too pleasing for the club's lawn tennis players, but nevertheless the Varsity Match remained there until 1921, when it was transferred to the new home of the game in England — Twickenham — which was opened in 1909. Interest in the Match continued to grow. The moves from The Oval to Blackheath and thence to Queen's saw steadily increasing numbers of spectators. A crowd of almost 8,000 was reported at Queen's as early as 1888, and by 1894 attendances had risen to 10,000. The reason for this growth in the popularity of the Varsity Match was, quite simply, that the Universities had been playing the most attractive and successful rugby to be found anywhere in the land.

For this pre-eminent position of University rugby in the game as a whole two men were largely responsible: Harry Vassall of Oxford and Charles Marriott of Cambridge. With their deep thinking, perseverance and the sheer force of their personalities they revolutionised rugby to a degree never seen before or since. Vassall started it all off during the 1880-81 season after he was appointed Oxford's hon. secretary. He immediately strengthened the organisation of rugby within the University, ensuring that college football was on a firm footing and that no players of potential were left unwatched. The following season he was appointed captain, and saw to it that promising players were not only seen but were given trial matches in which they were coached

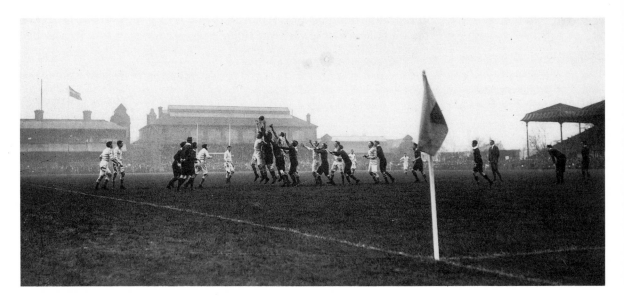

towards the high standards he had set himself. Vassall wrote that 'everybody with any sort of a reputation, either from his school or from his college, was given a chance of showing what he was worth. Men were tried in new positions: threequarters were made into backs or forwards. And, most important of all, constant coaching was going on throughout the game.'

Vassall, who had been at school at Marlborough, first played in the Varsity Match in the 1879-80 season at the age of 19. A forward of medium build, he weighed 15 st 9 lb, which was heavy for

Above: At the Queen's Club in 1910. The Club is now associated primarily with racket sports, but physically it has changed very little as the skyline shows.

The Oxford XV, 1881. Harry Vassall, who revolutionised rugby at Oxford, is in the centre of the front row.

those days, and judging by contemporary photographs had exceptional lower body strength. In his first game for England, against Wales at Blackheath in 1881, he scored four tries. It was his imaginative thinking and dynamic coaching that enabled Oxford to break out of the established mould of mauling and battering and to adopt a hitherto undreamed of style of quick, open passing by backs and forwards, with everyone lending support all over the field. Vassall was re-elected captain for the 1882-83 season during which Oxford played 13 matches and won them all, scoring 28 goals and 26 tries, and conceding only two tries and a dropped goal. The two tries against Oxford were both scored in their first match of the season, before the side was properly prepared, and the dropped goal in a match in which Oxford had already scored six goals and a try.

Of his time at Oxford, Vassall wrote: 'It was the development of the passing game which was the keynote to the success of the team. Short passing amongst the forwards had been adopted by other clubs before this date, but long passing, right across the ground if necessary, was a thing hitherto unknown ... opponents, who were not accustomed to these novel tactics, were completely non-plussed.' Oxford not only won the Varsity Match four years running between 1881 and 1884, but they also enjoyed an unbeaten sequence against all comers lasting more than three years, from November 1881 to February 1885. In that period they played 58 matches, winning 52 of them, and drawing six. They scored 110 goals and 110 tries and had only ten goals and 11 tries scored against them. Curiously, the last team to beat Oxford before this remarkable run of success began was Edinburgh University, the club which also brought the sequence to an end more than three years later.

Another mark of the dominant position of Oxford rugby in the game as a whole in this period is the fact that in the 1882-83 season there were 12 internationals in residence, plus four men who went on to win caps. Thus the influence of Oxford, and in particular of Vassall, who captained England, spread far beyond the confines of the University.

The great contribution of Charles Marriott to University rugby was the determined way he set about bringing Cambridge up to the unprecedented standards set by Oxford. Captain in 1883, he introduced an organisation to Cambridge rugby of the kind Vassall had given Oxford, and he persuaded Rowland Hill, then secretary of the Rugby Football Union, to travel frequently from London to Cambridge to coach his men. Marriott's efforts did not reap immediate reward — Cambridge lost the Varsity Matches of 1883 and 1884. However, his policies were fully vindicated in following years. Cambridge won four times on the trot and five times in the seven years between 1885 and 1891, and 13 members of the 1886 Cambridge team became internationals. Marriott went on to serve the Rugby Football Union as secretary for 17 years, a period which saw the purchase, development and establishment of the Twickenham ground.

Both Vassall and Marriott campaigned to get Blues awarded for rugby at their respective Universities, but with contrasting results. When Vassall arrived at Oxford, only rowing, cricket and athletics had Blue status, and in 1882 the University soccer captain, T.H. French, suggested to Vassall that the time was ripe for him to apply for Blue status for both codes of football. Vassall accordingly wrote to the president of the Boat Club, A.R. Patterson, who was the senior representative of existing Blues and who had played in the rugby teams of the three previous seasons. Patterson called a meeting of representatives of rowing, cricket and athletics for 29 November 1882 and wrote next day to Vassall that 'there are no objections to your adopting a Blue coat'.

At Cambridge the attitude among existing Blues was very different when a year later Marriott, accompanied by H.G. Fuller, who was in his sixth year in the XV, and by E.W. Pawson, the soccer captain, met with the presidents of the rowing and athletic clubs and the captain of cricket. The footballers' case was that, to quote Marriott, 'the Oxford teams, both rugby and association,

having been granted their full Blues the previous season, it was thought that the Cambridge men selected to oppose them were worthy of similar honour.' The Blues committee were jealous of their privileges, however, and after much discussion eventually came up with a rather feeble compromise: that a certain number of Blues should be divided among the players of the two codes of football. 'This suggestion', wrote Marriott 'could not be entertained by the football authorities.'

The matter was shelved until the following year when the Blues committee went no further than to come up with a similar compromise. 'At length,' wrote Marriott, 'the rugby players adopted the only course remaining to them, viz., to take their full Blue for themselves.' And this they did, appearing for the first time in Blue coats in the Rectory Field, Blackheath on 10 December 1884. This defiant action, not surprisingly, infuriated the Blues committee, which determined to put the rugby players in their place. To debate the subject, the committee chose as their forum the Cambridge Union, and a date at the end of the Lent term when interest in both codes of football would be at its lowest. The motion, put before the Union by the rowers, was 'this meeting regrets the resolution of the authorities of the CURUFC and the CUAFC to adopt the full Blue against the decision of the committee to whom they had submitted the question, and trusts they will yet find it possible to bring themselves into harmony with those unwritten laws by which the social relations of this University are governed.' Well over 1,000 members of the University attended the debate, many sitting on tables and on the floor, and it was reported that the Union had never been so full. After a long and lively debate the motion was lost by 466 votes to 707, a majority of 241. Thus the rugby and soccer clubs won their official right to a Blue.

In these days Cambridge were playing their home matches on the Corpus ground because they had been banned from Parker's Piece in the 1881-82 season — the municipal authorities claimed that rugby was doing too much damage to the turf. Oxford continued to use The Parks except for the occasional game. One of these exceptions came early in 1884, when a special match was arranged between the University and Yorkshire, unbeaten for three years. Since The Parks was public land, no gate money could be taken there, so this game was played at the Iffley Road athletics ground. A crowd of nearly 6,000 saw Oxford win by a goal to nothing. The Merton ground was also sometimes used for similar reasons, and it was not until 1899 that the present Iffley Road rugby ground was opened.

Two Varsity Matches stand out especially from the 1880s. In December 1883 Oxford scored seven tries and converted three of them while Cambridge managed just one goal, a margin of victory not exceeded for 26 years. A year later came one of those rare games in which the side that controls the forward play does not win. Cambridge pushed Oxford all over the Rectory Field, but the backs won the match for Oxford by three goals and a try to a try. Prominent in both these matches were Gregory Wade, an Oxford threequarter, and Alan Rotherham at half-back. In the 1883 game Wade scored three tries, one of them when his drop-kick at goal fell short and he regained possession, hurtling over before Cambridge could stop him. In 1884 he intercepted a Cambridge pass and raced 50 yards for the first try of the match. Altogether Wade played in three Varsity Matches and in eight games for England and was never on the losing side.

Yet Wade, who went to school at King's, Paramatta, New South Wales, might never have come to the notice of Oxford's rugby fraternity but for a letter to the OURFC from Paramatta asking what had become of their man who had already been in residence at the University for a year.

Charles Marriott (left), whose determination brought
Cambridge up to the standards set by Oxford, pictured in
later life as president of the RFU.

Harry Vassall promptly made enquiries and discovered that Wade was making a name for himself as an oarsman for Merton. Impressed by Wade's formidable bodywork and muscularity, Vassall gave him a trial which was quickly followed by outings in the Varsity team. So powerful a runner did Wade immediately prove that, on Oxford's recommendation, he was picked by England for their match against Wales at Swansea in December 1882. He justified the faith of Vassall and the England selectors by scoring three tries. Since the Varsity Match of that year had to be postponed from December to the following February, Wade achieved a rare distinction for a Varsity player: scoring three tries against Wales before ever playing against Cambridge. Wade went on to receive a knighthood and to become Prime Minister of New South Wales. More important for the development of rugby, he was an essential member of Oxford's threequarter line in February 1883 when, for the first time, three threequarters rather than two were deployed by both sides in the Varsity Match.

Alan Rotherham and Gus Grant-Asher, a Scottish international, were Oxford's half-backs in three consecutive Varsity Matches, and it is generally felt that they were the key players in the realisation of Vassall's revolutionary theories on open rugby. In those days the two half-backs did not have the separate roles of scrum-half and stand-off half as we know them today. They were both more or less scrum-halves, playing on each side of the scrum, and were very closely marked by their opposite numbers. The ability to break or to pass under pressure was the vital quality of a half-back. Rotherham was the ideal man for this job, and he scored many crucial tries for Oxford. Charles Marriott's brother, Bruce, once wrote of Rotherham: 'He was the greatest of halves ever seen, sharp as a needle, solid brawn and muscle. When running, his free arm was working like a piston, and when he handed you off, it was like the kick of a Brazilian mule. A very difficult man to stop'.

Cambridge likewise had an exceptional half-back in the early 1880s. Don Wauchope played 12 times for Scotland after being discovered at Cambridge by Charles Marriott. Marriott was walking across Parker's Piece when he became aware of a large and excited crowd. On investigation he discovered they were watching a game between Fettesians and Cliftonians in which one of the Fettesians was dodging his way over for try after try. Marriott was so impressed by Wauchope's ability as a deceptive runner that he put the Fettesian half-back straight into the University team the following Saturday. He played in two Varsity Matches and, but for injury, would have played in a third.

Both Universities have had their disappointing years, but the frustration of the 1890-91 season has probably never been equalled. The Varsity Match planned for December 1890 had to be postponed because of fog; moreover fog descended on Queen's on each of two further days for which the postponed game had been re-arranged. After three postponements the Varsity Match eventually took place on 3 March 1891, when it ended in a draw. The weather also came close to causing the 1899 match to be postponed. This time the trouble was snow which fell heavily overnight. However, the authorities at Queen's had the snow removed in the morning, and the pitch was found to be in good condition. Cambridge certainly thought so, for they proceeded to win by two goals and four tries to nothing, the heaviest defeat inflicted on Oxford in the 27 years of the Varsity Match.

Previous page: An artist's impression of the 1896 Varsity Match, printed in the Illustrated London News.

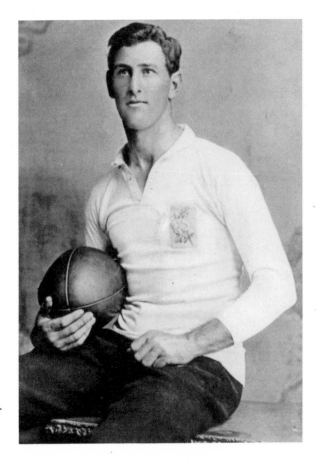

The versatile Australian Sammy Woods. He won 14 caps for England at rugby and represented his native country at cricket in Tests against England in 1888.

Cambridge in this match owed almost everything to their forwards, who were led by the formidable John Daniell and included 'Darkie' Bedell-Sivright, one of Scotland's greatest players. Seven members of that Cambridge pack were internationals, and the eighth subsequently played for his country. Bedell-Sivright, a powerful, forceful forward, went on to win 22 caps for Scotland and to captain the British Isles in Australia and New Zealand in 1904, while Daniell would probably have won far more caps for England than his seven over six seasons had not injuries and absence abroad ruled him out of consideration. Also a cricketer, Daniell captained Somerset for several seasons, and he later held the rare distinction of becoming an England selector for both rugby and cricket. He was an England rugby selector from 1913 to 1939.

Daniell was but one of the many versatile sportsmen to make his mark on Varsity rugby at this time. He was preceded in the Cambridge rugby and cricket teams and in the Somerset cricket team by another great all-rounder, Sammy Woods. Woods, a big, strong, exceptionally fast forward, was an Australian who went to school in Brighton. He played in three rugby Varsity Matches from 1888 and won 14 caps for England. At cricket Woods, a fast bowler, captained the University in 1890 and then played for Somerset for 24 years, for 13 of them their captain and secretary. While still at Cambridge, he played in Tests for Australia against England at Lord's, The Oval and Old Trafford in 1888.

The greatest all-rounder of them all, C.B. Fry, the England Test cricketer, international soccer player and holder of the world long-jump record, would have won a rugby Blue for Oxford had he not damaged a leg muscle while playing against Harlequins shortly before the Varsity Match of

1894. A centre or wing threequarter, he had played in all the earlier games that term. The same injury kept him out of an England trial, but he did play for the Barbarians. The Varsity Match he missed is notable for its brevity: the referee mistakenly blew the final whistle after 30 minutes of the second half, instead of the normal 35. Nor did he allow any injury-time. It was generally reckoned that the game was nine minutes short and, as Cambridge were pressing continuously in the late stages, many people felt that Oxford would have been beaten if the game had run its full course. As it was, the result was a draw at a goal each. There was another unusual incident in the Varsity Match two years later when H.T. Wallis, the Cambridge wing, went over the Oxford dead-ball line in running for a try. The referee consulted with Oxford's captain, Leslie-Jones, and since it was agreed that the dead-ball line had been marked too close to the goal-line, the try was allowed to stand.

Overseas players made an impact on the Varsity Match even in its early days: the first Oxford Blue from South Africa and the first from New Zealand both played in 1885. South African full-back James Sutherland hailed from Pietermaritzburg but was educated at Fettes. The New Zealander, John Hall, a son of the Premier of New Zealand, played at half-back and threequarter in his two Varsity Matches.

In 1886 another South African, Herbert Castens, won a Blue as a forward for Oxford after learning the game at Rugby School. When he returned to South Africa, he became a player and coach in Western Province and captained the Springboks in their first-ever international match, against the Anglo-Scots touring side of 1891. Three Tests were played on that tour, all won narrowly by the British. Castens was captain in the first Test, was dropped for the second and refereed the third, surely a unique experience. Three years later he captained the first representative South African cricket side to tour England. No Tests were played on that early cricket tour but in their most important match, against MCC at Lord's, Castens led his side to victory over a team captained by W.G. Grace.

5
Pre-War Splendour

The first Varsity Match of the new century produced one of those gallant fight-backs in the face of adversity that have become so much rarer since the introduction of substitutes. Early in the Match Oxford lost Crawfurd, a wing threequarter, through injury and had to play the rest of the game with only 14 men. Oxford also made the unorthodox decision not to bring a forward out to the wing to replace Crawfurd, because the Cambridge pack, still including John Daniell and Darkie Bedell-Sivright, was such a formidable unit. Not until they had reached half-time, the score at 0-0, did Oxford send out a forward to play wing threequarter. After the interval Cambridge, their forwards living up to their reputation, scored two tries and converted one of them for an 8-0 lead.

The beleaguered Oxford team, however, bravely took the only option left to them — they started a passing movement from near their own line. In his book on the Varsity Match Howard Marshall described the movement thus: 'Kershaw at half-back had whipped the ball to his partner, Walton. Walton shot it to Luce, who went through a crack in the Cambridge defence and sent Hammond charging up the field. Hammond passed it to Terry, the defence was spreadeagled, and Oxford had a glorious chance. Terry jinked like a hare for 20 yards, gave the ball to Luce again; Luce made ground, and there was the ubiquitous Walton on the Cambridge 25, up to take the final pass and race away to score a wonderful try, one of the finest in the history of the Varsity Match.' The try was converted, and then it was Cambridge's turn for bad luck: one of their wings, Jones, who was limping with a knee injury, failed to field an Oxford punt. Crabbie, who had been doing a great deal of steadfast tackling for Oxford, now grabbed the loose ball and raced away for a try. The conversion gave Oxford an astonishing victory by two goals to a goal and a try.

In the early years of the century the two Universities produced some of the most famous players in the history of British rugby, a fair proportion of them from Scotland. Darkie Bedell-Sivright, who continued in the Cambridge team for four years, as captain in the last two, was joined by his younger brother, J.V., who also spent four years in the Blues side and was likewise capped by Scotland while at the University. They were both from Fettes, as were two other remarkable brothers, L.M. and K.G. MacLeod, centre threequarters of contrasting styles and stars of the Cambridge team in those years. Louis was a robust, strong-tackling centre, while Kenneth was a real flyer who often played on the wing for this reason. Louis played for the Light Blues in 1903,

39

Above: The Bedell-Sivright brothers with their Cambridge team-mates of 1902. Darkie is in the centre (with ball) and his younger brother J.V. is on the far right of the same row.

Below: Cambridge captain Louis MacLeod heads for the try-line in 1905.

1904 and 1905 (when he captained the side), and Kenneth in four Varsity Matches from 1905 to 1908, leading the team in 1907. Like the Bedell-Sivrights the MacLeods played for Scotland while at Cambridge, Kenneth winning his first cap before his Blue. Indeed, Kenneth was so impressive at school that the headmaster of Fettes was approached unofficially to allow the boy, then aged only 16, to be available for Scotland. The head, perhaps wisely, said no. As it was, at the age of 17 and now at Cambridge, Kenneth played in the centre alongside Louis for Scotland against the All Blacks at Inverleith in November 1905. He went on to win ten caps before he was 21, retiring from the game at the age of 20 largely, it is said, because of the untimely death of Louis from appendicitis. In addition to his achievements on the rugby field Kenneth won Blues at cricket and athletics and played cricket for Lancashire.

Curiously, Kenneth MacLeod was only once on the winning side in his four Varsity Matches. This was in 1905 when the two brothers played together in the centre less than four weeks after doing so for Scotland against the All Blacks. Cambridge won by three goals to two goals and a try.

It is just possible that Cambridge scored more points than Oxford in Kenneth MacLeod's last Varsity Match, in 1908, which the records give as a draw of a goal apiece. It was another foggy day at Queen's and late in the game, with the scores level, MacLeod let fly with a drop-kick at goal from near halfway. John Daniell, who had coached the Cambridge forwards and who was running the line, later recalled: 'It was a frightful afternoon — thick West Kensington fog — no visibility at all higher than ten feet above ground level. I was one of the touch-judges, and when the game was being played on the other side of the ground, I could see nothing. Grunt [MacLeod] dropped at about halfway — it must have been an enormous kick — and the ball disappeared in the fog, not to be seen again until it was returned by someone in the crowd, who said it had dropped amongst them out of the muck. No one knew if it was a goal or not, the poor referee, Crawford Findlay, least of all. So he said to K.G. "How was it, Grunt?" "No goal" was the instant answer. The result was a draw.' As an experiment this Varsity Match was played on a Saturday, and a record crowd of 13,000 attended.

K.G. played in three Varsity Matches as a centre and once, in 1906, on the wing. On that occasion he scored a dashing try and created another with a slashing run through the middle of the Oxford defence. This Varsity Match, incidentally, started late because the referee did not turn up on time, and a substitute had to be found for him. This was also the game in which an already misty field was enveloped by a pall of smoke, one of the Queen's Club chimneys having caught fire. K.G. suffered the disappointment of seeing the side he captained in 1907 lose by 0-17, but Howard Marshall wrote of him: 'It is generally agreed that K.G. was one of the greatest three-quarters the game has seen. He had every attribute; a magnificent turn of speed, a baffling swerve, and a drop-kick or punt of tremendous length. He was very thickly built below the waist and thus difficult to tackle. Truly a superb athlete'.

That Cambridge did not have matters all their own way in the early years of the century was due partly to the fact that Oxford, too, had some exceptional players and partly to the influence of Adrian Stoop on Oxford's back play. Stoop, like Harry Vassall before him, was a man of vision and imagination who had entirely fresh ideas about the way in which the midfield backs should co-operate. Oxford in those days were still using the old half-back system and, even when Stoop captained the side in 1904, he and Pat Munro, another outstandingly gifted half-back, took it in turns to put the ball into the scrum. Stoop did not put his ideas fully into practice until he left the University and played for Harlequins and England — 15 caps between 1905 and 1912. It was then that he performed specifically as a stand-off and made sure that those around him had the understanding and the skills to make the most of his promptings from this position. Even so,

The referee's nightmare: a Varsity Match played in the fog at Queen's.

during his Oxford career he had a profound influence on thinking and tactics, which was to bear fruit in subsequent seasons. Howard Marshall wrote of Stoop: 'He had a remarkable natural instinct for the game, and he studied it and practised it with rare devotion and intensity. As a player he had great gifts, for he was beautifully built, a balanced runner with exceptional speed off the mark. His genius, however, lay in his original approach to the game, his refusal to accept conventional principles, his belief in swinging the direction of attack, his conception of planned surprise, and his attention to detail'.

Stoop had mixed fortunes in his three Varsity Matches. In 1902 the Cambridge forwards dominated, and Stoop was credited with having done much to secure a drawn match with his quickness in snapping up stray chances to run and with his deft punting. In 1903 Oxford had what is believed to be the lightest pack of forwards they have ever fielded — three men weighed less than 11 stone — but, inspired by the leadership of 'Lump' Cartwright, they managed to provide enough possession for Stoop and Munro to engineer a narrow victory by three goals and a try to two goals and a try. In 1904, when Stoop was Oxford's captain, the Cambridge forwards again dominated the match, and their side won by three goals to two. Stoop, however, managed to score one of the great individual tries in the history of the Varsity Match, running a full 50 yards through the Cambridge defence.

Pat Munro, another Scot, was just as effective a player as Stoop. A small, wiry half-back, he succeeded Stoop as captain for the 1905 Varsity Match and in that and the two following seasons won ten caps for Scotland. He then disappeared from rugby to work in the Sudan Civil Service, but when he returned on leave he would pick up the threads again so instinctively with London Scottish that the Scotland selectors gave him three more caps in 1911. By then, of course, he, like Stoop, was playing specifically as a stand-off half. The first Varsity Match for which Oxford gave specific roles to a scrum-half and stand-off half was in 1907, during the period from 1906 to 1911 in which Oxford were unbeaten in six Varsity Matches, winning five and drawing one, and scoring 29 tries to Cambridge's eight. It cannot be mere coincidence that this sequence came at a time when Oxford had two of their greatest centre threequarters, Henry Vassall and Ronnie Poulton.

Vassall, a nephew of the earlier Vassall, was the complete, classical centre. Howard Marshall says of him 'he was very quick off the mark, with a most deceptive body swerve, and he timed his passes perfectly, making beautiful openings for his wings. His tackling was magnificent and this, with his constructive methods, made him a tremendous asset to any side.' He was slightly built but long-legged with a deceptive turn of speed. In his first Varsity Match in 1906, Vassall scored a try and prompted others in Oxford's victory by four tries to a goal and a try. In his second, won by Oxford by a goal and four tries to nil, Vassall played a vital part in what E.H.D. Sewell described as one of the three best combined tries he had witnessed in over 40 years of watching rugby at every level.

Of this 1907 try Sewell, writing in 1944, said: 'It seems only last week to me as I see now almost every move in it. We were within about five minutes of half-time with the scoresheet blank when they formed down in Oxford's left-hand corner just behind the 25. From one to another, Williamson, Cunningham and Tarr, the passes were given and taken faultlessly against a high wind. The Old Uppinghamian, Tarr — and what a grand player he was, with splendid defence, good hands, pace and a "head" — bore out right-handed and gave to Vassall between the 25 and halfway with ample elbow-room. One felt now it was a cinch, as Vassall had the priceless knack of giving final passes which even an elderly lady wearing spectacles could have taken. He was in his stride when he took Tarr's pass and, with simultaneous effortless acceleration and outward swerve, he proved far too much for Coates, the Cambridge wing. Vassall was thus able to draw the back, R.C.C. Campbell, before he practically placed the ball into Martin's hands. The little man finished alone near goal'.

Vassall's third Varsity Match, in 1908, was one he should never have played in. He was suffering from a thigh injury, and the gamble of including him did not pay off. He went lame in the first five minutes and left Tarr to do a great deal of defending against the great K.G. MacLeod in the Cambridge centre. This Varsity Match, which ended in a draw of a goal apiece, was the only one Oxford did not win between 1906 and 1911. The irony was that Oxford that season had in residence six threequarters who were or were to become internationals. It is a measure of Vassall's skill that despite this abundant strength in reserve Oxford decided to include him for the Varsity Match, knowing he was by no means 100 per cent fit. The biggest irony of all was that one of those who was left out of that Oxford team was Ronnie Poulton, who was considered to be a genius by most of those who saw him later. He was a freshman from Rugby School in 1908, and he played in several games for the University before the Varsity Match, both as a centre and on the wing. The trouble was he was so unorthodox in seeking and finding openings that his team-mates could not combine with him. However, England picked him as a centre against France, Ireland and Scotland that same season, and for the 1909 Varsity Match Oxford found a place for him on the left wing. To say that Poulton then justified Oxford's belated faith in him would be the grossest of understatements: he scored five tries, which remains a record for either side in a Varsity Match.

*Ronnie Poulton scores one of his five tries for Oxford in the
1909 Match. His feat remains a record to this day.*

This game has always been referred to as 'Poulton's Match' and with good reason. After only three minutes the ball was passed along the Oxford threequarter line to Poulton who, feinting this way and that, ran for 50 yards through the Cambridge defence for a try at the posts. Seven minutes later a further series of passes involving all the Oxford backs created the chance for Poulton to score his second try. A few minutes after that Poulton was checked on the left, but he passed the ball inside, and a threequarter movement on the right sent the right wing, Martin, over for a third try. Oxford were 11 points ahead at the end of the first quarter of an hour and, with Poulton racing off for his third try, Oxford led at the interval by a goal and three tries to a try. In the second half Poulton scored two more tries and Martin three. In modern scoring terms the result would have been 44-4.

What makes the result, and the manner of Oxford's success, all the more remarkable is that one of their centres, Tarr, broke a collar-bone early in the first half and had to go off, leaving Oxford with only 14 men for most of the Match. The full-back, Buchanan, was switched to take Tarr's place in the centre, and a forward, Honey, later president of the National Olympic Committee of South Africa, deputised at full-back. Moreover for a time Oxford were reduced to 13 men by an injury to one of their forwards, Turner, who was not fully fit when he returned to the fray. All seven members of Oxford's back division that day were either already internationals or were to play for their countries that same season and their sheer quality was decisive. Howard Marshall wrote that 'many experienced observers considered that no finer exhibition of combined back play would ever be seen again'. A great deal of credit, however, must be given to the seven forwards who provided those illustrious backs with a chance to show their paces. Once more the Universities, in this instance Oxford, had shown the rest of the rugby world what could be achieved with imagination, daring, timing and skill.

In his second Varsity Match in 1910, Poulton played in the position he preferred, centre, and again had a major influence on the result. It was a game which each side in turn seemed bound to win. Oxford led 13-0 in the early stages, only for Cambridge to come back at them and lead 15-13 at half-time. Cambridge went further ahead to 18-13 and then had the misfortune to lose their left wing, Lewis, through injury. But it was the genius of Poulton that allowed Oxford first to draw level and then to win. In one attack he swung inwards for a try at the posts, and in another, just before the end of the Match, he swept outside the last of the Cambridge defenders and again scored at the posts for a final score of 23-18.

Poulton was captain in 1911, and he inspired Oxford to an astonishing start. Soon after the kick-off he scored a try, and he created two more tries in the first ten minutes of the Match. He then had the bad luck to tear a hamstring. He had to leave the field and, although he returned at the interval, he was unable to contribute much to the play, so Oxford were obliged to continue with a forward out of the pack to help the backs. Still, Cambridge were beaten by two goals and three tries to nil. In his three Varsity Matches Poulton scored eight tries, and had a hand in most of the others Oxford scored in those years. Howard Marshall said of him: 'There never was a player in the series, I suppose, who so hypnotised his opponents, running, as *The Times* correspondent put it in 1911, "swinging the ball from side to side as if he were rhapsodising on a concertina, compelling the defence to follow him spell-bound". A wonderful player and a remarkable personality'. He played 17 times for England.

There has always been a certain amount of confusion about Poulton because he appears in some records as Poulton Palmer. In fact he was related, on his mother's side, to the Palmers of Huntley and Palmer, famous for the manufacture of biscuits. In 1913 he came into an inheritance from the Palmer family, but a condition for accepting the inheritance was that he should change his name. In March 1914, therefore, he added the name Palmer to his own. For all his University and international rugby, however, except for his last game for England (against France at Colombes in April 1914), he was listed as Poulton.

It was in this period leading up to the First World War that Rhodes Scholars began to make their mark at Oxford. The first to win a Blue was W.W. Hoskin, a forward from St Andrew's College, Grahamstown, South Africa, who went on to captain the side in 1907. In the 1905 Match he counted three further South Africans — Gardner, Hoadley and Howe-Browne — in his pack. The first Blue from the United States, Donald Grant Herring, played in 1909. He too was a Rhodes Scholar. But the influx of overseas talent could not prevent Oxford's remarkable sequence of success coming to an end after Poulton had gone down. Cambridge, inspired by the captaincy of Jenny Greenwood, won the 1912 game by two goals to a try — their first victory since 1905. Seven members of Greenwood's outstanding team were shortly to lose their lives in the First World War along with 22 other Cambridge Blues, among them Darkie Bedell-Sivright. The War claimed the lives of 27 Oxford Blues, including six members of the record-breaking side of 1909 which had scored nine tries in the Varsity Match. Ronnie Poulton was among those killed.

6
University Rugby Rekindled

Writing of the contribution made by Oxford and Cambridge to rugby as a whole in the period up to the First World War, Howard Marshall said: 'We may justly claim that, but for the encouragement given by the Universities, rugby would never have become a game of international importance ... but for the fact that the game had become firmly transplanted from Rugby School to the Universities, it might have remained a curious traditional survival at Rugby, rather like the wall-game at Eton'. Right up to the War the Universities were leading the way, not just in the general standard of play but also in their imaginative development of tactics.

Upon the outbreak of War in 1914 the playing of rugby, at least at the top levels, virtually ceased. There seems to have been a feeling that it would be disloyal to be playing games while so many young men were losing their lives in the trenches. There must have been those who wondered how the game was going to be revived after the long years of inactivity on the fields of play. When peace came, both Universities found just the men to rekindle their rugby. At Cambridge Jenny Greenwood, who had won Blues in 1910, 1911, 1912 and 1913, captaining the side in 1912, and who had played nine games for England, returned to the University and devoted his energy to reorganising the rugby. He was appointed captain again for the first post-War Varsity Match in 1919, Oxford having granted him a dispensation from the rule limiting the participation of players to four Varsity Matches. He went on to play four more games as a forward for England in 1920, one of the few men who played for their countries both before and after the War. Cambridge owe a great deal to him for the way he rekindled their rugby. They won that 1919 Varsity Match by a dropped goal and a penalty goal to a goal — the first occasion on which a penalty goal was scored in a Varsity Match. With him in the pack Greenwood had Cove-Smith and Conway, who were to play many fine games for England, and Collis, who subsequently played for Ireland.

Oxford, too, had some experienced men, headed by Eric Loudoun-Shand, to rebuild their rugby. Loudoun-Shand had played for Scotland in 1913 before winning his pre-War Blue as a centre later that year, and when he returned to Oxford he was made captain.

Many years later, in his autobiography, *A Cap for Boots*, Greenwood explained that it was pure chance that enabled him to return to Cambridge after the War. After he was demobbed, he began taking an interest in rugby again and was concerned to hear that Cambridge were unlikely to have

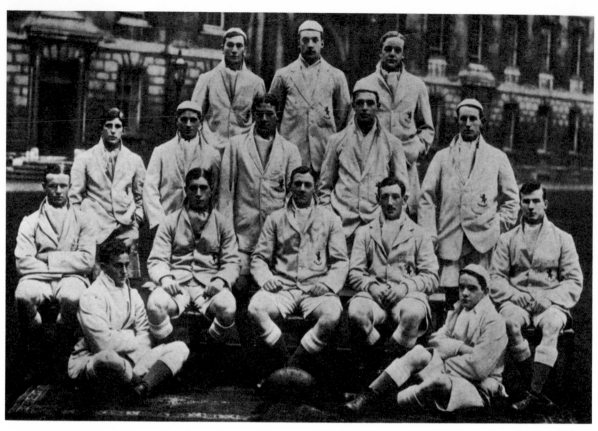

Above: Captain Jenny Greenwood (centre) with his 1912 Cambridge team.

Below: Jenny Greenwood and Eric Loudoun-Shand (right), the two captains, meet King George V before the 1919 Match.

a single old Blue to prepare them for the 1919 Varsity Match. He therefore arranged to meet Barry Cumberlege, the last Cambridge captain before the War, to discuss means of remedying this problem. Greenwood and Cumberlege were holding their discussion in a club when 'by an extraordinary coincidence who should walk in but Eric Loudoun-Shand, the new Oxford captain, and Bruno Brown, who had been the Oxford captain against me in 1912', wrote Greenwood. 'They were meeting with the intention of discussing Oxford prospects. Apparently Oxford were expecting four old Blues, and when I told Shand that it was doubtful we should have even one, he said "Why don't you go up again yourself?" I replied that there would not be much fun in getting a side together and then dropping out and not playing against Oxford. Greatly to my surprise Shand replied immediately that Oxford would not object to me playing a fifth time'. Greenwood then went to consult with the president of the CURUFC, H.G. Comber, who said he thought all would be well for Greenwood to play for a fifth year, provided the Oxford committee gave their consent in writing. This Oxford did.

'It was great fun playing for Cambridge as the first MA who had ever done so,' writes Greenwood. In fact, this was the second time Greenwood had been at Cambridge when, strictly speaking, from the academic point of view he had no business to be there. After captaining the University in 1912 he had gone down and had been articled to a firm of chartered accountants in London. But 'I got a great urge to play for Cambridge for a fourth time'. He borrowed money from his brother, as he did in 1919, played a term's rugby, and 'returned to the City directly after the Varsity Match'.

Greenwood cannot have had many regrets about returning to Cambridge in 1919 and playing in the Varsity Match. 'King George V came to the Match with Prince Albert, afterwards George VI, and Prince Henry, afterwards Duke of Gloucester. Eric Shand and I were presented to them, though I fear they did not see much of the game owing to the fog. Eric had his hand bandaged, which the King immediately spotted — he had been badly wounded on the Somme in 1916 — and asked him how he hoped to take a pass. Eric pointed to me and said "Look at him laughing, sir, he hopes I drop the lot".' Loudoun-Shand in fact had to have his arm amputated later.

The fact that Oxford were beaten did cause Greenwood some regret: he sympathised with his old school-mate. 'I was very sorry for my old friend, Eric, as it was through his sporting action that I was allowed to play in the match a fifth time.' Having seen Cambridge rugby through the immediate post-War period, Greenwood fully intended to retire from rugby following the Varsity Match. But it was not to be. 'A few weeks later I received a telephone call late at night from John Daniell, chairman of the England selectors, saying they were in a hole regarding a captain and leader of forwards for the England team and would I play again. He knew that I wasn't keen, but when he agreed that it would be for all four matches and that I should not have to play for my place, I accepted.'

Nor did Cambridge let Greenwood out of their sights. He immediately became the University's representative on the Rugby Football Union committee and served that committee for 36 years, being president of the RFU for two terms, 1935-36 and 1936-37. Moreover while he was the Cambridge man on the RFU he raised sides to play the University each year, the precursor of Steele-Bodger's match as we know it now.

Among those who helped Eric Loudoun-Shand to relaunch Oxford's rugby was Martin Parr, a lock forward who had narrowly failed to win a Blue in 1913. Parr used to tell the story of a chance encounter in France during the War in 1915 when he was leading his troops to relieve some others at the front line. Arriving at the front line, he recognised the officer he was relieving. It was David Bain, the 1913 Oxford captain, who had dropped him from the team to meet Cambridge after he had been a regular in the side that term. As the shells whistled overhead, Parr went straight up to Bain and asked him: 'Why did you drop me?' 'Because you kept holding the ball in the second row', Bain replied. 'That wasn't me!', expostulated Parr, 'It was the other bloke.' They just had time for a wry laugh and a handshake before returning to the business in hand. The following week Bain was killed in action at Festhubert. Back at Oxford after the War, Parr again missed out on a Blue.

There was a strong South African influence in the second post-War Varsity Match in 1920. Oxford's captain was South African Denoon Duncan, a forward good enough to have played four times for Scotland. In the few days before the Varsity Match, after the last game of the term, he was faced with the problem of having to find a new stand-off half, the regular man for that position, F.A. Waldock, having announced that he was not fit enough to play against Cambridge. Eventually Duncan made the extraordinary decision to switch another South African forward, Knoppie Neser, from the pack to play at stand-off. What made this decision all the more strange was that Neser, who had won his Blue in the pack the previous season, had never played at stand-off half. It is probable that Duncan knew Neser had been tried at stand-off half as a young prep schoolboy in South Africa, but all through his teens Neser had been coached as a forward, and he had arrived at Oxford with the reputation of being an exceptionally strong, powerful and technically well-equipped man of the pack. He had proved these qualities to the full in the 1919 Varsity Match. It was a tremendous gamble that Duncan now took.

It paid off — but only just — Oxford beat Cambridge by a goal and four tries to a goal and three tries. Neser played a vital part in the scoring. He launched the threequarter movement which brought Oxford their first try; he made the break which created their second and he scored the fourth himself. Furthermore this last try came from a classical stand-off half move from a scrum not far from the halfway line. Neser shot round the blind-side, drew the opposing wing, passed to his own wing and then was up for a return pass when his wing reached the Cambridge full-back.

No wonder then that this game is always referred to as 'Neser's Match'. Howard Marshall wrote of him: 'Neser was immensely strong — there can never have been a more powerful stand-off half. Although he had the physique of a heavy-weight boxer, he was also surprisingly quick off the mark, and he had beautiful hands. On the great day he played extremely well, as if he had always been a stand-off half, uncontaminated by experience of the myopic grovellings which are the lot of forwards'. Neser became an international referee on the 1924 Lions' tour of South Africa.

The 1921 Varsity Match was the first to be played at Twickenham, the ground having been opened in October 1909. There had been campaigns as early as 1911, when the number of spectators approached 16,000, to have the match moved from Queen's. Many people felt that, in spite of temporary stands, the facilities at Queen's were not adequate to cope with the increasing throngs attracted to the exciting displays of attacking rugby provided by Oxford and Cambridge. There was also the problem of the fog, which had the habit of swirling in on West Kensington in early December. However, in 1912 officials of the two Universities had decided to continue at Queen's, which had been the home of the Varsity Match since 1887, 'so long as adequate arrangements are made by the directors of Queen's Club'. When it came, the move to Twickenham cannot have been made without some pangs of regret, but the rapidly rising gates after the switch showed the wisdom of the decision. By 1923 the attendance had reached 30,000, and in 1925 it was 40,000. Such crowds could not possibly have been accommodated at Queen's.

The media's view of the two University teams of 1921.

It was in 1921 that Wavell Wakefield, who was in the RAF, arrived at Cambridge on a special Service course. Wakefield — later Lord Wakefield of Kendal and known to everyone in the game as 'Wakers' — had already made a name for himself as a formidable leader of the England pack. At Cambridge he joined two other England forwards, Cove-Smith and Conway. All three had served in the War and were the kind of mature players who had meant so much to Varsity rugby in the post-War rebuilding process. Also among the Cambridge forwards that year was David MacMyn, who was soon to play for Scotland. Howard Marshall described those Cambridge forwards as 'about the most powerful and menacing pack in the country'.

In an unusual tactical ploy Cambridge, having won the toss, decided to take the kick-off. Wakefield deliberately punted the ball directly over the touch-line, the idea being that Cambridge should give Oxford an immediate taste of their power at the subsequent scrum at the centre of the field. Oxford were duly sent back-pedalling for 15 yards. This indignity appears, however, to have inspired the Oxford forwards to play well above their reputation. Ewen Campbell played a real captain's game behind them, and Oxford eventually confounded predictions by winning by a goal and two tries to a goal. Wakefield himself wrote later that Cambridge would have won this match had they kept play among the forwards instead of repeatedly heeling to their backs, who lacked the understanding and class of Oxford's.

Great as Wakefield's contribution was to Cambridge as a player, it was as a thinker, planner and captain (in 1922) that he made his imperishable mark on University rugby. He invited many famous rugby people — among them John Daniell, Tommy Vile and Dicky Lloyd — to come to Cambridge to coach his side. He was not worried that his players might become confused by

Wavell Wakefield — 'Wakers' to one and all — takes a breather in the England trial match of 1923.

conflicting advice from his diverse panel of experts: he believed, on the contrary, that his men would come to appreciate all the options and would be drawn into using their imagination and intelligence. During his own career Wakefield played mainly as a loose forward or at lock, and it was for his insistence on scientific loose-forward positional play, both in attack and defence, that he became famous — some would say notorious — as an innovator. Some people still claim that Wakefield's loose-forward theories were responsible for the decline in open back play throughout the game, but Wakefield always maintained that there were ways to negate scientific loose-forward defence, notably by means of the cross-kick by the open-side wing threequarter.

In the preparation of his side for the 1922 Varsity Match Wakefield had some unusual theories. One of these concerned the habit of going for runs before breakfast. Writing several years later he said: 'It had become customary for probable members of the team to assemble and go for a training run together before breakfast. This practice I entirely cut out, for I consider it to be the most stupid form of training ever invented, except for those few mortals who make a daily habit of it.' Notwithstanding this view, Wakefield was also quite a performer on the track, according to former BBC commentator Rex Alston, who was himself an athletics Blue. 'He was first string for Pembroke College and I shall always remember him, a huge, bulky figure but very compact. He always made a wheezing, puffing noise when he ran, but he could run the 100 yards in something like 10.4 seconds. I don't suppose he did much training, but strength and guts got him there. He was tremendously fast, but the older he got the cannier he became, and he would play his rugby in bursts. He would have a rest in the scrum then suddenly make a break, pummelling away up the field with his scrum-cap on, handing people off. He was frightfully difficult to stop if he was anywhere near the line and was certainly an inspiring leader and a great thinker on the game.'

To general astonishment Wakefield also severely cut down on the number of training and coaching sessions in the two weeks before the Varsity Match. 'I drove the Varsity side as hard as I could in the first part of the season', he wrote. 'I believed that if the players were going to learn anything, they must learn it a considerable time before the Varsity Match. In the last ten days we had only one practice. The players were, in fact, during that time not allowed to change at all, except to go down to Fenners a couple of times for short sprinting. In my opinion there is a great temptation to over-train at the Varsity, and the most difficult task a captain has to tackle is to prevent his side going not so much physically as mentally stale.'

The match itself (the first for which the players wore numbers on their backs) was a triumph for Wakefield's planning and his tactics of aggressive defence. 'With several freshmen in our side, we were meeting a team of brilliant and experienced individuals. If we were to win, we had to rattle Oxford without being rattled ourselves ... We were at first content to let Oxford have the ball, so that we might get into their halves and threequarters good and hard ... If we heeled, Francis at stand-off half was to kick into touch immediately, partly because our backs, lying up as they were, were out of position for attack, and partly to give those of our team new to big football a chance to settle down.' By all accounts Oxford were shaken, both physically and mentally, by the fierceness of this early Cambridge tackling, so that when Wakefield suddenly switched his tactics to all-out attack, chinks appeared in the Oxford armour and Cambridge, with their freshmen now relishing the big time, swept to victory by three goals and two tries to a goal and a try.

It was to prove an exceptionally busy and successful season for Wakefield. In the New Year he captained the RAF to victories over both the Navy and the Army in the Inter-Services Tournament — the first time they had ever achieved this feat — and he played along with Cove-Smith and Conway in the England team which won the Grand Slam in 1923.

7
From Macpherson to Aarvold

Wakefield, whose course at Cambridge lasted only those two years, had every reason to respect the 1922 Oxford backs; the division already included three members of the famous all-Oxford three-quarter line who played together for Scotland in 1924 and 1925. Phil Macpherson, who, like Ronnie Poulton, did not get into the Oxford side in his first year, had already played four games for Scotland early in 1922 by the time he got his Blue as a centre. George Aitken, one of the 1922 wings, had captained the All Blacks against the 1921 Springboks in New Zealand as a centre, and Johnnie Wallace, the other wing, had played for New South Wales against New Zealand in 1921. That, incidentally, was in the days when New South Wales represented Australia as far as international matches were concerned; and Wallace went on to captain the 1927 New South Wales touring team (The Waratahs) that defeated Ireland in Dublin and Wales in Cardiff, winning 24 of the 31 matches they played in the British Isles and France.

The fourth member of Scotland's subsequent all-Oxford threequarter line, Ian Smith, was also in residence at the University in 1922, but he was then playing soccer, having been to school at Winchester which had not taken to the oval ball. The story goes that Smith was urged to play rugby by a girlfriend and that he promptly bet his father that he would get a rugby Blue in 1923. He won his bet and went on to gain 32 caps for Scotland, three times scoring four tries in an international. In his last international season, 1933, he led a young Scotland side to the Triple Crown.

Such was the talent available to Macpherson, the 1923 captain, that he could not find a place for Aitken against Cambridge even though Aitken played three times for Scotland that season. This was largely because of the arrival as a freshman of Jake Jacob, who had built a formidable reputation at Blackheath as a very fast, swerving centre. So Jacob, who played for England later that season, got into the University side in the centre, with Smith on his wing, while Macpherson himself played centre to Wallace.

Some seasoned observers believe this was the most dashing threequarter line Oxford have ever fielded. They relied on sheer speed and combination and, if their defence was sometimes a little fragile, Macpherson's philosophy was simply that his men would score more tries than their opponents. They arrived at Twickenham unbeaten, having defeated such sides as Bristol, Leicester, Gloucester, Blackheath and Harlequins, scoring 277 points and conceding only 77 in the process.

Wallace, on the left wing, was an exceptionally neat and tricky runner with the ability to leave opponents stranded by the use of his feint and jink. There was another Australian, Tom Lawton, at stand-off half. Lawton, a Rhodes Scholar, was a big, strapping man who had played for New South Wales against the All Blacks in 1920 and had earned Blues at stand-off half in 1921 and at full-back in 1922. He was destined to play international rugby with Wallace on the Waratahs' 1927-28 tour, to captain his country against New Zealand in 1929, to play against the 1930 Lions and to face the All Blacks again in 1932, once more as captain.

In spite of this plethora of talent, victory for Oxford in the 1923 Match was by no means a foregone conclusion. This was partly because their forwards were outplayed early in the game and partly because Hamilton-Wickes, the Cambridge captain and wing threequarter, scored a try which, according to Howard Marshall, 'must rank as one of the great individual efforts of the series'. Hamilton-Wickes received the ball near the touch-line, Oxford following up to bundle him into touch. 'Pivoting swiftly, he jinked inwards, slipping two tackles, and began to run with great determination diagonally across the field. This unorthodox behaviour by a wing threequarter caught the Oxford midfield players in two minds and on the wrong foot. Running across their bows to mounting Cambridge cheers, threatening to straighten up but continuing his slanting course, Hamilton-Wickes beat one pair of clutching hands after another and flung himself triumphantly over the line on the far side of the goal-posts to score a magnificent try.' This try actually gave Cambridge a lead of 6-5 but, with the Oxford forwards eventually doing enough to allow their gifted backs to make their presence felt, Oxford finished winners by three goals and two tries to a goal, two tries and a penalty goal. Among the Oxford forwards that day was an American Rhodes Scholar, Alan Valentine, who the following year won a rare gold medal for rugby at the Olympic Games in Paris, where the United States defeated France 17-3 in the final.

Scotland's all-Oxford threequarter line never did play together in a Varsity Match. Following the omission of Aitken in 1923, Smith was unavailable in 1924 because he had not recovered from injuries sustained on the Lions tour of South Africa earlier that year. The arrangement for 1924 therefore was that Macpherson and Aitken played in the centre against Cambridge with Wallace on one wing and Jacob on the other. As far as internationals are concerned the great moment for Smith, Macpherson, Aitken and Wallace came when Scotland, captained by Macpherson, defeated England 14-11 to win both the Calcutta Cup and the Grand Slam in the first match ever played at Murrayfield, on 21 March 1925. But for injuries the quartet would have played more than five times together as Scotland's threequarter line. As it was, they amassed between them 82 Scotland caps.

At Oxford, Macpherson has always been venerated in much the same way as Ronnie Poulton. Sir Andrew Noble wrote of him: 'He had a dancing swerve and side-step that often made it appear that the defence was getting out of his way, as Poulton, in a different way, had done in his day; this drew the defence towards him, and he timed his passes beautifully.' Even E.H.D. Sewell, who was hard to please, said: 'In his best years he was a nailing good attacking centre because he was a thinking one, with the natural ability and quick wit to translate thought into action.' Howard Marshall, too, laid emphasis on Macpherson's value as a thinker: 'His contribution to Oxford rugby was great, and always there was evident behind his play an exceptionally keen intelligence. He was another of the theorists, like Stoop and Wakefield, and he worked out the possibilities of midfield attack with the calculating precision of a watchmaker. Only the most observant and knowledgeable spectator could appreciate to the full the chessboard subtlety of Macpherson's moves in attack or defence. A beautiful and most gifted player, worth his place in any company'.

It says much for the direction the Universities gave rugby in the British Isles in these post-War years that Oxford in 1924 had in residence 13 players who were or were to be internationals, including two complete sets of threequarters. It also says much for Cambridge that in the Varsity Match they held Oxford to a score of a goal and two tries to two tries. In doing so, Cambridge owed a great deal to the instinctive understanding of their well-tried half-backs, Young and Francis. These two had played together as schoolboys at Tonbridge and they were now in their third year in the Cambridge side. Young had played for England and had been on the 1924 Lions' tour of South Africa. E.H.D. Sewell said of him: 'a real box o' tricks type, as slippery as an eel, with a tiger's courage. In every respect one of the game's greatest scrum-halves'. He went on to win 18 England caps. Francis played for England four times, but as a centre, Young's stand-off half on those four occasions being the Oxford 1924 stand-off, Kittermaster.

It was thanks to the combined running of Young and Francis that Cambridge scored the opening try of the 1924 Varsity Match. Almost immediately, however, Oxford got the ball out to Macpherson who 'feinted and swerved like a ballet dancer through the centre' before giving a scoring pass to Jacob. Many years later Howard Marshall wrote: 'I can see Macpherson now, with his head up and that jigging run of his, melting past the clutching Cambridge hands, and whenever he had the ball Cambridge were in mortal peril.' In fact he made another try for Jacob before the match was over. While Oxford had eight actual or future internationals in their 1924 side, Cambridge had ten. These included wing threequarter Rowe Harding, who won seven caps for Wales before earning his Blue, and forward Bill Tucker, whose leadership in 1925 was to initiate four consecutive Cambridge victories in the Varsity Match. Tucker's men made sure that Oxford's Macpherson era was well and truly at an end, for in the 1925 Match they scored nine tries and won the game 33-3, which in modern scoring values would represent 42-4. Yet Oxford still had Jacob, now captain, and Wallace in their threequarter line, and boasted five Old Blues in their pack to Cambridge's three. Moreover they had acquired a very talented and experienced full-back in Dan Drysdale, who had already played 12 times for Scotland and who had been on the 1924 Lions' tour of South Africa, playing in all four Tests against the Springboks.

Strong, Oxford's scrum-half, really should not have played in this match — he had a shoulder injury which slowed his passing. This slowness must have been all the more marked considering that Cambridge had discovered Wilf Sobey, who was soon recognised as one of the quickest passing scrum-halves of his time. It cannot be a coincidence that in the two Varsity Matches in which Sobey played Cambridge scored 17 tries. He was to play for England and to tour New Zealand and Australia with the 1930 Lions, though an injury on tour cut short his career.

The main reason for Oxford's shattering defeat, however, was that Tucker got his team, and especially his forwards, on to the pitch at Twickenham in exactly the right frame of mind. He and his pack rampaged about the field with infectious confidence from the start, and Oxford became demoralised. Devitt, on the wing, scored three of Cambridge's nine tries. Wavell Wakefield asserted that it was only in this match that the coaching and organisation effected in his day really began to bear fruit. If Oxford men thought this startling upsurge in Cambridge fortunes might be a flash in the pan, they were in for a shock on 14 December 1926. With a wet ball Oxford scored the first points of the game with a try which was converted, and Cambridge led by no more than a goal and a try to a goal at half-time. In the second half, however, Cambridge ran riot, scoring six more tries, and won by 30-5. Thus in two consecutive Varsity Matches Cambridge scored a total of 17 tries to Oxford's two.

The architects of this handsome 1926 victory were the Cambridge half-backs. Sobey had now been joined by Windsor Lewis, already a Welsh cap, and the stand-off half's quick eye for an opening and his subtle changes of direction thoroughly bemused the Oxford defence. It was the genius of Windsor Lewis that created the first Cambridge try when he slid deftly through the

Oxford midfield, and he himself scored the second by wafting his way between the defenders. Thereafter his constant probing destroyed Oxford's confidence, so that openings were created for the rest of the tries.

Rhodes Scholars had always been a boon to Oxford because, in most instances, they were older, stronger, more experienced and more mature than the home-bred product, having already been to a university in their home countries. But did Cambridge reap the benefit of a backlash? Wavell always maintained that the presence of Rhodes Scholars at Oxford led many schoolmasters to encourage their best players to go to Cambridge, where their path to a Blue would not be blocked by seasoned men from overseas. Wakefield held, in particular, that this was the explanation

Left: A.T. Young of Cambridge, 'as slippery as an eel, with a tiger's courage', went on to win 18 caps for England.

Right: The teams poised for battle in 1928. The Match was by this time firmly established at its present home, Twickenham.

behind the arrival at Cambridge of so many talented Welshmen in the 1920s and 1930s. Cambridge certainly owed a great deal to Windsor Lewis in 1926 — and indeed for many, many years thereafter as an advisor — and by 1927 five of the seven Cambridge backs were Welshmen. Four of those five — Windsor Lewis, Morgan in the centre, Rowe Harding, the captain, on the wing, and Roberts, the full-back — had already played for Wales, and centre Harry Bowcott was soon to do so.

Oxford this year welcomed a formidable recruit. The great John Bannerman, who had already played 28 games in Scotland's pack and who was to play in all Scotland's matches between 1921 and 1929, winning 37 caps in total, came into residence at the University on a two-year course in agricultural economics. Probably because of his experienced presence the Oxford forwards gave a far more convincing display than in the previous two years with the result that they scored the same number of tries, four, as Cambridge. Oxford, however, gave away two penalty goals, and Cambridge eventually won by 22-14, despite being handicapped by an injury which deprived them of Sobey. This and the improved performance of the Oxford forwards meant that Windsor Lewis had far fewer opportunities than the year before. All the same, with little more than a quarter of an hour to go and with only three points between the sides, Windsor Lewis received a pass from a line-out and ran so deceptively that he created a timely and vital try.

The Oxford forwards, with Bannerman still exerting much influence, put up another grand fight in 1928, but could not prevent Cambridge achieving a fourth consecutive victory, albeit by the narrow margin of 14-10. Cambridge this year were captained by Carl Aarvold, the England and 1930 Lions threequarter, who was in his fourth year in the side. He thus achieved the distinction of playing in four winning teams in the Varsity Match. (The only other player to have

THE FIFTY-THIRD STRUGGLE OF THE BLUES UNDER THE RUGBY CO

*J. W. G. HUME
Mill Hill and Merton (½ back)

H. H. TURCAN
Rugby and Trinity (½ back)

N. M. S. MACPHERSON
Fettes and Trinity (½ back)

J. A. ADAMSON
Durham and Keble (back)

*J. M. BANNERMAN
Glasgow High School and Balliol (f.)

E. T. BENSON
Blundell's and Merton (½ back)

W. ROBERTS
Cardiff High School and Brasenose (½

*E. G. TAYLOR (Captain)
Loretto and Trinity (½ back)

S. HOFMEYR
Cape Town and University (forward)

P. C. HORDERN
Brighton and Wadham (forward)

*T. W. GUBB
Grahamstown and University (forwa

A. E. C. PRESCOTT
Marlborough and Christ Church (forward)

M. J. B. MOLOHAN
Cheltenham and Trinity (forward)

A. G. CRIDLAN
Uppingham and Worcester (forward)

D. S. TROUP
Uppingham and St John's (forward

THE OXFORD UNIVERSITY FIFTEEN.

This week saw the fifty-third Rugby encounter between the Universities of Oxford and Cambridge, and pictures of last Tuesday's play at Twicken ham will be found on page 725. Up to this year Oxford had won 23 matches and Cambridge 20, 9 being drawn. For the last three year Cambridge has proved successful. The Cambridge side was this year made up of eight Old Blues, while the Oxford team had four, these player

*A gallery of Blues published during the
build-up to the 1928 Match.*

60

THIS WEEK'S OXFORD AND CAMBRIDGE TEAMS AT TWICKENHAM.

*J. ROBERTS
H. Sch. and St. Catharine's (back)

R. SMEDDLE
Durham and St. Catharine's (¾ back)

*W. G. MORGAN
Christ's, Brecon and St. Catharine's (¾ b.)

F. M. HEYWOOD
Haileybury and Caius (¾ back)

*G. M. BOWCOTT
H. Sch. and St. Catharine's (½ b.)

C. E. M. WIGGINS
Mill Hill and Trinity (½ back)

*G. R. COGHLAN
Rugby and Clare (forward)

*G. A. McILWAINE
ndrew's, S.A. and Selwyn (f.)

*P. T. COOPER
Marlborough and Caius (forward)

*F. H. WATERS
Loretto and Pembroke (forward)

*C. D. AARVOLD (Captain)
Durham and Emmanuel (¾ back)

D. CRICHTON-MILLER
ettos and Pembroke (forward)

A. M. DIXON
Dulwich and Clare (forward)

J. J. A. EMBLETON
St. Paul's and Caius (forward)

F. W. P. BROOK
Whitgift and Emmanuel (forward)

WINNERS BY 14 POINTS TO 10 : THE CAMBRIDGE UNIVERSITY FIFTEEN.

marked on the above pages by an asterisk against their names. Although it is fifty-seven years ago since this Inter-University match was instituted, the
had been played for many years previously at both Universities. This season the Light Blues had given promise of obtaining a fourth consecutive
y. It was felt that Oxford's best chance was on heavy ground, but that with a dry ball Cambridge would very probably score again.

equalled this feat was Grant-Asher, the Oxford half-back, in the years from 1881 to 1884.) In his first Varsity Match Aarvold played in the centre, in his second at full-back, and in his third on the wing. He reverted to the wing for the 1928 Match, a game remembered chiefly for the brilliant start made by Cambridge and for Oxford's gallant fight-back which all but turned the tide. It was largely thanks to the dashing play of Aarvold that Cambridge scored three tries in the first quarter of an hour, enough to demoralise most opponents. Bannerman, however, led rush after rush for Oxford as they battled their way back into the match. Smeddle, Aarvold's Durham partner on the wing, scored three of the four Cambridge tries, and his captain the other.

Thus Aarvold, who was capped 16 times for England and later knighted, established a winning record which has not been bettered this century. All of which is perhaps a little surprising for a man who decided to go to Cambridge only in his final term at school, and hadn't given any thought to playing rugby there. He explains, 'I played rugby at Durham, and having had a very good coach I suppose I learned some of the tricks of the game. I hadn't come to Cambridge with any idea of playing rugby, the idea was to come up to learn what life was about. Then I had the sheer good fortune to play in the Freshmen's Match and I had a write-up in *The Times*. It was enough to make one laugh oneself stupid and of course to mistrust journalists from that day on, but it was quite a good write-up and a couple of days later I was asked to go up to Grange Road to practise with the Cambridge side'. Suddenly the North Country lad found himself at centre in the Cambridge side, travelling up to London to play the likes of Harlequins, all of which proved tremendously exciting for the young Aarvold. As the first Varsity Match approached he was enjoying himself so much that he refused to be overawed by the occasion, and regarded playing for the side as one of the luxuries of being at Cambridge. 'In the first game I was playing in the centre with Tim Francis, who had all kinds of odd code-words for different moves. For example, when he shouted "bananas" it meant that the fly-half was going to shoot off to the right as if he were going to take the pass from the scrum-half. The opposition naturally thought the ball was going to go that way but instead Wilf Sobey would flick the ball to Tim Francis, who was going the other way. It was all good fun but it worked.'

Aarvold was to score the first of his three Varsity Match tries in that first game, something which he maintains owed much to the reputation of his wing partner, Rowe Harding. 'He was a magnificent wing, very speedy, and he had already played for Wales. Oxford had come up with the idea that Harding was the man to watch and that we would play to him. But suddenly the ball came out of the scrum and shot to Colin Bishop at fly-half. Rowe Harding was on the wing outside me, and the whole of the Oxford team, sensing that Rowe was the danger-man, shot for the touch-line to stop him scoring. They had forgotten that miserable little Aarvold was hanging about in the centre with the ball in his hands, not knowing quite what to do. Suddenly I looked ahead and there was no one there, so really all I had to do was to walk over the line to score. For a chap playing in his first Varsity Match to score in the first ten minutes was a bit of a boost, while poor old Rowe had the whole of the Oxford side round his shoulders and didn't know what the hell was happening. It was tremendous good fortune as far as I was concerned.'

Oxford had lost their whole Scottish international threequarter line, while Cambridge had some fine players. Apart from Harding on the wing and Francis as his centre partner, there was the half-back partnership of Sobey and Bishop. 'Sobey was a magnificent scrum-half, tough and wiry, quite superb. He had the misfortune to wreck his knee in the first match against New Zealand when we went on tour. Bishop was also first-class and we had Tom Devitt on the wing who I think is still the only wing threequarter to have scored three tries in a Varsity Match. Skipper Bill Tucker was a superb enthusiast. I remember going up to Grange Road to practise before one match. It was one of those days when the snow was falling heavily and the pitch was covered in about six inches of snow. We couldn't go out to practise, and old Bill was dejected but he said "never mind, we'll go to the Caius ground because I know there'll be no snow there". "But Bill", we said, "that's only 100 yards away." "Never mind", he said, "we'll go", and we did — but of course we couldn't play there either.'

In his second year Aarvold became secretary of the side but during the course of the term he did not play well and found himself dropped from the team. The last fixture before the Varsity Match was against a side led by Jenny Greenwood, including the legendary Wavell Wakefield. During the match the Cambridge full-back, Witham, was injured and because it was a friendly game the Cambridge skipper 'Punch' Barlow was allowed to bring on a replacement in the shape of Spencer Block. But at the beginning of the second half he too was injured, and in desperation the skipper asked Aarvold to come on at full-back, a position he had never played in his life. 'In the course of that half, old Wavell came roaring up with the ball at his feet and kicked it ahead, but it went a little too far. I still believe that he did it on purpose because the thing came bouncing up to me at full-back. It bounced into my hands and not really knowing what to do I set off running. Barry Cumberlege was the opposing full-back and I knew he would go steaming out to the touch-line and then come back inside. I saw him head off towards the touch-line so I promptly changed direction. There was no one in the way and I scored a try from well inside my own half. I was quite lucky, but as a result Punch put me at full-back for the Varsity Match even though I'd played less than half a game there!'

Left: Carl Aarvold, the England and 1930 British Lions threequarter, who played in four winning Varsity Matches for Cambridge, captaining them in his last year.

Aarvold's second Varsity Match was a quite different affair from the first. To begin with it was a horrible day, pouring with rain, and Oxford put the first points on the board. 'Oxford were pressing close to our line and the ball came out to one of their forwards, Taffy Landale. There was only me between him and the line so I hurled myself at his feet. I got a boot on my nose for my trouble and he went over to score a try. I stayed at full-back with a broken nose and blood pouring down me, wet and perishing cold. For the rest of the game I saw the ball only once when someone kicked it to me and I kicked it back into touch.' Oxford's domination of the Match gained them six tries, and they won 30-5.

For his third Blue Aarvold found himself in yet another position in the Cambridge line-up. Captain Rowe Harding had two good centres in Bowcott and Morgan, so Aarvold was played out on the wing. Although he had had only a couple of outings there, he didn't really mind where he played at this stage as long as he was in the team. 'Sobey had been injured a couple of games before the 1927 Varsity Match and we were all very depressed about that, but it never occurred to me that we might lose. We had Windsor Lewis, who was quite a fly-half. We had a damned good side and were on top for most of the game. I scored but I don't remember much more about it.'

For Aarvold's last match, in 1928, he had been made captain, leading a side which he considered to be as good as any. They lost only one match prior to the Varsity Match, and even that defeat, by Swansea, was a quirk of fate. As captain he was able to revert to his favourite position of centre, but picking the team from the talent available posed its problems. 'I had a number of wings to choose from, including Bill Smeddle, who came up from Durham where I had been. I was in a slightly delicate position because it must have looked like favouritism to a lot of people, but he was a damned fine player who fitted in marvellously so I put him in. On the other wing was Bartlett, who had played for Wales the year before, but I had my eye on a chap named George Heywood, whom I thought was first-class and who again fitted superbly into the side. So I picked him in preference to the Welsh international, and they both proved to be excellent performers.

'It was a very tight match, but we really started off with a roar. I think, left to our own devices, we would have put up a record score but, rightly or wrongly, I felt the Oxford scrum-half came round offside practically the whole of the ruddy game and there was nothing I could do about it. Tommy Vile, the referee, was a dear fellow and I travelled all over the place with him but he did like a rugby match to be a close thing not a runaway affair. This was obviously going to be a runaway affair; so I think he was a little lax in stopping the chap coming round and waiting for us to heel it — I thought he was miles offside. It never occurred to us that it was going to be an easy contest. The Oxford side had two damned good centres in Joe Hume, who was a Scottish international, and Henry Turcan. Towards the end, when things were getting a little tight, we really had to put in everything we had. I think I tackled old Joe Hume by hurling myself at him and hitting him just in the right place. It must have taken all the wind out of him — it did me! Towards the end there was a very great danger that we were going to lose and I think everybody put the sort of effort into their tackles that I had put in myself. But I feel it would have been most unfair if we had lost.' Thus Aarvold scored a try in his final match and had the satisfaction of seeing his gamble of playing his Durham colleague Smeddle on the wing pay off. Smeddle scored a hat-trick in the 14-10 victory and was selected for England soon afterwards, while Aarvold's name went into the record books for his four successive wins.

8
Varsity Rugby in the Vanguard

At this time the Varsity Match was seen very much as an extra national trial, such was the proven ability of the Universities to produce talented players; to coach them, to help them reach an unrivalled peak of fitness, and to encourage them to apply their intelligence in devising and implementing fresh methods and tactics. The England side of 1924, for instance, included five consecutive Cambridge captains — Conway, Cove-Smith, Wakefield, Hamilton-Wickes and Young. Nor was it only England selectors who gathered at Twickenham for Varsity Matches: following Scotland's all-Oxford threequarter line of 1924-25, there were three current Welsh caps in the Cambridge team of 1934 — Wilf Wooller, Cliff Jones and Arthur Rees. Such was the attraction of Oxford for young men from outside England that there were only four Englishmen in Oxford's 1929 side, and in 1932 the seven Oxford backs comprised a South African, a New Zealander, a Welshman, an Irishman, an Australian and two Scots — not an Englishman among them. And it was no coincidence that when Oxford at last turned the tide of four consecutive Cambridge victories, in 1929, there were five Rhodes Scholars in the Oxford pack and two more in the backs. In addition Roberts, the stand-off half, had by now been capped by Wales. Oxford won that 1929 game only 9-0, but this was the start of a sequence in which they were to remain undefeated in the Varsity Match for five years, from 1929 to 1933. The only check to Oxford's winning progress in those five years was a draw in 1930, the first draw in the fixture since 1908.

Even draws can be exciting, however, and this one in 1930 is remembered as a grand match, given spice by three particularly notable moments. The first incident came after John Tallent, the Cambridge centre, later to play for England, had raced through for a try near the Oxford posts. At this time the man taking a conversion kick had to have the ball placed for him by another member of his side. The placer would hold the ball just above the ground until the kicker was ready to run up. Opponents were not allowed to charge until the placer had put the ball down on to the ground. In this instance there was confusion as to whether Simpson, the Cambridge scrum-half and placer, had put the ball down. Oxford thought he had, and so they charged out from the goal-line. Williams, the Cambridge kicker, did not think so, and he therefore stood back, waiting for the referee to disallow the Oxford charge. The referee, Bob Jeffares of Ireland, agreed with Oxford, who continued their charge and booted the ball upfield. Since the final score of the match was only 3-3, the two conversion points that went by default could have made all the difference.

The second memorable feature was the manner in which Oxford acquired their three points. Smeddle, playing on the wing for Cambridge in his third Varsity Match, was caught in possession and then penalised for lying on the ball. The kick was from the touch-line and well into the second half on a typically gloomy Twickenham afternoon in December, but Chook Henley, a forward and a Rhodes Scholar from New Zealand, sent the ball cleanly over the crossbar. The third talking point was that later, with Cambridge on the attack, the referee inadvertently blew the whistle for no-side eight minutes early.

This match marked the Varsity debut of Vivian Jenkins, who played for three years in the Oxford centre, although he was to make a wider reputation as an international full-back and a rugby writer. A product of Llandovery School, which had a tradition of Oxford Blues, he went up to the 'Welsh' College, Jesus, to study Classics with an eye to getting a Blue. Jenkins was given a taste of Oxford tradition upon his arrival. 'There was a scout, who was like a valet or batman, and he used to look after every floor of undergraduates and would bring tea in the morning and a jug of hot water to wash in. I remember our old scout, Hatton, telling me that the room I was in used to belong to Alban Davies, who later became a reverend and led the Welsh pack which became known as the "terrible eight". I felt it a great honour to have the same room as this chap.' At school Jenkins had been keener on rugby than on cricket, and in the holidays he had played for Bridgend. At 17 he had already faced several Welsh clubs. Although he had played scrum-half, stand-off half and centre at school he had a hankering for the full-back position and indeed had had a Welsh Schools trial in that position.

Once at Oxford he put his name down for the Freshmen's trials at full-back. 'There were about 80 players in all and there were two matches. The one in which I played was won 35-3 by our side and I don't think I touched the ball once. I then went back to college and didn't hear anything for a month. Well, the term was only eight weeks long, so when Bridgend came up to play the Greyhounds, Oxford's reserve XV, I played for them. In those days if you couldn't get into the Varsity side you could play for any club and I'd already played for London Welsh a few times. So I played against the Oxford side for Bridgend. Anyway, we beat them and I must have had a good game because about a week later I had an invitation to play for the Greyhounds.'

One of the Varsity centres at the time was Tommy Hart who, although a freshman, had already been capped by Scotland. However, he was injured, and Jenkins was invited to play. 'I think my first game was against the Old Alleynians, a 16-16 draw. The next match was against Blackheath and I was marking Carl Aarvold. We beat them by 30-odd points and my wing scored three tries.' But Jenkins didn't make the line-up for the Stanley match, because Tommy Hart was to be tried once again. In those days one was invited to play in the Varsity Match a month before the game, although one didn't actually become a Blue until one had played the game. Hart was injured once again and was destined never to pick up that elusive Blue.

'I remember the secretary, Bill Roberts, and skipper Steve Hofmeyr coming to me one autumn night to ask me if I would go down to Eastbourne with the team on the off-chance that Hart wouldn't be able to play. It was one of the greatest moments of my life: after they had gone I walked around the college quad in the dark for about 20 minutes clenching my fists to the stars before I eventually calmed down and climbed the staircase to my room.' It was traditional for the Oxford team to go down to Eastbourne on the Thursday before the Varsity Match for a change of scene and a change of air. On one occasion the air almost proved too much as Jenkins and Percy Minns decided to save some money by accepting a lift in a car belonging to a flanker called Kelly. 'It was a cold night in December and the car was an open tourer. We arrived there at tea-time and were so cold that we went up and got into a hot bath and sat there for two hours to thaw out.'

Members of the 1935 Cambridge team enjoy a moment of relaxation during the Varsity Match build-up on the sea front at Brighton.

The players had to pay for themselves and in the 1930s a few nights at the Grand Hotel meant a hefty bill. 'I think the hotel bill was five pounds — which was a colossal amount of money in those days, probably the equivalent of £200 today. I got it from somewhere, I think I borrowed it from an uncle. We trained at the Eastbourne College school ground, and they provided a pack of forwards, but really the trip was more for relaxation. We'd been training for months, with two or three games a week; it was very intense. Every generation that comes through says that they didn't train in the old days like they do now. We said the same about the people who played 50 years before us. We used to practise scrummaging and line-outs but always worked with the ball. In the threequarters we would practise quick passing, trying to get the ball to the wing when he was in midfield, not on the touch-line. We trained every day, so when we went down to Eastbourne we used to relax and play rounds of golf at the Eastbourne club. We always stayed at the Grand Hotel, which had become famous on radio through Tom Jones and his Palm Court orchestra. The hotel was luxurious; I'd never seen a hotel like it and I'd never seen a meal with so many courses which cost so much money. It was 12/6d — the most expensive meal I'd seen anywhere. No one told us anything about diet and we were young, so we just got stuck in. We did have to go to bed early, but all that sea air made us tired anyway for the first few days.'

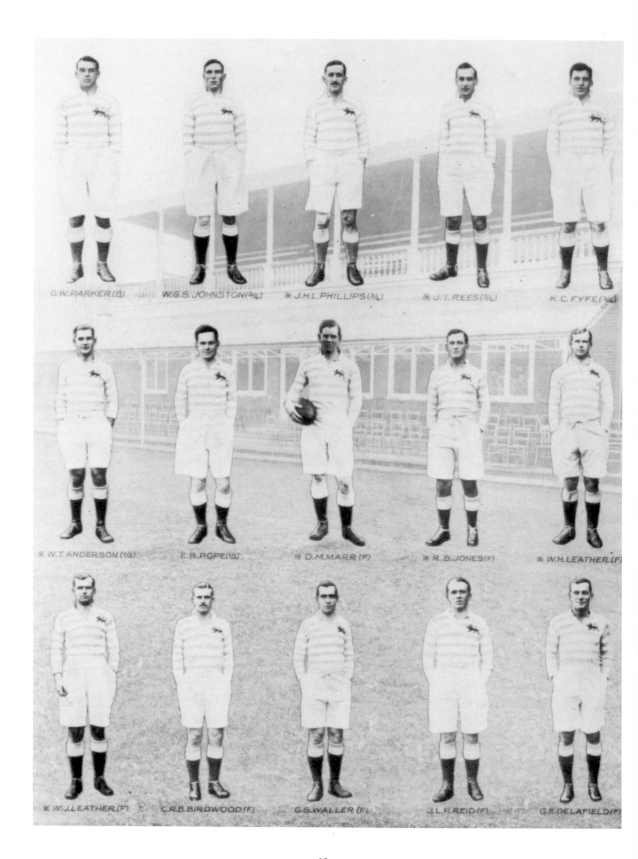

G.W. PARKER (8)   W.G.S. JOHNSTON (3/4)   J.H.L. PHILLIPS (3/4)   J.I. REES (3/4)   K.C. FYFE (3/4)

W.T. ANDERSON (1/2)   E.B. POPE (1/2)   D.M. MARR (F)   R.B. JONES (F)   W.H. LEATHER (F)

W.J. LEATHER (F)   C.R.B. BIRDWOOD (F)   G.S. WALLER (F)   J.L.R. REID (F)   G.E. DELAFIELD (F)

H.G. OWEN-SMITH (B)   ✳ V.G.J. JENKINS (¾)   H.O.B. LORRAINE (¾)   ✳ P.C. MINNS (¾)   S.L. WAIDE (¾)

K.L.T. JACKSON (½)   ✳ N.K. LAMPORT (½)   C.A.L. RICHARDS (F)   ✳ E.S. NICHOLSON (F)   M.F. PEACOCK (F)

A.E.S. CHARLES (F)   ✳ K.W.J. JONES (F)   R.E. PRESCOTT (F)   J.B. BOWERS (F)   H.M. KELLY (F)

On the Monday the team would get the train up to London and spend the night before the match in the Richmond Hill Hotel. 'I remember the newspapers being full of the match — it was one of the greatest thrills of my life to be chosen for the Varsity team. The following day we got into Rolls Royces decked out with dark and light blue ribbons to go to the match. As for the game itself, I remember it as being very fast — not as tough as other matches, but twice as fast as any international because we'd been training so hard and it meant so much.'

In that first game, which ended in a 3-3 draw, Jenkins well remembers Tallent scoring the first try for Cambridge and then the legendary mix-up over the conversion. 'Williams was to take the kick and Frank Simpson was to hold it for him. In those days you couldn't charge till the ball had been placed on the ground. Well, we charged because we believed that the ball had been put down but Williams just stood there as much as to say "don't be silly, it hasn't been put down." The referee, Jeffares, allowed play to go on so we booted it away and the try went unconverted. I had a letter from Williams a year or two ago, and it was obvious that the incident had worried him for the rest of his life. In it he said that he couldn't believe a man like Simpson, with whom he'd done all his goal-kicking, would ever have put the ball down without being told to do so.'

Even though the result was only a draw the scale of the celebrations was immense. They began with dinner at an exclusive restaurant, each team dining separately. 'It was just the 15 players, the touch-judge and Tommy Vile, who used to come up from Wales not to coach us but to criticise us. He would come to watch a couple of games during term and then give a long seminar telling us what we should and shouldn't do. We learned a tremendous amount. Every one of us had a magnum of champagne, and personally I had never had a drink before. Hardly anybody finished the meal and there was a hell of a row from the RFU later because the bill came to £147.'

The team then went to the theatre and there proceeded to wreak havoc. Apparently the done thing among the students was to try to stop the show, so when barracking didn't achieve this two of the students stood up in the aisle and staged a mock fight, which seemed to do the trick. Then it was on to the Park Lane Hotel to meet up with the opposition, and the following day Oxford travelled up to Scotland for a tour.

Oxford continued to benefit from the presence of gifted recruits from overseas, particularly in their back division, and in 1931 fielded one of their most multinational threequarter lines. The

England wing R.W. Smeddle opens the scoring for Cambridge in the 1931 game but Oxford's talented threequarter line eventually secured a 10–3 victory.

Previous page: The line-up for the 1932 encounter.

centres were Welsh and South African, and the wings a New Zealander and an American. Vivian Jenkins' partner in the Oxford centre in 1931 was Stanley Osler, a brother of the famous Springbok stand-off half and captain, Bennie Osler. The two brothers had played together for South Africa against the touring All Blacks in 1928, but when Bennie Osler brought his 1931-32 Springboks to Iffley Road, the brothers played against each other. Stanley, a Rhodes Scholar, was a tricky runner but prone to injury. He missed three Tests against the All Blacks in 1928; he was hurt in Oxford's match against his brother's Springboks, and an injury in the 1931 Varsity Match put an end to his playing career.

Both the wings were Rhodes Scholars. Percy Minns hailed from Auckland University, and Frederick Hovde was an American Footballer from the University of Minnesota, who threw the ball in from touch torpedo-style·with a flick of the wrist. To add to the multinational flavour of the Oxford backs, Roberts, the Welsh international, was still at stand-off half — and in his fourth year was captain — and the scrum-half, Lamport, was yet another Rhodes Scholar, this time from Sydney.

The Cambridge backs of 1931 included three current England internationals; Askew at full-back, Smeddle on the wing, and Tallent in the centre, while the other centre, Idwal Rees, subsequently won 14 caps for Wales. Cambridge scored first at Twickenham, Smeddle racing for a try after a break by Tallent, but Roberts, running, passing and kicking cleverly, took charge of Oxford's tactics. His short, diagonal punt made a try for Minns, and then he dropped the goal which gave Oxford a half-time lead. Both sides attacked and tackled with all they had in a stirring second half, but the only further score was a try for Oxford by Hovde after a Cambridge attack had broken down.

Vivian Jenkins collected his second Blue in this game and recalls the tremendous performance by Bill Roberts. 'He dropped a goal, about the only one he scored in his life, I think, and scored a try and made a lot of marvellous runs. I played centre to Percy Minns, a very good, hard-running wing from New Zealand, who still holds the record of six tries in a Ranfurly Shield match, which he set against Southland before he came to Oxford. In that side we had the American Freddie Hovde on the wing. I couldn't understand why everyone got so excited about the appearance of Dawkins, "the yank at Oxford" in 1959, because all this had happened 30 years earlier with Hovde. He was an all-American quarterback who could throw the ball from one side of the pitch to the other. He wasn't all that big, but a brilliant runner. He later became head of Perdue University. Adrian Stoop refereed one game in which Hovde played and saw him making these long passes. After the game Stoop went out on to the pitch with a ball. He came back into the pavilion a little later and went up to Freddie. "Ah, Hovde, I can see how you do that now, I've got the idea", he said. Freddie replied: "Well done, Mr Stoop, you're mighty quick. You got it in 20 minutes whereas it took me eight years."'

It was in 1932 that Oxford discovered one of their great full-backs, Tuppy Owen-Smith. He was a Rhodes Scholar from Cape Town who had always played stand-off half at home. Indeed, when he arrived at Oxford, he was best known as a cricketer and a boxer. He had toured England with the South African cricket team in 1929 at the age of 20 and had played in all five Tests, making a century at Headingley. He won cricket and boxing Blues in his first year, 1931, but only came on to the rugby scene when he helped to make up the numbers for a Greyhounds tour of Germany. Having begun his career at full-back in Germany, he went on to play in two Varsity Matches, won ten England caps in this position and, in 1937, captained England to their first-ever win at Murrayfield, a victory which gave them the Triple Crown. He was still in England at that time, continuing his medical studies at St Mary's Hospital after leaving Oxford.

The great Vivian Jenkins gets the ball away to his Oxford wing partner, S.L. Waide, despite having taken a tumble in the 1932 Match.

Viv Jenkins says, 'Tuppy and I played cricket together at Oxford in my final term. I used to keep wicket and he used to field at cover point and would throw in at me like a bullet. I remember playing against him at Twickenham, when I was full-back for Wales and he was full-back for England. It was 0-0 at half-time and we had been trying to outdo each other all half. As the referee blew to start the second half I happened to catch his eye across the pitch from about 30 yards away. He threw his lemon at me exactly as he would have done from cover point and I caught the thing like a wicketkeeper, then off we went to play like hell for the second half.'

Owen-Smith was a small man but wiry and very strong. Howard Marshall wrote of him: 'He had an instinctive positional sense and beautifully sure hands. His boxer's footwork, his quick intelligence and cool head enabled him to escape from the most threatening situations with almost casual care. Although he was not heavily built, he was wonderfully tough and could take any amount of punishment. Oxford never had a more reliable player at full-back.' He played a prominent part in keeping Cambridge at bay in the 1932 Varsity Match which Oxford won by a goal and a try to a try.

And in 1933 Owen-Smith was the chief reason why Cambridge did not win. Vivian Jenkins, writing nearly 50 years after the event and with a lifetime of watching international rugby all over the world behind him, said this of Owen-Smith's performance that day: 'The 1933 match was the first after I had gone down, and it featured what I still regard as the finest exhibition of classical full-back play I have seen. Cambridge attacked for three-quarters of the match but lost 3-5, almost entirely because of a superlative display by Owen-Smith for Oxford. Time and again he

The tall, long-striding Cambridge centre Wilf Wooller, who was capped by Wales while still at Rydal School. Wooller dropped one of the most colossal goals ever seen at Twickenham during the 1934 Varsity Match.

cleared his lines with glorious spiralling touch-kicks of 50 yards and more, his catching was immaculate, and his tackling saved at least a couple of tries.' It was just as well for Oxford, who won this Varsity Match by no more than a goal to a try, that their full-back had the game of his life. For Cambridge that year had nine actual or future internationals in their side, among them those two great Welsh backs, Wilf Wooller and Cliff Jones.

Wooller, a tall, long-striding centre, had been capped by his country while he was still at school, so he joins the select band of players who were capped before earning their Blues. Howard Marshall wrote of him: 'Wooller was beyond doubt one of the outstanding centre threequarters in the history of the Varsity Match, with his tremendous pace and stride and his siege-gun kicking, and his ability to win a game on his own by some sudden gargantuan thrust'. Wooller began his rugby at Rydal School, Colwyn Bay, as a forward, which is hardly surprising since he was over six feet tall. But after a while his headmaster said: 'Wooller you're too fast for a forward, you'd better move into the backs and learn to pass the ball'. He was hoping to go up to Cambridge in 1932, at the age of 18, but there was, he remembers, a slight obstacle. 'Unfortunately you had to have Latin to get in in those days and I was hopeless at it. So I had to stay on at school for an extra year to concentrate on Latin.' Thus, instead of winning a Blue, he became one of the very few schoolboys to win a Welsh cap.

Because his school was in a predominantly soccer area, Wooller went off to play senior rugby at Sale where his cousin played. Upon making the first team he found himself alongside Welsh international Claude Davey. Davey became something of a mentor to the young Wooller, who had already distinguished himself for the Welsh Schoolboys in a North versus South match, earning praise for his performance in the *Western Mail*. Davey drew the attention of the Welsh selectors to Wooller, adding that if they weren't quick England would snap him up — he qualified to play for England. He was duly brought down for a final trial at Swansea, where he had an extremely good game for the Possibles, and was promptly promoted into the Welsh team to face England at Twickenham. Wales had never won at Headquarters, and it had become a bit of a 'bogey' ground for them. The 1933 match proved to be a momentous occasion as Wales won there for the first time, and Wooller went on to play in all the internationals that season.

He managed to overcome his problems with Latin and went up to Cambridge in 1933. The future looked bright for Wooller, but unfortunately there was a cloud on the horizon. 'I was injured playing for Sale in the Manchester Sevens and ended up with water on the knee. It was badly handled by a local doctor — if I'd had proper treatment I would've been back on the field in three weeks. Instead I was laid up and my muscles atrophied. Consequently, when I went up to Cambridge I was very slow. In fact I was very fortunate to make enough impact to get into the Cambridge side, whereupon my muscle strength did start to improve.' But the cloud had a silver lining, which was to make Wooller an even better player than he had been when capped for Wales. 'I had always been very fast and was able to make breaks and get away with it without letting the ball do the work. But because I'd slowed up by the time I arrived at Cambridge this method wouldn't really work any more. Fortunately we had a very good coach in Windsor Lewis, who concentrated on back play. We had to give and take a pass in two strides, running flat out, and get the ball to the wing before his opposite number could get to him. So the back play was of a very high standard and I learned how to give and take a pass. That part of my game improved and it became really important. Being at University made all the difference to my career, because it turned me from an individual into a team player. It also taught me how to train other people.'

It should be remembered that certain aspects of play were quite different in those days. For instance, the offside law stated only that the opposition had to stay behind the ball. So at a scrum, the flankers and threequarters were often on top of their opponents as soon as they got the ball. 'The secret was to get the hooker to heel the ball straight back as quickly as he could and the scrum-half had to be very fast to get it out. The outside half had to be taking the ball flat out and the ball had to be moved along the backs quickly. In a tight game like an international or a Varsity Match one had only two or three scoring chances and so the passing and backing-up had to be perfect. That was the pattern of play and there's no shadow of a doubt that the backs of pre-War days were very much more direct and very much faster in their giving and taking of a pass. They had to rely on being able to beat a man with speed, swerve and side-step.'

Wooller's centre partner, Cliff Jones, proved to be a master at all three. The pair used to train together at Cambridge, using spikes on a cinder track behind the pavilion to improve their speed as well as working on drills to help them beat a player. 'Cliff was really a superb player and could jink his way through a whole pack of forwards. I remember once he was jinking about in a match against South Africa when two great forwards came to sandwich him. He stepped out of it like a ballet dancer and they both crashed together and fell to the ground, much to the amusement of the crowd.'

Wooller had seen his first Varsity Match in 1932, the year before he went up, and had been struck by the pace and intensity of the contest and the 'do-or-die' attitude. By going up to Cambridge, he was entering a fitness and training regime which was decades ahead of both club and international rugby. 'The Cambridge build-up and training was totally different to preparation for internationals — we trained three afternoons and played two games a week. We were highly trained and highly specialised. For internationals, the team did not even meet up until the lunch-time of the day before the match. We would go out for an hour but it wasn't an arduous session at all, it was more about getting to know each other and putting little moves together. The remainder of the moves and any other tactics were formulated during the actual game. In comparison with club rugby the international game was faster and tougher, whereas the Varsity Match didn't quite have the same strength but was very fast, and the tackling was superb. Players would project themselves at runners going flat out. Also, you endeavoured to win by open play. Kicking and ten-man rugby didn't exist as far as we were concerned. It was not the way to play rugby football and certainly not the way to win a Varsity Match. Even though it may have been a low-scoring game there was plenty of handling: the tackling was good enough to stop people scoring. If you went to see a Varsity Match you could bet your life you were going to see a jolly good game.'

Wooller eventually won 18 caps for Wales, and only pressure of work prevented him from going on the 1938 Lions tour of South Africa. He played cricket for Glamorgan, captaining them when they won the County Championship in 1948, and subsequently became their secretary.

Cliff Jones, in terms of his style of play, was the antithesis of Wooller. A small man with short legs, his footwork was nimble and he had the ability to dart through the smallest gap. Whereas Wooller tended to kick the ball with awesome power, Jones directed it with neat precision. Jones won 13 caps for Wales but, like Wooller, was not available for the 1938 Lions tour. He was a Welsh national selector for 20 years, on five occasions chairman of selectors, and he was president of the Welsh Rugby Union in their centenary season, 1980-81.

In the 1933 Cambridge threequarter line with Wooller were three men, Fyfe, Dick and Johnston, who were already or later became Scottish internationals, while behind them was Graham Parker, another well-known cricketer, who was England's full-back in 1938. The only back of the 1933 Cambridge team who did not become an international was the scrum-half, Jack Bowcott, a brother of Harry Bowcott who had won Blues in 1927 and 1928. Jack, like so many other aspirants for national honours, was unlucky in that his path to the very top was blocked by someone else, in his case Wick Powell, who won 27 caps for Wales. However, Oxford's back division contained more actual or future internationals in 1933 than that of Cambridge. Indeed, all seven Oxford backs of that year played international rugby at some time or other: Owen-Smith, Warr and Cranmer for England; Lorraine and Jackson for Scotland; Rees-Jones for Wales and McShane for Australia. But in the pack Cambridge had the pull; Jones was already a Welsh international, Rees about to become one and Murray later played for Scotland. Oxford's only forward in this category was Ted Nicholson, who was England's hooker in 1935 and 1936.

That made a total of 17 current or future internationals in the two 1933 sides. Nicholson, who played in four Varsity Matches, had the distinction of scoring Oxford's try in 1933. Cranmer, the burly England centre, broke through and, when faced by Parker, the Cambridge full-back, kicked ahead over the Cambridge line. To the surprise of many spectators it was a hooker, Nicholson, who was there to touch the ball down for the try. Jackson's conversion proved to be the decisive score, because when Dick ran through for a try for Cambridge, the conversion kick proved too difficult for Fyfe, and there was no further scoring — mainly because of Owen-Smith's impeccable defence.

Wooller says: 'It was remarkable for the incredible performance of Tuppy, who is one of the finest all-rounders I've ever seen. We were up against a strong side and a very powerful Oxford back line, and we were unfortunate in that our captain, Jones, was injured in the first 20 minutes when he dived to stop a kick and took it in the side. It split his spleen and he was carried off, so we had to play with 14 men. Otherwise, I think we would have won. Unfortunately with only seven forwards we didn't get enough of the ball, but it was Tuppy who stood out in that Match. We made many breaks from which we thought we must score, but somehow he managed to thwart us. I remember one particular incident in which I made a break on the right flank and tapped ahead over the centres' heads. The ball was heading to drop just short of Tuppy and I was coming on to it flat out. There was only him in the way and he couldn't reach the ball because it was dropping just short. He then trapped it in an extraordinary way with one hand on the ground, picked it up with the same hand, side-stepped me and kicked the ball a good 70 yards back on to our 25-yard line. It was incredible — I've never seen it done since. When that ball went sailing over my head and I had to go back another 50 or 60 yards I remember thinking "we're never going to win this match". We had done everything but score and Tuppy had turned up in all sorts of places. It remains to this day the finest exhibition of full-back play I've ever seen. He caught, picked up, tackled, and kicked without flaw or semblance of concern. Wave on wave of Light Blue attacks cracked and dispersed on the Owen-Smith breakwater.'

It was in the following year, 1934, that this talented Cambridge side really did themselves justice at Twickenham. With only four changes from the previous year's team, they scored six tries to none against Oxford and thus recorded the first Cambridge victory since 1928. Fyfe, on the left wing, scored three of the Cambridge tries, and Wooller dropped a famous goal from near halfway and out towards the touch-line. Vivian Jenkins always maintained that this was the most colossal dropped goal he ever witnessed — the ball landed full toss in the enclosure underneath the North Stand. Wooller rates the 1934 Cambridge backs as the best set he ever played with in his long career.

'We had Graham Parker, who was a very sound player, at full-back. Johnny Johnston had matured as a strong wing, while Ken Fyfe was a very fine runner indeed. The big difference was Peter Candler, who came in at centre. He was a very good passer of the ball and had a beautiful pair of hands. Then we had Cliff Jones at fly-half. Our scrum-half, Oscar Browning, was a very interesting player because he did one thing well. He couldn't make a break or anything like that, but he was a very good passer of the ball. He could get the ball to his fly-half with great speed, which was just what Cliff Jones wanted. However, about a month before the Varsity Match he cracked an elbow. The Cambridge doctor, Salisbury-Wood, who was brilliant, treated him and strapped him up before the game. So Browning played in the Match and did extremely well, but broke down later and never played again. Windsor Lewis had us moving the ball from the base of the scrum to the wing every day, back and forth, until we could do it absolutely perfectly. By the time we got to the Varsity Match we were moving with absolute precision. We also had a good pack that day, very well led by Arthur Rees, and the ball was coming along the line beautifully.'

Wooller was up against his old friend and rival Peter Cranmer in the centre. Although Cranmer was a good defensive player, Wooller worked out that instead of tackling him head-on he would let his opponent go half round him and then take him from the side. This suited Wooller because at the speed he was going when he got the ball he was able to go half round Cranmer and also to half-commit the Oxford wing, Warr, who moved off his wing in the belief that the Cambridge man was going to break through. Wooller then transferred the ball to Fyfe, who scored and eventually ended up with a hat-trick. With things obviously going well, and with a few points on the board, Wooller thought he would try for a dropped goal. 'I used to practise my drop-kicking all the time. I remember practising in the prefect's room at school because there were always a few balls around there. I'd throw the ball up in the air and get into position as it dropped. I would practise for hours and it paid off — I think I still hold the record for dropped goals at Cardiff with 13. I was a long kicker, and when I got the ball early inside my own half during that game I thought I'd have a go. So I let fly and I watched it go way over the posts and drop into the front row of the stand. I don't know why the devil it went so far but I remember Peter Cranmer turning to me and saying, "You cheeky bugger!"'

The most famous of all the talented backs who played in the Varsity Matches of the 1930s represented Oxford. Prince Alexander Obolensky, who won his first Blue on the wing in 1935, was the son of an officer in the Czar's Imperial Horse Guards, who brought him to England as a baby to escape from the turmoil of the Russian Revolution. The young Obolensky was educated at Trent College where he made a name for himself as a sprinter. At Oxford Obolensky found a natural niche on the right wing, and he set about trying to make himself as fast on the rugby field as he was on the track. He used to have coffee most mornings at Elmer Cotton's sports shop in The Turl, demanding ever lighter and thinner boots. The Cotton family did their best to meet these demands, but Obolensky's boots were often so delicately made that they would split in the course of a match.

E.H.D. Sewell wrote of Obolensky: 'He was one of the most graceful runners in our game, gliding along with something of the easy sinuosity of movement of an antelope at full speed'. While the 1930s were years of depression for most people in Britain, Obolensky is said to have made a habit of eating a dozen oysters before taking the field for any match in the London area. He was at Oxford for three years, but played in only two Varsity Matches, in 1935 and 1937. Some older watchers of present-day rugby tend to scoff that hamstring injuries are a modern phenomenon and largely in the mind of the player. It may be salutary for them to recall therefore that Obolensky missed the 1936 Varsity Match because he had pulled a hamstring. Oddly for a player of his talents and fame, he did not score a try in either of his two appearances against Cambridge.

His place in rugby history rests rather on the eccentric try he scored for England against the All Blacks at Twickenham in January 1936, the day the New Zealanders were defeated 13-0. The English backs were attacking to the right, and the All Blacks were covering to that side of the field when Obolensky, without the ball, turned inwards, took a short pass, and raced diagonally leftwards with all the New Zealanders taken by surprise and on the wrong foot. He hared along a channel through the defence and scored on the left.

This try has remained one of the most famous ever scored at Twickenham — or anywhere else. It was not, however, the only one Obolensky scored against those 1935-36 All Blacks: in fact, he scored another earlier in this same match, albeit a rather more orthodox one. For this try he was given an edge near the right touch-line and raced 40 yards, rounding the All Blacks' full-back on the way. It was probably the pace and ease he showed in scoring this first try that made the New Zealanders cover across so determinedly when England launched their subsequent attack to the right — the movement which eventually brought Obolensky's second, wrong-footing, try. Only a few weeks earlier, in November 1935, Obolensky had scored a marvellous try for Oxford against

The dashing Russian Prince Alexander Obolensky seen in action tackling an Old Blue while playing for Rosslyn Park. Obolensky was one of the most famous threequarters ever to appear for Oxford and became the first rugby international to lose his life in the Second World War.

the All Blacks at Iffley Road. For this try, in spite of heavy rain and a slippery foothold, he tore 75 yards across the ground. Oxford lost this match by only 9-10. Obolensky, who also played for Rosslyn Park and the Barbarians, was the first rugby international to lose his life in the Second World War. Serving in the RAF, he was killed in March 1940 when the fighter he was piloting on a training flight crashed on landing.

Vivian Jenkins remembers Obolensky very well. Although he didn't play alongside him in a Varsity Match he played against him for Wales against England. We tend to think that intense study of the opposition's strengths and weaknesses is a modern invention, but before he faced the Russian prince, Jenkins had done his homework thoroughly enough to satisfy any current gridiron coach. 'I didn't see the two tries he scored against New Zealand because I was playing in a Welsh trial, but I had read all about it. He was due to play for England against us two weeks later at Cardiff, and I didn't know anything about the tries. So I went to a little news flick in the Strand where you paid a shilling and had an hour's cartoons and news. They had the England match on the newsreel and I was able to see the two tries.

'I sat down at one o'clock and had to sit through all these damned Mickey Mouse cartoons until it came on. But when it did it all happened so quickly that I knew I had to have another look at it, so I waited until it came round again. I did that four times and had to sit through four hours of cartoons.'

Despite that ordeal, he now had the tries and the manner in which they had been scored imprinted on his mind. The first, which Jenkins actually considered the better of the two, was a classic wing threequarter's try. 'He went round the blindside of the scrum and then had the New Zealand full-back Gilbert to beat. Gilbert was coming across so Obolensky moved inside and stopped him dead, then went outside him, which is the classic way to beat a full-back. For the second try, which has become famous, there was a movement across the field; Peter Cranmer broke through and gave the ball to Obo with the right-hand corner staring at him. My instinct watching the film was that he should just have gone straight for the corner flag but he didn't — he stopped because there was someone coming across and instead cut inside, continuing to cut inside defenders. He went through the lot until he scored over on the other side.'

Jenkins made up his mind that whatever happened he wasn't going to let Obolensky swerve outside him as he had done in his first try against New Zealand. So a fortnight later at Swansea, he got together with his centres, Cliff Jones and Wilf Wooller, and worked out a plan. He told the pair that if he allowed the England wing to feint inside and then accelerate outside they would never catch him, so whatever happened he would just keep going towards the touch-line and they would have to do the covering if Obolensky did cut inside. 'Obo had only one chance in the game: he broke clean through and I'll always remember the tremendous mental effort it took not to stop when he veered into me. I did eventually tackle him and put him in the straw which surrounded the pitch. When I finally got up, there underneath me was little Cliff Jones, who had come across to cover as we had planned. Anyway, we got him and the match ended in a 0-0 draw.

'Obo wasn't a great rugby player but he was strong, and a very fast, powerful runner. He was also a lovely bloke and great fun, a real White Russian Parisian type who loved to celebrate — truly one of the lads. Arthur Rees was learning to fly in the RAF at the same time as Obo. They were playing in some early Wartime match and discussed flying, and apparently Obo said, "One thing I just cannot get the hang of is landing". Of course, he was eventually killed in training, landing a plane at RAF Martlesham near Ipswich.'

It was curious that, when Oxford had Obolensky and Cambridge still had Wooller, Fyfe and Cliff Jones, the 1935 Varsity Match should end 0-0, the first scoreless draw since 1892. By all accounts, however, it was a far from dull game, remembered by many for the way Obolensky raced across to the opposite side of the field to tackle the Cambridge wing, Rawlence, into touch a foot from the Oxford line. Wooller remembers it as a very tight game with few scoring opportunities, mainly because the Oxford pack were playing extremely well. 'Although there was no score in the game there was a lot of open play. I missed the upright two or three times with drop goal attempts; it was just one of those days. However we did have one good chance to score and should have won the game. I made a break in the second half and got clean through. I came to Stuart-Watson, the Oxford full-back, and passed to Rawlence on the wing. This put him clean away out on the right flank. He was about 25 yards out and going for the line, and there was no one near him. Of course, Oxford had Obolensky, who was the fastest wing of the day and he had come across from the other wing. Now, if Rawlence had been more experienced he would've looked to his left to check what was happening. He would have been bound to score because he had so much room — he could have checked or stopped, but he just went tearing for the line. He must have been within five feet of it when Obo caught him and hit him into touch with a magnificent covering tackle which saved the match, but Rawlence just didn't realise Obo was there. It looked a try from the moment I gave him the ball, it was one of Obo's great moments.'

Wooller, too, had another gigantic drop at goal but this time just missed. Oxford were without their elected captain, Scottish international stand-off half Kenneth Jackson, because of injury. His role as captain was taken by Mac Cooper, a Rhodes Scholar from New Zealand, who was to lead the side in his own right the following year. Jackson won Blues in 1932 and 1933 but he in turn missed the 1934 Varsity Match through injury.

In retrospect the Cambridge side of 1936 could be described as presidential. Tommy Kemp, the England stand-off half, subsequently became president of the Rugby Football Union, and among the Cambridge forwards were Cliff Wilton, president of the Scottish Rugby Union in the 1980-81 season, and Owen Chadwick, later to become president of CURUFC. Perhaps the qualities of authority and efficiency shown by these three men in their more mature years were already with them in 1936. In any event, Cambridge won the Varsity Match by two tries to a goal, and it is recorded that Wilton took part twice in the movement which led to his scoring the first of the Cambridge tries.

Chadwick had gone up to Cambridge in 1935. His father had also been at Cambridge, and his was probably the last generation to know that from a very young age they would follow the same path. Chadwick had already excelled at rugby, having played hooker for the English Public Schoolboys against Scotland, and he was looking forward to his rugby at Cambridge. 'I went up to Cambridge to play rugby not to pass exams', he recalls. 'I hoped I might eventually get a Blue. I had seen that marvellous game in 1934 and thought Cambridge must be a wonderful place — Wilf Wooller was a particular hero of mine. The following December I went up to take my entrance exam. Some friends then took me out to the Dorothy café for coffee and there at the next table sat Wilf Wooller, so I really thought Cambridge was the place to be.'

In 1935 Cambridge had a sitting tenant at hooker in the shape of Ray Lord. Chadwick soon became his first reserve and spent that season honing his skills and gaining first-class experience with Blackheath. His performances aroused the interest of the selectors who were putting together a British touring party to go to South America. One was on hand to witness an outstanding performance by Chadwick in a college cup final, and as a result he was taken along as one of the young hopefuls. The tour fitted in perfectly with the Cambridge vacation and provided invaluable experience for Chadwick. When he returned he was an obvious candidate for the Cambridge team of 1936. 'The 1936 season was very special because we only had one Old Blue left and that was the captain, Charles Laborde. At the beginning of the season all the newspapers predicted that Cambridge wouldn't do anything that year. I remember our first match, against the Old Boys of the Leys School, which was usually fairly easy. We drew 3-3 and the whole of the press said that was that.

'Then we went down to Twickenham the next Saturday to play 'Quins and, my goodness, how their tune changed! For although we had only one Old Blue there were some real players in that team. It was in this game that fly-half Tommy Kemp made his name. Outside him in the centre was a young freshman who looked about 16. None of us had ever heard of him and had no idea why he was there, his name was John Forrest and he had just come up from Strathallan. "Springy" Forrest was like a gazelle and became one of the great Scottish wing threequarters, although he played centre for us in 1936. At fly-half Cambridge had been used to the Cliff Jones-Bleddyn Williams type of player, who was a great individual and did it all. But in Tommy Kemp we had a man who could really use threequarters. This meant that players like Harry Roden, who was a big, tall centre, were getting the ball at exactly the right moment. We had John Rawlence on one wing and MacDonald on the other.'

Cambridge had a good season leading up to the Varsity Match, but they were up against an

Oxford team which was particularly strong in the forwards and included players of the calibre of Mac Cooper, Mike Marshall and John Brett. They also had a top-class full-back in Trilby Freakes and the famous Micky Walford at centre. In the event Cambridge won the Match by scoring two tries to a solitary goal by Oxford, but the game is best remembered for one incident involving Cambridge wing MacDonald and Oxford full-back Freakes. Five minutes from the end Mac-Donald intercepted and Chadwick remembers: 'He was clear and had no one to beat but Trilby Freakes who, like the good full-back he was, was shepherding him quietly into touch. But at about the halfway line Johnny suddenly stopped dead and so did Freakes. They both looked at each other, then Johnny set off and swerved past Freakes, who was totally wrong-footed, to score the winning try. It was an amazing incident, quite unforgettable, and almost comic to watch'.

'Trilby' Freakes was another South African full-back and a Rhodes Scholar, and he followed Owen-Smith into the England side before captaining Oxford in 1938. But for the 1937 Varsity Match Freakes was asked to play in the centre with the specific task of marking John Forrest, the elusive Cambridge centre who was soon to play for Scotland. Freakes and the rest of the Oxford side tackled so fiercely and relentlessly that, although the Cambridge forwards won the ball almost continuously from the set pieces, Oxford won the match by 17-4 with five tries to a

The 1937 Oxford side that beat Cambridge 17–4 thanks to a remarkable display of tackling. Controversy still rages about a tackle by Oxford centre Freakes on the Cambridge danger-man Forrest, which knocked the Light Blue centre out and set the pattern for the game.

dropped goal (worth four points in those days). It was one of rugby's most remarkable defensive victories, Howard Marshall commenting that 'no side ever heeled the ball so regularly as Cambridge did yet lost the match'. 'That match was an absolute disaster', recalls Owen Chadwick. 'We had a jolly good record prior to the game and everybody was talking about a Cambridge win by 30 points, which was fatal. We still had some good backs, including Rab Bruce Lockhart, who was already a Scottish international, at fly-half. They had Obolensky, of course, but on that British tour of South America he had had a terrible time and wasn't even picked for the Test Match, so we didn't consider him too dangerous. We still had Roden, and a good pack which included Newton-Thompson and Young. We went on to the field in the belief that we would win easily.'

Cambridge's game plan was very simple: the forwards would win the ball and the threequarters would run up a large score. But that plan was soon shattered. 'Oxford were naturally afraid of Forrest and at the first scrum we duly heeled the ball back and it went out to him. The ball and Freakes arrived at Forrest at the same time. There has been a long argument ever since about whether Freakes arrived before the ball, but I am convinced that they arrived simultaneously and therefore that it was a perfectly fair tackle. But it knocked Forrest out and he was never quite the same for the rest of the game. Whether it was the injury or the fact that he was keeping half an eye on Freakes I don't know — it was a tremendous tackle. So here we were, a side who could win a lot of ball; I could get it in the tight and Christopher Newton-Thompson could win it in the line-outs, yet when we gave it to the backs they could do nothing. We had no other plan. Perhaps if we had had a captain who understood forward play he would've told us to hold on to the ball in the forwards and try to hold their back row in, but instead we just went on heeling the ball, letting it out and losing the match.

'Oxford won thanks to a magnificent display from their back row and their scrum-half, Paul Cooke. Pat Mayhew played a storming game at wing forward. I remember one particular moment of horror when I hooked the ball with a very quick heel. It went out and by the time I got up from the scrum Pat was dribbling the ball in our 25, miles behind where the scrum had been. I knew Paul Cooke because we'd shared a room on the tour to South America. He had a magnificent game that day — I still shudder at the memory of that match.'

Freakes' centre partner that day was Micky Walford, one of the great all-rounders, who won Blues at rugby, hockey and cricket. He never quite managed an England cap at rugby, but he played many times for his country at hockey, and at cricket he was a splendid batsman for Somerset over a number of years, his schoolmaster's duties at Sherborne permitting. Freakes and Forrest both lost their lives in the Second World War, as indeed did seven members of the 1937 Oxford team.

Freakes was but the latest in a long line of talented South Africans to serve the Oxford cause: largely because of the Rhodes Scholarships many more South Africans have won Blues at Oxford compared to about a dozen at Cambridge. One of the few at Cambridge was Chris Newton-Thompson, who was in the pack in 1937 and again in 1938, when the Cambridge forwards, now captained by Chadwick, put up a rousing performance in a match distinguished by tremendous tackling. Chadwick remembers having problems in picking his team for that match; the disappointment of the previous year was still very fresh in his memory. 'We were over-frightened of Trilby Freakes. We'd seen him devastate our centres, particularly Forrest, in whom we had a star. The problem was how to use him without Freakes killing him. Therefore it became an axiom that Forrest must be on the wing and I think that was his best position. But that meant we had to find two first-class centres.

Action from a 1941 unofficial Wartime Varsity Match held at Grange Road.

There was no shortage of support for the Wartime games, as these massed ranks of boatered spectators at Iffley Road show.

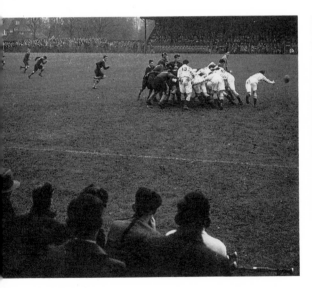

Cambridge mount an attack during one of the 1944 encounters on their own ground.

Cambridge captain Newton-Thompson is about to release the ball to team-mate Steeds during the first Wartime Varsity Match at Cambridge, which Oxford won 15–3.

'Bruce Lockhart was a natural fly-half but in order to supply Forrest with inside men we had to play him at centre and bring in a brilliant but very young and inexperienced fly-half, Pat Sherrard. Jim Parsons was at scrum-half, and although he later played for England it was a difficult choice because we had another very good scrum-half. The other centre was Keith Downes who, despite having played at full-back in previous years, was a natural centre. Joe Swanson, on the wing, was not a natural. He was a vast chap who wasn't very fast but he was a wonderful tackler and a great defender. At full-back we had a freshman, Keith Geddes, who was very inexperienced but a fine player. The scrum was nothing like as strong as the previous year. It included people such as Marcus Dods, who later became a famous conductor. But the main question was whether this little fly-half Sherrard would stand up to the treatment that Oxford were sure to give him. Oxford, for their part, had lost Charlie Grieve at fly-half and had Watts there. We were not unduly worried about him. They also brought in South African Dick Luyt at centre and they still had a formidable pack.'

Watts kicked two penalties to give Oxford a 6-0 lead but Geddes replied in kind for Cambridge to cut the lead. Skipper Chadwick remained confident: his team were having most of the play and he felt that sooner or later they would breach the Dark Blue defence. Ironically it was Forrest who set up the only try of the match. He took the ball at tremendous pace, went round his opposite man and was then confronted by the fearsome Freakes, now captaining Oxford from full-back. Forrest kicked ahead and Rab Bruce Lockhart, whose father J.H. (Rufus) Bruce Lockhart had been the Cambridge fly-half in 1910, touched down to make level the scores at 6-6. The young full-back, Geddes, then put the Light Blues ahead with a magnificent touch-line conversion. Chadwick's agony was by no means over as soon afterwards Oxford were presented with their only scoring chance of the match.

'I don't know whether it was an interception or a bad pass, but Dick Luyt got clean away and there in front of him, somewhere around our 25, was Keith Geddes. They were in the middle of the field, so Keith couldn't shepherd him into touch. Dick later told me what went through his mind at that moment. He thought the right thing to do would be to kick over Keith's head and run for the line, but he'd noticed that following up on his left was one of his forwards, Joe Coles, with no one near him. Dick thought that if he didn't pass 50,000 people would think him selfish, although he knew that Joe Coles was so slow that if he did pass he might not reach the line. He knew he would be blamed by the crowd for not passing so he did, and it happened as he feared — we easily caught up with Joe. Dick always cites this as his greatest failure of character. He had done the wrong thing because 50,000 people thought it was the right thing.'

Three minutes from the end, Chadwick suffered desperation once again as there was a scrum in front of the Cambridge posts with an Oxford put-in: a situation that was tailor-made for a stand-off half to try a dropped goal. A tremendous burden rested on the Cambridge hooker and skipper. 'I thought the only way I could lose this match was to have a penalty awarded against me for a foot up, yet I knew that if they won the scrum there was a 50-50 chance of a dropped goal. It was a tense moment, but luckily the Oxford hooker lost the ball and we managed to clear the danger.'

The outbreak of the Second World War in September 1939 meant that no official Varsity Matches were played until December 1945. The standpoint on the playing of games in Wartime was, however, different from the attitude that prevailed in the First World War. Now it was generally agreed that no harm could come from the continuation of competitive sport, and so rugby went on, if on a limited scale. Oxford and Cambridge agreed to meet in unofficial Varsity Matches, and indeed there were two such games in each of the six years of the War. The record was nine wins to Cambridge, two to Oxford and one draw.

9
The 1940s: The Post-War Years

The trend of the Wartime meetings was soon reversed when the Varsity Matches became official again in 1945. Cambridge won that year, but of the first seven post-War games Oxford won five and Cambridge two. In fact, when Oxford won in 1951 for a fourth consecutive year, they had achieved a lead of seven over Cambridge in the overall series since 1872 — a lead which was to be usurped by Cambridge in the 1980s.

Students from the Commonwealth continued to play an integral part in the Dark Blues' success: the famous overseas influence at Oxford has seldom been stronger than it was in the immediate post-War seasons. Ossie Newton-Thompson, from South Africa, was captain in 1946; Jika Travers, from Australia, in 1947; and Nelles Vincent, from South Africa, in 1949. The 1946 Oxford side included seven overseas players — four South Africans, two New Zealanders and one Australian. In 1947 there were six players from overseas, in 1948 five and in 1949 six.

At Cambridge the influence from outside England in this period, as in the 1930s, tended to come from Wales. John Gwilliam, lock forward, and Clem Thomas, wing forward, went on to captain Wales, and Glyn Davies, an elegant stand-off half, played for Wales before he got his Blue, as indeed did Thomas. As was the case after the First World War, in the immediate post-War period most of those participating in the Varsity Match had seen Wartime service. Their average age was pretty high, and Sir Andrew Noble records that of the 1946 Oxford side eight were married, two divorced and only David Swarbrick, the England wing threequarter, had not been in the Forces. Gilthorpe, the hooker, was 36, and two other members of the team, Bevan in the centre, and Sutton at lock, had been at the University in 1937. Bevan had to wait nine years for his Blue, and Sutton eight.

The Universities soon started to attract the attention of national selectors again. The 1946 sides included eight Oxford men and seven Cambridge men who were soon to play for their countries, and in 1949 Oxford fielded nine players who were or were to become internationals. In the first Cambridge side after the Second World War were three forwards who subsequently played for England — hooker Henderson, Bance at lock, and Steele-Bodger at wing-forward — and in the centre was Logie Bruce Lockhart who subsequently played both in the centre and at stand-off half for Scotland. Bruce Lockhart was another son of J.H. Bruce Lockhart, the 1910 stand-off half, and brother of Rab, of the 1937 and 1938 Cambridge teams. The Bruce Lockharts were thus

Micky Steele-Bodger captained Cambridge against a powerful Oxford side in 1946. Despite his try his side were beaten 15–5 in one of the most compelling Varsity clashes.

remarkable for the fact that the father and his two sons all won Blues and Scotland caps at stand-off half.

Typical of the mature students to be found at the Universities in 1945 was Ossie Newton-Thompson, the Oxford scrum-half. He had served in the War from 1941; flying Spitfires, winning the DFC and reaching the rank of Wing Commander. A Rhodes Scholar, he quickly settled back into playing rugby and was capped by England the following season. Two of the 1945 Oxford loose forwards were also to win caps, C.D. Williams for Wales, and Philip Moore for England. In the 1980s Moore was a private secretary to the Queen, while Williams was still closely involved with the Cardiff club. The full-back, Sampson, who had been a prisoner of war, was a son of H.F. Sampson who had played in the same position in the Oxford sides of 1910 and 1911, and was yet another South African Rhodes Scholar.

Sir Andrew Noble records that after the 1945 game the Varsity Match came close to being switched from Twickenham to Wembley. Oxford, he says, were dissatisfied with the financial arrangements offered by the RFU and, with the agreement of Cambridge, made enquiries at Wembley, whose officials came up with considerably more favourable terms. In the end, however, the RFU improved their offer, and the teams returned to Twickenham in 1946, when Micky Steele-Bodger captained Cambridge. He was to win the first of his nine caps for England that same season, and later to serve rugby in many different capacities from chairman of the England selectors, president of the Rugby Football Union, and chairman of the Four Home Unions Tours committee to chairman of the International Board. The 1946 Varsity Match was notable for the tactics of aggressive defence devised and directed by Steele-Bodger against one of Oxford's most formidable teams.

Oxford arrived at Twickenham having won all their 11 games of the season thus far with a record of 53 tries to three and a points difference of 260 to 22. Such a record emphasises the example set by the two Universities in galvanising rugby in the immediate post-War years. Six of that Oxford side were to play for England, together with four from Cambridge. In addition, three of the 1946 Cambridge team were to play for Scotland, and two of the Oxford side similarly went on to win Scottish caps. Oxford were now captained by Newton-Thompson, whose meticulous attention to detail and thorough planning had much to do with his team's successes. His partner at stand-off half was Martin Donnelly, the New Zealand Test cricketer, who had been in residence the previous season but who had declared himself insufficiently fit to be considered for a Blue. Donnelly, an Army major in the War, was a neat, balanced runner with clever footwork. He had a quick eye for an opening, a cricketer's hands and a penchant for dropping goals. 1946 was his only year in the Oxford side, for the next season both he and Newton-Thompson gave up regular rugby in order to concentrate on their studies. Incidentally, Newton-Thompson, like Donnelly, received a cricket Blue, as did Sutton and Travers from the same 1946 side.

A crowd of 40,000, at that time a record for the Varsity Match, turned up at Twickenham, and Donnelly duly obliged them by opening the scoring with a left-footed dropped goal. But although the Oxford pack were on top, Steele-Bodger's tactics began to pay off, and he himself pounced for a try, following a powerful run up the right wing by Martin Turner, later to serve a long stint in administration with Surrey and the Rugby Football Union. In the end, though, Oxford's all-round excellence was not to be denied, and Cambridge were beaten 15-5 in a match fit to rank among the most compelling of the series.

The 1947 Varsity Match was played on the last Saturday of November instead of on an early Tuesday in December. The choice of a Saturday provoked protests from London clubs, who felt that the big game at Twickenham would drastically reduce their own attendances. In fact the Varsity Match crowd was slightly smaller, 38,000, than the previous year. It had never been the intention of the University authorities to interfere with London club rugby — the impetus for the change came from the Home Office, who were anxious to cut down on midweek sport during the current industrial crisis. As it turned out, this was not one of the more spectacular Varsity Matches, Cambridge winning by no more than two penalty goals to nil. What is more, the man who kicked those goals, Lloyd-Davies, promptly signed up with a Rugby League club soon afterwards. On one of their wings Cambridge had a rare recruit from Argentina, Barry Holmes. He played at full-back in the following year's Varsity Match and then in the same position for England in all their four games of 1949. Back home in Buenos Aires, he played for Argentina against France; a rare instance of a man playing for two different countries in under 12 months. Tragically, Holmes died shortly afterwards of typhoid fever.

The 1947 Oxford captain, Jika Travers, who hailed from Australia, also had an unusual experience at international level: he played for England against his compatriots, the 1947-48 Wallabies. Nor did Travers, a flanker, spare himself against his fellow Australians. Denzil Batchelor, a well-known journalist of the period, wrote of Travers: 'I don't think I ever saw a mightier game played in his position than that he turned out for England against Australia, his native land'. Travers, a Rhodes Scholar who had served throughout the War in the Australian Infantry, was a man who thought deeply and widely about the game and preached his theories to his Oxford side. Soon after his Oxford days he wrote one of the first of the detailed rugby coaching manuals, *Let's Talk Rugger*. While he was writing it, he persuaded the Harlequins to let him play at full-back so that he could put to the test some of the theories about back play he was including in the book. By all accounts he did not let the Harlequins down. Certainly his book became the most widely-read rugby textbook of its time.

It is ironic that, with such a knowledgeable man at the helm, Oxford did not score a single point in the 1947 Varsity Match. They came close, in the sense that the current England full-back, Syd Newman, a Rhodes Scholar from South Africa, failed with four penalty kicks at goal and Clive van Ryneveld hit a post with another. Van Ryneveld, who was later to play in the centre for England, had joined his elder brother, Tony, a loose forward, in the Oxford side, and they were to play in two Varsity Matches together. Both brothers were Rhodes Scholars, and Clive captained the University and South Africa at cricket. The Varsity sides that year included six men who had already played for their countries. Oxford fielded wing forward Jika Travers, centre David Swarbrick and full-back Syd Newman, who had all played for England, as well as lock George Cawkwell, a New Zealand Rhodes Scholar who had played for Scotland. Cambridge had lock Vic Perry and hooker Peter Henderson from the previous season's England pack.

By the time of the 1948 Varsity Match, the international ranks had expanded further still. John Gwilliam, the Cambridge lock, had played for Wales and Cambridge had acquired Glyn Davies, an elegant stand-off half, who had played for Wales and was to win 11 caps in all. Oxford meanwhile had welcomed Lew Cannell, who had played in the centre for England earlier that year and who went on to gain 19 caps. Moreover, each side in the 1948 Match fielded a future president of the Rugby Football Union. Cambridge had J.V. Smith in the centre and Oxford John Kendall-Carpenter at prop. Smith was to win all his England caps on the wing, and Kendall-Carpenter was to earn most of his in the No 8 position. Each side also included two future Scotland internationals: Cambridge had Arthur Dorward at scrum-half and Laurie Gloag on the wing, while Oxford fielded Gully Wilson, their captain, at lock and Peter Kininmonth at No 8. Kininmonth was to play 21 games for Scotland, yet he arrived at Oxford as a threequarter and had only played four games as a forward when first chosen for the University.

In common with many of his contemporaries at the University J.V. Smith had come to Cambridge via the Army. He had played in all the back positions while at school and gained first-class experience with Stroud, Gloucestershire and the Army before going up to Cambridge in 1948. However, he was very lucky to be playing any sport at all, having fractured his spine during a training accident with the parachute regiment. On leaving the Army he had been advised to try for Cambridge even though at that time there was a tremendous backlog of people trying to gain a place. Out of 2,000 who applied to St Catharine's only 124 were accepted, and one of these was Smith. While in the Army he had played centre because his favourite position of fly-half was held by Welsh international Glyn Davies, who also went up to St Catharine's that year, and the pair soon found themselves in the Cambridge team.

They were both tremendously fit, because of their Army training, and the intense regime at Cambridge suited Smith who, in the course of his club, county and Army commitments had once played six times in seven days. At that time Windsor Lewis and Tommy Kemp were overseeing activities on the rugby field and every once in a while the legendary Wakefield would come to watch and then march into the dressing-room to deliver his forthright views on the game. John Smith recalls one such occasion: 'We were playing Leicester at Grange Road and after the game Wavell strode into the dressing-room and went straight to our hooker, who had been completely outplayed that day. His name was Doherty, and his father, Bill, had played for Ireland. "Young Doherty," said Wavell, "I'll tell you this. Your old man wouldn't have let them walk around the front row like that, he would've given them the leather."'

Smith remembers his first Varsity Match as a fine, open game of rugby. 'I think Oxford led right from the word go but we managed to pull back from 11-0 to 11-8 and were attacking. Then a movement broke down and I think it was van Ryneveld who got his foot to the ball and booted it up the field. It was then kicked all the way to our goal-line where someone fell over it to bring the score to 14-8 and that was the end of the game. But it had been very even and could have gone either way. Oxford were favourites because they had a lot of good players, including Springboks and New Zealanders who were very strong.'

The 1949 game was less memorable but it included what is probably the most famous incident in the history of the Varsity Match, in which Smith had a chance to cover himself in glory. Oxford were winning 3-0 with just a few minutes left. From a loose scrum in their own half they had managed to move play upfield, deep into the Cambridge half to the right-hand corner of the field, about 15 yards in from touch and some 35 yards from the Cambridge line. 'Dorward was the scrum-half and Glyn Davies, the fly-half, moved to the open-side ready to receive the ball. We won the ball from the breakdown and Dorward got it and went to pass it open to Davies. Just then he caught sight of me and heard me shout. So he swung round and passed it to me in a blind-side breaking fly-half position. The first chap I saw was the left wing, who came in towards me. I sold him a dummy and he moved out to take my wingman. I now had a gap on the blind-side. Some-one, I suspect it was Small, the Oxford blind-side flanker, came up to me and I went outside him. I can remember him diving to try to take my ankles. Now I was up the field with a long way to go. I can remember seeing in the corner of my eye the Oxford No 8, Curtis, and Rittson-Thomas, the open-side, coming across, and I had the Oxford full-back in front of me. I went to come inside to hold him back, and then swerved outside him. Now the line was about 40 yards ahead.

'Suddenly I saw Kendall-Carpenter and I thought, "Good God, what on earth is he doing?" because he was coming across very fast, almost at a right-angle behind the full-back. I looked to cut inside but there were Curtis, Small and Rittson-Thomas coming across and there was no way I could, I would have been tackled about 25 yards short. It was probably this moment's hesitation that cost me the try. Carps had seen this and just carried on, while I went to speed round him. I knew I'd be about five yards short so I thought my only chance was to go hard at him and hope that the momentum would carry me over the line with the tackle. But his weight and speed and the angle he was coming at meant that he tackled me into touch about five yards short.'

What makes the incident even more startling was that Kendall-Carpenter was playing prop that day, although he made his name as a No 8 for England. Smith has his own theories on how the Oxford man managed to be in the right place at the right time. 'I'm convinced he was left over from the previous movement or he was tying his bootlaces. There was no reason for him as a prop to be there. He should never have been in that position and yet in all the years since, when I've said, "Come on, Carps, tell me the truth", he just laughs. We would have won that game but for him.'

John Kendall-Carpenter first went up to Oxford in 1944 on a naval short course. On being demobbed he went back in 1947 and spent the first term 'learning the game' with the Grey-hounds. He was an open-side wing forward, very fast and very fit, and had already played for Cornwall, but such was the wealth of talent at Oxford, particularly from overseas, that he was unable to get into the Varsity Match side in 1947. But the standard of the Greyhounds was very high, he had a good term, went on tour and played for the Varsity side after Christmas. It was then that the first seeds were sown of a campaign that was to take him into the front row. 'An Oxford hooker called Gilthorpe saw a tour photograph of me and said "those shoulders ought to

*John Kendall-Carpenter became an Oxford folk hero in
1949 when he brought off a magnificent cover tackle in the
dying minutes of the game to deny J.V. Smith a try that
would have levelled the scores.*

be in the front row", and that's how it all started. I was lucky enough to be selected as a non-Blue for the Oxford and Cambridge trip to Argentina, where I played in the first Test in the back row and the second at lock. When I came back I was plonked in at tight head prop although the following week I had a trial with England at No 8. Places in the back row were at a premium so I settled down in the front row for Oxford and England and it wasn't until my third Varsity Match that, being captain, I managed to emancipate myself and played in the back row.'

Oxford came to the 1949 Varsity Match with an impressive record. They were unbeaten and had a formidable try-tally to their credit. But on the big day they froze and didn't turn in anything resembling the performance of which they were capable. Nick Gent had managed to drop on to a kick over the line to score and Oxford were desperately hanging on to their 3-0 lead as the match entered the final few minutes. Kendall-Carpenter recalls how he saw the scene leading up to his legendary try-saving tackle. 'I remember our full-back, Hofmeyr, using his left foot to kick for touch somewhere near the West Stand between our 25 and the halfway line. He didn't find touch and so had to go up. Meanwhile, I had been screaming for the ball because I had a good left foot. When he kicked someone had to stay back and in those days it was the No 8's job. Although I was playing prop, I was still a No 8 by instinct so I stayed back. I was pretty fast in those days — over the length of a pitch J.V. couldn't actually keep up with me.

'Anyway, the ball was picked up by the Cambridge backs and went out to J.V., who set off in an arcing run towards the north-east corner. I set off on a line to cover the situation and Ian Botting, the wing, did the same. The interesting thing was that J.V. couldn't quite come inside me and ought to have gone outside. But he hesitated and I think our eyes met. I saw a hunted look and I knew then that he was my captive. I eventually tackled him into touch. We were lucky because, quite honestly, Cambridge deserved a draw. As far as that incident is concerned I think my long name helped commit it to the public memory. If it had been Smith v Brown instead of Smith v Kendall-Carpenter, I'm sure it would have sunk a long time ago!'

Despite coverage of the match on the newsreels, it was so dark by that stage of the game that it is almost impossible to see the movement clearly. After the Match Smith learned that that particular incident had caused Prime Minister Clem Attlee to lose his hat. Apparently Attlee wore a black Homburg to the game and when Kendall-Carpenter pulled off his tackle, being an Oxford man, he threw it up into the air shouting 'We've saved the day!'. The incident in itself was noteworthy, but the fact that it happened in front of such a large crowd with just three minutes to go, and came from a breakout in the Cambridge 25 for what looked for all the world like a match-winning score, has ensured its place among Varsity Match folklore.

With so many talented players about, it is not surprising that the crowd for the 1948 Varsity Match reached 45,000. The spectators were rewarded by a marvellous game — won 14-8 by Oxford — which is probably one reason why the following year's fixture attracted a record attendance of 59,400. That 1949 match is remembered chiefly for the spectacular clash between those two future presidents of the RFU. Alongside Smith in that 1949 Match were several accomplished footballers. His partner in the centre was John Williams, who subsequently played for England; at wing forward was Clem Thomas, who had already been capped by Wales at the age of 19, and Cambridge No 8 Peter Young later won nine caps for England. However, Oxford were in an even stronger position, possessing a real embarrassment of riches, especially among their backs. They still had Lew Cannell and Clive van Ryneveld, who had played together in the centre in all England's matches the previous season, and now there was also Brian Boobbyer, who had arrived at the University with a tremendous reputation as a schoolboy centre. The solution to this problem was to play Cannell and Boobbyer in the centre and to move van Ryneveld to stand-off half. The standard of Boobbyer's play can be judged from the fact that he and Cannell played together in all England's matches that season, van Ryneveld having decided to concentrate on his studies after the Varsity Match. To accommodate these changes, the 1948 stand-off half, Murray Hofmeyr, another South African Rhodes Scholar, was switched to full-back, in which position he, too, was capped by England that season. Furthermore Ian Botting, a New Zealander, who had just taken part in the 1949 All Blacks tour of South Africa, turned up at Oxford. He took the right wing position in the University side and also in that season's England team. All this meant that there was no room in the Oxford side for Trevor Brewer, who played on the wing for Wales against England at Twickenham that season, or for Chris Winn, who went on to play on the wing in eight internationals for England.

All three of Oxford's loose forwards of 1949 subsequently became internationals. Harry Small, a South African Rhodes Scholar, played for England that season, while Brian Curtis played for Ireland and Chris Rittson-Thomas won three caps for England in 1951. In fact, six of the 1949 Oxford side played in England's opening match that season, against Wales at Twickenham: Hofmeyr, Botting, Cannell, Boobbyer, Kendall-Carpenter and Small. With such strength at their disposal, it is hardly surprising that Oxford arrived at Twickenham with a record of having won nine of their ten games to date, the only blemish on their record a 0-0 draw with Cardiff at the

Oxford's trial match of 1950. Harry Small leads out his team followed by Lew Cannell and Ian Botting (right). For the opposition, Chris Winn follows Doug Baker (below). All five men won England caps.

Arms Park. They had scored 38 tries and had had only three scored against them. Cambridge did well to hold such a formidable team to a score of 3-0.

For Clem Thomas, the disappointment of losing was tempered by the fact that he had gained his elusive Blue in his final year. With a former Cambridge Blue, Graham Parker, as his rugby master at school and having seen such Welsh greats as Wilf Wooller, Cliff Jones and Harry Bowcott all play with such distinction for Cambridge, he went up to the University in 1947 determined to follow in their footsteps. But post-War University life had changed slightly since their day. 'When I went up, only five per cent of the students had, like myself, come from school. The rest of the guys were all from the Services with grants, demob payments and gratuities. Consequently those three years were real salad days — there was a lot of money swishing round. There were people like Jika Travers, who was a colonel in the Australian Army, and we had majors and captains, in fact anybody below the rank of first lieutenant was hopelessly outranked, so we had a lot of hoary old veterans. The post-War years also saw the enormous influence of Rhodes Scholars at Oxford, people like van Ryneveld, Hofmeyr and Newman. We often felt at quite a disadvantage at Cambridge because they did have some superb players. To a young boy up from school it was very daunting because we weren't competing with our own age group, but with war veterans who were physically more powerful. You may think you're very strong and fit at 18, 19 and 20, but you're not as hard as these men. This was one of the problems I found it very difficult to overcome and, if I remember rightly, in 1947-48 very few of those who had come up from school played for the Varsity.'

In his first year he found himself alongside two internationals and a dozen or so county players. But being a Welshman and steeped in the game, he found some of the tactical appreciations and knowledge of rugby among some of his team-mates rather questionable. 'I remember one training session in which we were working on coming away from a scrum. They asked me to turn inwards and then come out which was ludicrous. I found that even people who had played for England didn't appreciate the finer points of the game and I had a certain amount of contempt for them.' It was this approach and commitment to the game that led to him missing out on a Blue in that first year. 'We were playing London Scottish, who had a terrible man at hooker called Sampson. He was really roughing things up, and I let go a fist at him, but missed and instead caught my own captain, Eric Bole, on the chin. Bole was also captain of England and a Christian Scientist and he dropped me, saying, "We're not going to have any dirty Welsh tactics here".

'In my second year I was injured two games before the Varsity Match and although I was fit to play they refused to risk me. The following week I played against Cardiff, and we relieved them of their unbeaten post-War ground record. Cardiff were *the* club in Britain at that time and had 11 internationals in their side. I happened to score a try under the posts in that game and was selected for Wales later in the season.' As did so many great players both before and since, Thomas revelled in the commitment and enthusiasm that was demanded of Varsity rugby players. The training every day and the high level of fitness required made a big impression on him. 'One thing that University rugby teams do have is this tremendous closeness. For instance, Peter Young, who later captained England, was a fantastic character, and we used to go on tours all over the place. We were very closely-knit as a rugby community at that time and those friendships prevail right throughout one's life. I spent the most pleasant three years of my life there — it was a great experience.

'If I meet, anywhere in the world, any of the guys I played with in that Varsity Match, as I do quite often, immediately one is back to 1949. You don't talk about the old days as much as other people you were involved with at the time. You find out how well they're doing and catch up with

Mark Thomas follows in the footsteps of his famous father Clem by stepping out at Twickenham in the Cambridge colours.

all the news and this runs right through your life. It happens at every level of rugby but I think there's a particular bond between the Varsity Match players because you have been so close and involved with each other for those eight weeks leading up to a Match. Everything is channelled towards beating Oxford and you're eating it, sleeping it and breathing it. That's why I think the Varsity Match has survived. There have been times when it has been a poor spectacle but I'm glad to say that it has improved over the last few years.' The intensity of life and the friendships forged made it all the more sad when tragedy struck. 'I remember Barry Holmes, who played full-back for England. He was a marvellous man and a great footballer. He decided to go back to Argentina to do National Service. He was stuck out on a frontier post where he caught typhoid and died. I'll never forget playing against Guy's Hospital in 1949 — I was sitting in the bath after the game when someone came in and told us he'd died. It depressed us enormously.'

In 1949 Clem finally got his Blue, but in the lead-up to the big day he was terrified he would be injured and miss out as so many had done. He found the actual match a nerve-wracking experience and a strange game to play in. 'I've heard this said many times since, that the game is so fast and furious that it is difficult to make an impact. I felt I never got into the game or made my presence felt in it and yet I probably did as much as anybody. When you get on to the pitch you want to beat Oxford more than anything else in the world — everything else pales into insignificance. That whole term, that whole year had been geared towards this one Match and when you get out there you're at peak fitness. Everything has to be done as a reflex action, almost instinctively, and I came off disappointed because it wasn't as great a moment as one would have wished and I could recall very little. Of course, that was the match in which John Kendall-Carpenter made that incredible tackle on J.V. Smith which denied us the game. It was particularly annoying for me as it turned out to be my only Varsity appearance. It was quite different to any other game I had played in. The general level of skills was not perhaps as high as in international matches but the pace and ferocity would equal that of any international. I found the rucks and mauls terribly fierce — one just had to steel oneself to take it and give it, that's the whole mood of the game, and it's very difficult to catch up with the ball. In later years when one plays in internationals, one is far more composed and aware of what is going on, but the Varsity Match is such a blur. Certainly, if you are a forward there's not much time to consider anything but getting stuck into Oxford!'

Thomas believes that gaining a Blue is a tremendous experience and the attitudes it forges can be of real help in later life. 'When you leave University you feel a tremendous sense of personal fulfilment and getting a Blue does give you a bit of extra confidence. I think it's a great asset for a young person to have a degree and a Blue. If two candidates apply for a job and they're academically equal but one has a Blue, I think the employer will assume he's a pretty vigorous kind of guy. I don't think it takes you any further than that. It gives you a good start and no more. Anyone who tries to trade on it is wasting his time. I imagine if you traced the relative success in life of the intellectuals compared to that of the good, balanced all-rounders, the all-rounders would come off best. Most of these guys have been extraordinarily successful, but unfortunately the University authorities don't seem to see it that way — they did after the War, because sport was very important. It was the rugby at Cambridge which financed the other sports to a very large extent. The receipts from the Varsity Match were very important. In 1949 we had a record gate and that sort of money was vital. Those were the days when University sport was very strong but I think it has lost its way a little in later years. I remember Wilf Wooller saying, "Thomas, the likes of you and me would never get up to Cambridge these days". I replied, "You speak for yourself!" I feel that Cambridge in the last 20 years have suffered from not having this proper balance of the intellectual and the good, average all-rounder. I think the Universities are beginning to relax a little and a few rugby players are being accepted, but there was a period when sport could have died and I think the spirit of the Universities would have suffered a great deal.'

Clem was to relive all his Varsity Match emotions nearly 40 years later when his son Mark went up to Cambridge. In his first year Mark was due to play stand-off half in the Match but injured his knee badly in the Steele-Bodger's game and was ruled out of the Varsity side. 'I drove home that night with a very heavy heart because I'd been in that situation myself and I knew exactly what it meant to him. There's enormous sympathy when someone can't play. When I was at Cambridge a man called Archer failed to get a Blue for three years because of injury. In many ways I think it is unfortunate that one can only get a Blue by playing in the Varsity Match itself. I've always thought there was an injustice there, because a man could play his heart out for three years and still not get his Blue. I think if someone has played in most of the games during the year he should be awarded his Blue.'

The following year, 1986, Mark played only three games yet managed to get his Blue playing at full-back, albeit on the losing side. In 1987 there was no prouder person at Twickenham than Clem Thomas when he saw his son, now playing on the wing, score the try which clinched victory for Cambridge in a thrilling match. He still believes that the Varsity Match is a great source of talent both on and off the field and is vital to British rugby. 'Cambridge and Oxford are tremendous breeding-grounds for great players because they learn to commit themselves wholly to a game and do the same for their clubs and countries afterwards. They build up discipline and ambition. The influence of the Varsity game on rugby in this country is enormous — you only have to look at the RFU and the number of Varsity men who are involved. It's the same in Wales. It's important that we have this breeding-ground for this type of man.'

Ten of that 1949 Oxford team were available the following year, and by now six of them were full internationals. Botting, Cannell, Boobbyer and Winn made up the threequarter line; Hofmeyr reverted from full-back to his 1948 position of stand-off half and Kendall-Carpenter, Small and Rittson-Thomas were still in the pack. Kendall-Carpenter, now captain, moved himself from prop to No 8. Contemporaries speak warmly of the qualities of Ralph Green, who was in his third year as Oxford's scrum-half. He must have been good to have fought off the opposition of Derek Ashcroft, who had had England trials, Brian Gale, who played for the Barbarians and Ken Spence, who was to captain the University in 1952 and to play for Scotland in 1953. Another indication of the strength of Oxford rugby in this period was that Doug Baker, although in residence from 1949, did not get his Blue until 1951. He subsequently went on the 1955 Lions tour of South Africa as deputy stand-off half to Cliff Morgan and played in the last two Tests of that series as full-back. In addition, 13 of Oxford's 1950 side played for the Barbarians. Again, Cambridge, who had only two internationals, Glyn Davies, the stand-off half and captain, and J.V. Smith on the wing, did well to restrict Oxford to one try in the Varsity Match. This was scored by David Emms, a prop, who somehow managed to be in position to support a break by Boobbyer.

Oxford won again in 1951, but their fourth consecutive victory marked the end of this particular spell of Oxford dominance, and indeed of any dominance by either University. Oxford could still call on three international threequarters — Trevor Brewer of Wales, Brian Boobbyer of England and Ian Coutts of Scotland — and they had the redoubtable Ken Spence and Doug Baker at half-back. Two of their forwards, Bruce Thomson and Mike Walker, were later to play for Scotland. The Cambridge team was notable for the award at last of a Blue to Ricky Bartlett at stand-off half. He had previously been kept out of the side by the excellence of Glyn Davies, but subsequently played seven times for England.

10
On the Attack

Oxford men looking back at the 1950s tend to remember chiefly the machinations of the Brace-Smith half-back partnership of 1955 and a host of outstanding internationals like Paul Johnstone, Malcolm Phillips, John Young, John Willcox and Richard Sharp in the backs; and Peter Robbins, John Currie, Robin Davies and Frans ten Bos among the forwards. Cambridge men recall a string of talented international half-backs such as Ricky Bartlett, Tommy McClung, Andrew Mulligan, Phil Horrocks-Taylor, Gordon Waddell, Stephen Smith and Ken Scotland. Then there were wings like Arthur Smith, who captained the 1962 Lions in South Africa, and Jim Roberts, who won 18 caps for England, and forwards like David Marques and Roddy Evans, who both went on the 1959 Lions tour of New Zealand and Australia, Vic Harding of England, R.K.G. MacEwan of Scotland and David MacSweeney of Ireland.

This was another period in which mature students featured strongly. Although the Second World War had long finished, there was still compulsory military service which most men underwent between leaving school and arriving at university. The Universities' ability to produce or attract international players continued. Between 1951 and 1959 Oxford had 31 current or future internationals and Cambridge had 28. Fourteen of the 30 players who took part in the 1957 Varsity Match were or were to become internationals, and the 1958 Cambridge side included ten men who played for their countries at one time or another. And yet, the 1950s produced some rather dour games at Twickenham, which is why Oxford men, at least, like to look back at the brilliance of the Brace-Smith match of 1955.

The two captains, Roy Allaway, the Oxford hooker, and Jeff Clements, the Cambridge wing forward, met before the game and agreed to play positive, attacking rugby at Twickenham, which is what they proceeded to do. Oxford's trump card was the switch play of their half-backs, scrum-half David Brace, who subsequently played for Wales, and stand-off half Mike Smith, who later played for England and became better-known as England's cricket captain. Smith was an orthodox, long-legged stand-off half, but Brace was an exceptionally active running scrum-half. Brace's chief ploy was to run flat across the field, passing or dummying to his fellow backs, none of whom knew which of them was to receive the pass.

Brace's appearance in the Oxford colours owed much to the far-sightedness of skipper Roy Allaway. After leaving Gowerton School in 1952 Brace, who was known as David east of

*Ken Spence (right), later Scotland's scrum-half, moves for
the ball in the 1950 Oxford trial while his team-mates
frustrate the efforts of Giles Bullard (in scrum-cap).*

Chepstow and Onllwyn west of it (or just plain 'Onkers' to his friends) went to Cardiff University and began playing on Saturdays for Aberavon. Coming as he did from a humble Welsh background, it had never entered his head to consider the lofty academic environment of Oxbridge until fate took a hand. 'In my third year at University I broke my nose during the Easter term and found it difficult to get back into the Aberavon side. At the same time the Newport scrum-half had broken his jaw so one night a committee-man came round to my digs and asked if I'd play for Newport. Oxford were on the Newport fixture list and we played them in the Hilary term in 1955 at Rodney Parade. I had a particularly good game and in the bar later I ended up chatting to Roy Allaway, the newly-appointed Oxford skipper. He asked me what I intended to do after finishing my degree and I told him I was going on to Loughborough to do a degree course in physical education. He suggested I go up to Oxford, so I sat the entrance exam and went up to do a diploma course in public and social administration.'

Allaway had seen something in young Brace's style that he felt Oxford could use as part of an exciting brand of rugby. It was a style which had been nurtured at school and developed at Newport. In terms of build and application Brace was probably more from the mould of a stand-off half than that of a scrum-half; indeed he had played a fair amount of his school rugby there. He was quick on his feet, liked to run and refused to be a slave to getting the ball out. He was always looking to make a break or exploit an opening and this was the game he took to the first-class scene.

When he went to Newport Brace was fortunate to team up with a stand-off half who was quite happy to follow his wanderings around the field and they worked out a whole host of moves and reverse passes. Allaway was suitably impressed, while for his part Brace was impressed by the approach to

100

rugby at Oxford. 'The application of the players to their game was far greater than anything I had ever been involved in, even in the first-class game in Wales. It suited me because I was a thinker on the game and a fitness fanatic, and here were 14 others with the same sort of attitude. The first training session would be with a magnetic blackboard. We would go through the previous Saturday's game in minute detail. The next hour would be taken up by fitness training and then skeleton rugby, which was the big thing then. We would end up with a session on the tackling bags. We had a big contraption like an enlarged goal-post from which hung a bag like a big boxing punch bag. The captain would shout a number and you'd have to hit it as hard as you could.' Once a week they would dine at Vincent's or some other restaurant, a meal that would often end up with the players on the floor working out moves with salt cellars. 'It wasn't just a question of the captain telling you what to do, he invited everyone to participate, and I think that's what struck me about the whole environment. There was a Musketeerish attitude — all for one, and one for all.'

Allaway was committed to raising the level of entertainment in the Varsity Match after three years of poor fare, and following the recruitment of Brace he decided on another bold move. In 1954 M.J.K. Smith had played at full-back, but the next year Allaway decided to pair him at half-back with his Welsh prodigy — a decision that showed extraordinary vision for a captain who

David Onllwyn Brace leads the Oxford side out at Twickenham in 1956. In the previous year Brace, together with his half-back partner M.J.K. Smith, had bamboozled Cambridge but in 1956 he carried an injury and was unable to inspire his team to victory.

played hooker. Brace maintains that it was an inspired choice. 'Smith was a superb ball-player, as befits a man who captained England at cricket and played rugby for England. He was in the English mould of fly-half, tall with long legs, and was a beautiful handler of the ball. But he was almost blind without his glasses — I don't think he ever saw a ball thrown at him until it was within a radius of two or three yards. So it really became a matter of telepathy between us. Nonetheless he had great ball-playing ability and a cricketer's reactions. Mike was also prepared to fit into what I call the Newport style of play, which meant adapting to the odd variable that I introduced. We certainly weren't conventional in our approach and we had a captain who actually applauded and encouraged us. I had a penchant for running across the field selling dummies. Sometimes I'd release the ball to the fly-half, sometimes to the centres, and sometimes I would run all the way across depending on the mood of the occasion.'

Using these unorthodox methods, Oxford won ten games in the term leading up to the 1955 Varsity Match, including a 23-6 thrashing inflicted on Cardiff at the Arms Park. Brace pays tribute to the players he had around him, particularly the forwards. They entered into the spirit of this unorthodox play, and in players such as John Currie and Peter Robbins Oxford had some of the best forwards to be found anywhere. 'John Currie was probably the best line-out jumper in England while Peter Robbins was perhaps one of the all-time great open-side wing forwards; tremendously strong, fast and a great ball-handler. The forwards complemented each other well and were willing to cover when things went wrong.' But as the Varsity Match loomed large this highly successful team were faced with a dilemma. It had long been a tradition for the Cambridge team to be invited to watch the Stanley's match and the Oxford side to see the Steele-Bodger's

Four Oxford undergraduates in a final training session at Iffley Road before their international debuts in the England v Wales match of 1956. Pictured (left to right) are Peter Robbins (England), Mike Smith (England), Onllwyn Brace (Wales) and John Currie (England).

game. Roy Allaway had declined the invitation to Steele-Bodger's, but his opposite number and the rest of his team were keen to witness the Stanley's encounter to see what all the fuss was about. Brace recalls, 'I remember sitting down after a training session one evening and the captain saying, "They are on the way down to see us playing Stanley's. Are we going to show them our tricks?" A vote was taken but the consensus was that we should let them see everything and let them worry about it, so that's what we did. Well, we shared 44 points in that game, and at one stage we kept the ball in our possession for one minute and 20 seconds, which is a remarkable length of time in a rugby match. The basis of all this was switch rugby, not only between the half-backs but the whole team; centres, wings, full-back and even second rows. It was total 15-man rugby.'

With just three weeks to go before the Twickenham game the team was virtually settled. Allaway had selected Mike Allison, who was really a scrum-half, to play on one wing. Apart from providing cover for the slightly-built Brace in his first Varsity Match, Allison was also an expert at throwing-in at the line-outs, which was vital if Oxford were to get the best out of John Currie. But the captain couldn't decide who should play on the other wing so, in keeping with his unorthodox ways, he devised his own selection test. Brace relates: 'He decided to call all the college wings to a training session one afternoon. He lined them up on the goal-line and told them that the first one to reach the opposite goal-line would get a Blue. That's how Campbell Walker got into the team.'

At Twickenham all these well-laid plans suffered an early set-back. Soon after the kick-off, Brace went off on one of his famous runs but the ball was nudged out of his hand and Kershaw, the Cambridge wing, gained possession of the loose ball to score under the posts. Jim Hetherington, later to become England's full-back, converted and Oxford were 0-5 down after just ten minutes. According to Brace, it was then that Allaway showed his true leadership. 'Many captains would have been ultra-conservative and quietened things down for a while, but Allaway's words behind the posts were, "OK, let's put that behind us, we still go out and play our normal game". That was the sort of encouragement someone like myself needed at the time. After all, we had just given five points to the opposition in a crucial game which we'd been building up to for two months. But we stuck to our plans. I don't really know who called the shots, to tell the truth. I suppose I called 70 per cent and Mike 30 per cent, but he was quite happy. He was deceptively fast with those long legs; once he had run the first three yards he was very quick, as people who have seen him running between the wickets will testify.' It turned out to be a tremendous game of rugby which, thanks to Brace's machinations, resulted in an Oxford victory. Campbell Walker and Ian Reeler added tries to an earlier penalty to give them a 9-5 win.

Both captains received much praise for their positive approach to the game and for their persistence in maintaining their high-risk rugby. Four of the 1955 Cambridge forwards, David Marques, Jeff Clements and John Herbert of England and Roddy Evans of Wales later played for their countries. Of the Oxford pack, John Currie and Peter Robbins went on to play for England, and Robin Davies for Wales. One of the most notable recruits to Varsity rugby in the 1950s was Paul Johnstone, who arrived at Oxford in 1952 after taking part in the 1951-52 Springboks tour to the British Isles and France. He played in all five internationals of that tour — all of which the Springboks won, including the famous 44-0 victory at Murrayfield — and he later went on the Springboks 1956 tour to New Zealand, winning four more caps. He was really a wing, but Oxford used him as a centre in the 1952 Varsity Match. Conversely, one of the Cambridge centres was Jim Roberts, who was later to win 18 caps for England as a wing. Also in that Cambridge side was Ian Beer, who subsequently played as a loose forward for England and went on to represent his University on the Rugby Football Union committee for many years. Oxford fielded Ken Spence, the captain, and Doug Baker at half-back for a second consecutive year, and their pack included four men later to play for Scotland — hooker Gurth Hoyer-Millar, Bruce Thomson at prop, Ewen Fergusson at lock, and Chick Henderson at loose forward. Henderson came from South Africa and was later to make a name for himself as a sports broadcaster in his home country. Fergusson, at one stage of his career, was British Ambassador to South Africa. His lock partner in the 1952 Varsity Match was Dudley Wood, later to become secretary of the Rugby Football Union, and one of the loose forwards was Alec Ramsay, subsequently president of the RFU. This was the match in which Cambridge turned the tide of four consecutive Oxford victories with a 6-5 win.

Dudley Wood had arrived at Oxford in 1951 from Luton Grammar School. He had almost followed in the footsteps of his elder brother, who went to Cambridge, but he missed the Cambridge entrance exam through illness. Dudley found a group of Oxford colleges that held exams at Easter, and was subsequently offered a place there. A keen rugby player, he had already played for Bedford and had had a couple of games for the Army during his National Service. However, at the Freshmen's trials he was in for quite a surprise. 'It was very strange because at that time Varsity rugby was very much dominated by South Africans. I packed down with so many of them that often they would speak to each other in Afrikaans and I felt totally out of it. I must have had a poor trial so I thought I'd just play for my college during my time at Oxford. This I did for the first term until another trial was held at Christmas, which is when the teams change over. They were short of forwards for the following year, and this time I had a good trial, so I went into the Varsity side after Christmas.'

Oxford found themselves firm favourites to take the 1952 Match. They had won the previous four and had had a string of good results including a win over Cardiff. But they were over-confident, and Cambridge won 6-5. Dudley remembers it as a desperately disappointing game. 'Cambridge played very well — it was the typical underdog story. The first 20 minutes were very fast, as always, then the game settled down and we gained a fair amount of possession, but resolute defence on the part of Cambridge kept us out. I could only get into the side at lock, although I usually played No 8, and I was in the second row with Ewen Fergusson, who is now British Ambassador in Paris. At one point we thought we had scored a pushover try when Chick Henderson touched down. I remember E.W. Swanton's report in the *Telegraph*, in which he said that when the referee blew his whistle he thought it was for a try because Henderson got up with the ball. But he gave a five-yard scrum instead.'

The influx of overseas students into the Oxford side reached another peak in 1953 when Alec Ramsay's pack included five such players, and there were a further four behind the scrum. The nine were made up of one Rhodesian, one New Zealander and seven South Africans. At prop was Pom-Pom Fellows-Smith, the South African Test cricket all-rounder, who also played cricket for Northamptonshire.The stand-off half was Ricky Winn, a younger brother of 1950 Blue Chris. Paul Johnstone played in his proper position on the wing, as did Jim Roberts for Cambridge. All three of Cambridge's loose forwards, Ian Beer, Jeff Clements and Peter Ryan, subsequently played for England. Dudley Wood was one of only four Englishmen in the Oxford side, indeed the South African presence was so great that they were nicknamed 'Springboxford'. Their record prior to the Varsity Match had been poor, with the exception of a good performance against the touring All Blacks. They lost that game 14-5, but the match had been much closer than the final score suggests. So Oxford went into the Varsity Match in good spirits, and came away with a 6-6 draw.

Cambridge's David Marques and Oxford's John Currie, who were to become one of the greatest partnerships in English rugby, first played opposite one another in the 1954 Varsity Match, and

*Cambridge lock David Marques soars up to win a line-out
for England during their 1958 international against France.*

were to meet in the fixture on four consecutive occasions. They were first capped as England's locks on the same day in 1956 against Wales at Twickenham while undergraduates, and they went on to play 22 consecutive games together for England, Marques eventually winning 23 caps and Currie 25. The 1954 Twickenham game was also notable for the first appearance in major rugby of Peter Robbins, who was to play in four Varsity Matches for Oxford and in 19 internationals for England as a strong, clever and skilful wing forward. On the Cambridge side Arthur Smith, one of the most graceful of wing threequarters, made the first of four Varsity Match appearances. He eventually played 33 times for Scotland in addition to captaining the 1962 Lions in South Africa. In the Cambridge loose forwards Ian Beer and Jeff Clements were joined by John Herbert, another England international in the making. Cambridge won this Varsity Match by a penalty goal to nil. Beer captained Cambridge and Paul Johnstone, playing out of position at stand-off half, led Oxford.

Oxford made another unexpected switch of positions in 1956 when David Brace, the star turn of the 1955 match and now captain, played himself at stand-off half instead of in his Welsh international position of scrum-half. 'I had been injured in a game against Gloucester about three weeks before the Varsity Match,' explains Brace. 'I broke two ribs but, in retrospect rather foolishly, I decided to play at stand-off half with the aid of painkillers. I really shouldn't have played, but I felt obliged to because I was captain. Such is the intensity surrounding the game that you want to disregard injuries, but you can't afford to be less than 100 per cent fit for a Varsity

The Oxford forwards win a line-out in the 1955 match. It was from such possession that half-backs Brace and Smith were able to weave their magic and secure a 9–5 victory.

*A.A. Mulligan, the Cambridge scrum-half, gets the ball
away during the 1957 match despite the attentions of
Oxford's John Currie.*

Match. I was only 50 per cent effective on the day, and that playing in what had become a strange position. It just didn't come off.'

Brace was unable to bring the best out of a dashing new centre, Malcolm Phillips, later to play 25 times for England. Cambridge, on the other hand, were particularly well served at half-back by Andrew Mulligan, who had already played for Ireland and who was to do so on 22 occasions in all, and by Phil Horrocks-Taylor, who went on to win nine England caps. Mulligan and Horrocks-Taylor both went on the 1959 Lions tour to New Zealand. In his first Varsity Match Horrocks-Taylor scored 11 points with a try, a conversion, a dropped goal and a penalty goal in Cambridge's 14-9 win.

That game also marked the debut of Geoffrey Windsor Lewis, son of the president of the CURUFC, who later went on to play for Wales. There can have been no one more steeped in Cambridge rugby traditions than Windsor Lewis. As a small boy he had had a teddy bear dressed in a light blue blazer and in fact it was the young Geoffrey's light blue number that became the prototype for the famous Cambridge blazer — an artefact which is now on display at Grange Road. He remembers the family home being full of rugby players or people talking about rugby. 'The old man was always bringing back people after University matches, the likes of Wilf Wooller, Bleddyn Williams, Rex Willis and Tommy Kemp, so from the age of about nine or ten the influence was there. In the days before coaching was officially accepted my father used to go up and talk to the Cambridge teams and I think everyone gained from his knowledge. He was one of the few people who watched the games on Wednesdays and Saturdays and who thus saw the very best rugby players in their formative years.

'Father encouraged the Cambridge captains to invite four or five ex-players to come down at different times in the term to watch and then to talk to the team next day. This was a good formula: they were not subject to the vagaries of one coach, who might have become either very popular and gone over the top, or unpopular, adversely affecting the side.' Geoff attended the Leys School in Cambridge and then went into the Army to do his National Service before going up to Cambridge in 1956. Although essentially a stand-off half, he soon realised that he would be

Peter Robbins in action for an England XV against London Scottish at Twickenham in 1958.

unlikely to displace Horrocks-Taylor and so he switched to centre. He remembers playing just a very small part in the success of the excellent 1956 team, his prime objective being to get the ball out to wing Arthur Smith. 'The first Cambridge try was the result of something we had practised and practised and it came off to perfection. I was exactly where I should have been, with the result that Alan Barter dummied me and finished up under the posts.'

The following year Cambridge began the Varsity Match as hot favourites, mainly due to the ten victories they had accumulated during the term. These included a 30-3 win over Leicester and a 13-8 defeat of Gloucester. They also beat Harlequins 33-5 and the touring Wallabies 13-3. They had also acquired two loose forwards of outstanding merit in David MacSweeney, who had already played for Ireland, and Keith Bearne, later to represent Scotland. But it was not to be their day. As Windsor Lewis remarks, 'This Cambridge team had probably scored more tries than anybody since the War but we just couldn't get off the ground in that Match. The ball simply wasn't coming back and the half-backs didn't play particularly well. It was a big upset. We were probably a better team than we had been the previous year, but we lost on the day to Peter Robbins in full flow in the Oxford back row'. Horrocks-Taylor was closely marked by Robbins who, as the new captain, had also coached his pack to slow the Cambridge heels from the scrums. The only score of this 1957 Varsity Match was a try for Oxford from Stephen Coles, the scrum-half, in support of a dashing run by John Young, the AAA sprint champion, who was playing on the wing and who was to go on to win nine England caps.

Two more famous Scots came into the Cambridge side the next year: Ken Scotland and Gordon Waddell. Scotland, the full-back, and Waddell, the stand-off half, had already played for their country and both were to become Lions. Scotland was a frail-looking full-back but a very gifted, attacking runner, Waddell orthodox and sufficiently strongly built to ride all but the firmest tackles. An important recruit in the pack was Vic Harding, a lock, who had gained a lot of experience with the Saracens club and had taken part in England trials. He was later to win six caps for England. The Oxford side in 1958 included a relative rarity, an Australian Rhodes Scholar, at stand-off half. Ross Sheil had played for the Wallabies against the Springboks in 1956, but at Twickenham he seemed intent on trying out an embryonic version of crash-ball tactics. He frequently ran headlong and was caught in possession. Unfortunately for Oxford, it was usually Cambridge who plundered the loose ball; the Light Blues scored four tries and won the Match 17 to 6, their widest margin of victory since 1934.

As captain in 1958, Windsor Lewis drew on his experiences in the two previous games. He was at centre with Haydn Davies, who also later played for Wales, but dropped several Blues from the previous year's team. Then he devised a plan he was determined they would stick to. 'The first two tries came from rehearsed moves, and when the team realised that what we had been practising was working, their confidence swelled and they became half a yard faster, enabling us to beat a very good Oxford side. Looking back, one of the great innovations of that year was to bring full-back Ken Scotland into the moves. He was certainly as quick as anyone in the side and I had this great theory that he shouldn't appear in the line until the second half when, as players slowed up a little, the surprise value would be greater. He was really the first full-back to be accepted into the line as an attacking player. I still have a picture from that match of Ken coming in outside me and feeding Pat Mills, the wing, who went over to score.'

There was another Australian international in the 1958 Oxford side: wing Tom Baxter, who had played for the Wallabies against the All Blacks earlier that year and had had the unusual experience of being converted into a wing forward for the Varsity Match of 1959. It was also in 1959 that three especially notable players made their first appearance for Oxford at Twickenham

The victorious Cambridge team of 1961 clap a gallant
Oxford side off the pitch. In the run-up to the match the
Light Blues won all their 14 fixtures scoring 249 points.
Oxford did exceedingly well to restrict them to a 9–3 win.

— Richard Sharp, John Willcox and Pete Dawkins. Sharp was a most elegant stand-off half with long legs and a superb outside break. He played 14 times for England and will always be remembered for the marvellous individual try he scored against Scotland at Twickenham in 1963 when he was captain. Willcox, who played in four Varsity Matches, eight games for England and joined Sharp on the 1962 Lions tour to South Africa, was a fearless, almost suicidal full-back who appeared to like nothing better than to field the ball, put his head down and take on the whole of the opposing pack. Dawkins, a big wing threequarter from the United States, had never played rugby until he arrived at Oxford; he was, however, a distinguished all-round athlete, having played ice hockey and basketball for West Point and having been an All American footballer. He took readily to rugby and won his Blue as a freshman. His torpedo throw-ins over the top of line-outs became famous, and two of them in the 1959 Varsity Match went straight to Malcolm

All-American footballer Pete Dawkins prepares to launch the ball torpedo-style into a line-out for Oxford in the 1961 Match. Dawkins had never played rugby until he came to Oxford but won three Blues.

Phillips, his captain, in the centre. Back home he rose to the rank of general, having been much decorated for his services in Vietnam.

For Cambridge, Ken Scotland moved from full-back to stand-off half, and Tony Lewis, of cricket and cricket commentating fame, came in at full-back. This turned out to be another Varsity Match in which the defences were too good for the attack, a disappointment for the crowd of well over 50,000. Kicking proved decisive — John Willcox scored three penalty goals from four attempts while Keith Bearne succeeded with only one from five. There were no other scores.

11
Varsity Match Blues

It is often said that the standard of play at the Universities declined in the 1960s and that most of the Varsity Matches in this period were unspectacular, leading to a fall in the number of spectators who turned up at Twickenham. As far as unspectacular play is concerned, this was not confined to the Universities; this affliction blighted much of the rugby played at every level of the game at this time. It is true, however, that apparently fewer students were interested in playing and watching sport. And yet, at least in the early 1960s, both Oxford and Cambridge continued to produce many international players. The Cambridge side of 1960 included ten men who either were or were to become internationals, and the number of such players in their 1961 team was only one fewer. And throughout the decade there remained players of exceptional ability. Cambridge continued their tradition of fielding international players at stand-off half: there were Gordon Waddell, Mike Gibson, Billy Raybould, Ian Robertson and Roger Shackleton. There were six Oxbridge men on the triumphant 1971 Lions tour of New Zealand — Mike Gibson, John Spencer and Gerald Davies from Cambridge, and Bob Hiller, Mike Roberts and Peter Dixon from Oxford. And it was during the 1960s that Tommy Bedford, the Springbok loose forward, and Chris Laidlaw, the All Black scrum-half, captained Oxford.

Cambridge won all the first four Varsity Matches of the 1960s, and in 1964 they seemed bound to do something neither University had ever done before, namely to record five consecutive victories. Cambridge were favourites because they had enjoyed the better record during the term, in particular they had defeated Blackheath 25-11 and Harlequins 13-8 whereas Oxford had lost conclusively to both these opponents. In the event Oxford, inspired by their Scottish captain and stand-off half Ronnie Lamb, scored four tries and won by 19-6.

The Cambridge team that won 13-0 in 1960 was a formidable unit. Ken Scotland, the captain and full-back, and stand-off half Gordon Waddell had already played for Scotland and the 1959 Lions in New Zealand, and John Brash, one of the wing forwards, was to play for Scotland that season. Two other backs, centre Mike Wade and scrum-half Trevor Wintle, were soon to play for England. In the pack were three future England internationals, props David Wrench and Bev Dovey and lock Vic Harding. The other lock was Brian Thomas, who was to play 21 times for Wales before making a name for himself as manager of Neath in the 1980s, and the No 8 was Roger Michaelson, who likewise subsequently played for Wales. Against this array of talent

Fly-half Gordon Waddell had already played for Scotland and the British Lions before he made his Varsity Match debut for Cambridge in 1960.

Oxford fielded three men who had already played for their countries — Joe McPartlin, the Scotland centre, Richard Sharp, the England stand-off half, and Frans ten Bos, the Scotland lock — and three who were soon to become internationals — John Willcox, the England full-back, Pat Burnet, the Scotland centre, and No 8 Colin Payne, who won his ten caps for England as a lock. So of the 30 players on the field at Twickenham in 1960, 16 were or were to become internationals.

Peter Stagg, recruited by Oxford in 1961, was almost certainly the tallest man ever to play in the Varsity Match. Standing 6ft 10ins, he enjoyed an obvious advantage at the line-out but he was more than a line-out specialist, becoming a very useful all-round forward. Scotland capped him 28 times, and he went on the 1968 Lions tour to South Africa, playing in three of the four Tests against the Springboks. Two Cambridge newcomers were Nick Drake-Lee at prop, and John Owen at lock, both of whom played for England in their 1963 victory at Cardiff Arms Park, when Drake-Lee was still at Cambridge. It is a sign of the continuing influence of the two Universities that the 1963 England side at Cardiff included eight current or former Oxford and Cambridge men: Light Blues Jim Roberts, Simon Clarke (the 1962 Blue), Bev Dovey, Nick Drake-Lee and John Owen and Oxford's John Willcox, Malcolm Phillips and Richard Sharp.

Cambridge's run-up to the 1961 Varsity Match was unusual in that they won all their 14 fixtures, scoring 249 points and conceding only 49 in beating such opposition as Cardiff, Coventry, Leicester, Gloucester and Newport. Oxford, captained by John Willcox, who was knocked out twice but remained on the field, did well to hold this fine Cambridge side to a score of 9-3.

This strong Cambridge side of the early 1960s was soon augmented by the arrival of one of the finest players ever to appear in the Varsity Match, Mike Gibson. Few young players have excited the critics as Gibson did when he appeared at Cambridge in 1963. He had played for Ulster and had had an Ireland trial, but he was generally unknown on the English side of the water. He was seen at once to be a stand-off half of exceptional ability: he had a quick brain, perfect technique and the confidence to use his footwork and his dummy to create gaps in the sternest of defences. Before the 1963 Varsity Match he had already displayed his talents against the All Blacks on their visit to Grange Road. He scored a try in that game, and another against Oxford, asserting his authority in the second half, to lead the way to a fourth consecutive victory for Cambridge at Twickenham, by 19-11.

Gibson played in three Varsity Matches, captaining Cambridge in the 5-5 draw of 1965. He won his first cap for Ireland in that 1963-64 season and went on to play in 69 Irish internationals, starting at stand-off half, moving to the centre and latterly playing on the wing, between 1964 and 1979. He went on five Lions tours, to New Zealand in 1966, 1971 and 1977 and to South Africa in 1968 and 1974, playing in 12 Tests. His total of 81 international and Test appearances remains a world record. It was on the 1966 Lions tour of New Zealand that Gibson was moved to the centre so that his talents could be combined with those of David Watkins, the Welsh stand-off half, and in New Zealand in 1971, together with John Dawes of Wales, he made a perfect centre complement to the genius of Barry John. Many experienced judges maintain that Gibson was the most complete midfield back ever.

Gibson's captain in his first Varsity Match appearance in 1963 was Dick Greenwood, who went on to lead England in 1969. Greenwood had the misfortune to injure an eye playing squash on the eve of the French match that year, missing the game and never playing for England again, though he did become England's coach in the 1980s. A notable recruit to Oxford in 1963 was Ken Jones, who had been a centre on the 1962 Lions tour to South Africa, and who played 14 times for Wales.

In 1964 Cambridge were hot favourites — and with every justification, according to Vivian Jenkins. 'We thought Oxford had the worst side ever. Scotsman Ronnie Lamb was captain and the team hadn't done anything all term. I had a bet with Windsor Lewis, who was president at Cambridge and an old friend of mine. I told him he had to give me some odds this time, so he gave me 10/- at 2-1. Blow me if Oxford didn't win and I got a cheque for a pound from Windsor. It was such an unbelievable surprise that I didn't cash it but instead put it in a frame and gave it to Ronnie Lamb as a memento which he always kept on his desk.'

Besides Gibson, the 1965 Cambridge team had another seasoned Irish international in Mick Doyle, who was later selected for the 1968 Lions tour of South Africa. He was one of the Light Blue wing forwards, the other being Martin Green. They met again as rival national coaches in the 1980s when Ireland played England. Oxford's wing forwards were Tommy Bedford and Tony Bucknall, who was later to captain England.

Oxford had a remarkable string of outstanding full-backs in the 1960s. After Willcox (1959-1962) there was Stewart Wilson (1963-64), who played 22 times for Scotland and was the Test full-back for the 1966 Lions in New Zealand. Wilson was followed by Bob Hiller (1965) who captained England and went on two Lions tours, to South Africa in 1968 and to New Zealand in 1971. Hiller, also a cricket Blue, was an exceptionally accurate goal-kicker, scoring more than 100 points on each of his Lions tours. Hiller's year of 1965 marked the arrival at Oxford of Tommy

Peter Stagg, the tallest man ever to play in a Varsity Match, looks suitably dominant for Oxford during this line-out in the 1961 game.

Bedford, who had already played for the Springboks as a loose forward and who was later to become their captain. He captained Oxford in his second year and stayed on for a third year under the captaincy of Bob Phillips, the stand-off half. Bedford was not in the traditional mould of South African forwards, who were usually big, solid, and forceful: he was just 6 ft tall and weighed little more than 13 st, and was loose-limbed rather than compactly built. Yet he moved swiftly, and his footballing intelligence directed him to the right place at the right time. He had a flawless technique, and his experience, together with his own deep thinking about the game, had a big influence on the University's rugby during his three years at Oxford.

Another who won his first Blue for Oxford in 1965 was Nigel Starmer-Smith, who went on to play for England at scrum-half and to make a name for himself as a television commentator on the game. Before anyone had heard of him I went to report a match between Preston Grass-hoppers and the Greyhounds, who were on tour in the north-west of England. I was much impressed by the play of the Greyhounds' scrum-half, listed in my programme as Stammer-Smith, and praised his performance in my report. At the Greyhounds' next match, against New Brighton, some time before the kick-off a polite young man approached me. 'Excuse me, sir,' he said, 'are you the man from the *Guardian*?' I acknowledged that I was, and he continued: 'Oh well, sir, we very much appreciated what you wrote about our game at Preston, but may I point out that the name is not Stammer-Smith but Starmer-Smith?'

Going up to Oxford and winning a Blue was something of a dream come true for Starmer-Smith because Oxford University had been his local club. He grew up in the town and actually went to Magdalen School in Iffley Road. 'I always went along and sat on the duckboards for the big matches. I can remember as a schoolboy watching people like Malcolm Phillips and the American Pete Dawkins with his amazing style of throwing. But I think the man who impressed me most was Andy Mulligan, when he played for Stanley's — I still think he's the best I've ever seen in that context. Usually we watched a winning side full of internationals. They were certainly on a par with everyone they came up against in terms of status and talent, and we avidly followed Ron Grimshaw's pieces about the team in the *Oxford Mail*.'

Starmer-Smith had been in a successful school side but didn't make an immediate impact at Oxford, and played mainly college rugby to begin with. In fact he was making more of a name for himself as a hockey player, when, at the end of the first year, he was selected for the Greyhounds tour. Finally, in 1965, he made the Varsity team under the captaincy of Fred Craig. Oxford had

The first black player to win a Blue, J.B. Coker of Oxford, is hurled into touch just short of the Cambridge line in 1965.

had a poor season leading up to the Varsity Match and Nigel was less than enthusiastic about the training methods adopted by his captain. 'Training amounted to flogging your guts out day after day in the most appalling pain — most people were on their knees by the end of it. It was so boring and unimaginative; it consisted of sprinting up and down Iffley Road and doing press-ups. We never saw a ball. But it was what had to be done if you were to win your spurs.'

The Varsity Match ended in a draw that year but the play was dull and uninspiring. Everything changed the following year when Tommy Bedford took over as captain and blew a breath of fresh air into the team and its preparations. 'The following season was an antidote, for which I will always be immensely grateful to Tommy Bedford. So much depended on the captain — he was all-powerful, being the selector, coach, manager, the lot — and if you didn't have someone of the right calibre it could be a problem, because he would spend more hours working with the team than any coach anywhere. 1966 was enjoyable principally because Bedford brought such a refreshing aspect to rugby and training. He was obviously influenced by Izak van Heerden and he used us as his experiment, which made for an attractive approach. The forwards were at last

Springbok forward Tommy Bedford on the ball for Oxford against London Scottish. Bedford was one of the game's great thinkers.

handling the ball and we were using a ball in training, and what we did in training we did in our matches. We were young and enthusiastic and had some good players, such as Phillips and Gabitass. It was a kind of rugby I hadn't experienced before and it was as enjoyable as any I had played. We had a good back row in Bedford, Tony Bucknall, who was a tremendous unorthodox flanker, and Hadman, who was the hard man. We had a useful front five which meant that the scrum-half was much more involved in working with the back row — we had about ten different back row moves. Training was fun, shorter but more intensive, and Bedford had learned about coaching and knew what he was doing.'

The new skipper also introduced a different philosophy. He was determined that while the Varsity Match remained the most important game his side were going to make their name playing good rugby against the clubs, and that University rugby would again be respected. 'That year we could have won every game. We had some superb matches and only just lost to Cardiff 14-8. Even when we didn't win we played good rugby. Bedford put the whole thing back into perspective, taking each game as it came. Sure, we were building up a side, but what we did along the way was

Nigel Starmer-Smith performs in front of the cameras, play-
ing scrum-half for Oxford in the 1966 Varsity Match.

Scotland centre Joe McPartlin, who led Cambridge to a 14–0 victory over Oxford in 1962.

Cornishman Richard Sharp, who won three Blues for Oxford and was one of England's finest fly-halves.

important. The Varsity Match itself was very exciting. I remember one of our tries was a back row effort which was something we'd worked on. It was a hard but clean game, and as I recall it was reported as having been the antithesis of the previous year, which it certainly was.'

Seldom can a Varsity Match have aroused as much controversy as that of 1967, which Cambridge won by a try and a penalty goal to nil. It was agreed by everyone that it was, from the spectators' point of view, a dull match. The point at issue was whether the Universities had a duty to provide the crowd with spectacular entertainment. I have always felt, and still do, that because they are amateurs the players can get on with the game in any style they like. Spectators are welcome at the Match but they have no right to demand their money's-worth of spectacle. It would be different if rugby ever became a professional sport: professional sport is part of the world of entertainment. In recent years rugby has gathered round it such trappings as hospitality boxes for businessmen and their clients. The same applies to them: they take a risk. The match may be deadly dull, but as amateurs the players must be more concerned with trying to win the game by whatever means they consider most suitable than with attempting to entertain the multitude, however much money the multitude may have paid for the privilege of being present.

The 1968-69 *Playfair Rugby Football Annual* condemned the 1967 Varsity Match in no uncertain terms: 'The University Match at Twickenham has been the subject of considerable discussion over the last few years because, as a spectacle, it has noticeably depreciated in entertainment value. The match in 1966 gave new hope, for it was described in the *Rugby Annual* as having redeemed the good name of rugby football. In 1967, however, this redemption was well and truly cancelled out in a match which, to the onlooker, was probably the poorest that this long and traditional rivalry has ever produced.' *Playfair* went on to excuse to a certain extent the

Martin Green of Cambridge is held by Holroyd of Oxford during the 1966 match. The following year produced the worst-ever spectacle, and as skipper, Green went into print to defend the players.

tactics used by the two captains, Bob Phillips of Oxford and Martin Green of Cambridge, but it continued: 'The really disturbing feature of this match was not so much the utterly defensive tactics used but the general lack in the basic skills of the game ... Today the Universities aim to turn out boffins and the like. They turn a blind eye to the immense character-building that sport at the top engenders ... The upshot of all this, of course, with a lowering of standard, is that the crowd at Twickenham will continue to diminish each year as it has been doing over the years. Whether the 30 players on the field each time can be wholly blamed is a moot point. They are, perhaps, rather caught up in the emotions and the way of life of contemporary England.'

The 1967 Cambridge captain, Martin Green, bravely went into print in the following year's Varsity Match programme. 'The Varsity Match is more of a players' game than any other game in the Rugby Union calendar', he wrote. 'The physical and mental (and nowadays academic!) demands made upon the player are extreme in the eight weeks before Twickenham. To present 14 individuals with the prospect of anything but "victory at all costs" at the end of their labours, in my opinion, represents an inadequate appreciation of the psychology of the game ... All this does not mean that Cambridge were unconcerned with the game as a spectacle last year, but simply that the circumstances of the preparation and of the game itself led to the adoption of a system that, although effective, was the most deadly to observe except to the most partisan of eyes.'

That those close to the game thought none too ill of this episode is proved by two facts. Green went on to become England's national coach, and Bob Phillips, the 1967 Oxford captain, was, most unusually, elected captain for a second consecutive term of office. Moreover, the 1967 Cambridge stand-off half, Ian Robertson, was to prove a most successful Cambridge coach and an apostle of 15-man rugby in later years, as well as a widely respected radio commentator on the game in general.

It is ironic, then, that the man largely responsible for making Cambridge synonymous with talented running threequarter play should have been involved in what is widely held to be one of the worst Varsity Matches ever staged. Ian Robertson had been at University in Aberdeen and had already been a reserve for Scotland and had played for the Barbarians. In his final year he was given an ultimatum by his professor: either give up rugby and get a degree or keep playing rugby and lose his degree. He settled on a compromise and announced that he would no longer play for the University side, which pleased the tutors. However, unbeknownst to them he went off to play for Aberdeenshire, under the name of David Donald, and teamed up with one of the all-time greats, Ken Scotland.

It was Scotland who suggested that Robertson should go to Cambridge after his final year at Aberdeen. 'Coming from my kind of background it had never remotely entered my head that someone like me could get into Cambridge. Ken said he'd write to a certain Dr Pratt at Christ College, who, he said, was a wonderful fellow who was always taking in rugby players. Looking back I was so wet behind the ears that it was quite frightening, but I went down for the interview knowing that my one link with Cambridge and a Blue was Dr Pratt. I knocked on the door and went in and there was an old man sitting behind a desk who said, "What can I do for you?" I said, "My name's Robertson and I'm down to see Dr Pratt for an interview". He replied, "Oh yes, it's very sad isn't it, poor Dr Pratt dying last week, and you've even missed the funeral. That's pretty worrying isn't it? I could give you an interview but I'm strictly an academic man. I suppose you were thinking you'd get in with a pair of football boots?" "Oh no," I said, "I really want to be a teacher". "You haven't got a prayer," he replied, "because you're going to have to read and write before you can get in. Bad luck, I hope things work out well for you", and he showed me out and slammed the door.

'I was absolutely destroyed, my whole world had crumbled. I went out of the building and 'phoned home. My father said that as I was in Cambridge I had better go and see if someone else would give me an interview. I went back to the secretary's office where I was told: "Oh, Dr Pratt's in room 216". I said that I had already been there but I was assured that Dr Pratt was indeed there and told not to worry. Sure enough, I came upon the same man. "Hello," he said, "what's your name?" "Still Robertson," I replied. "Steele Robertson, is it? Right, just stand over in that corner." And he picked up a rugby ball and flung it at me, which was meant to be his way of conducting an interview. Not only did I catch it but, left-footed, I dropped kicked it straight into his wastepaper basket. He rushed across the room, flung his arms around me and said, "An honours student, I see", and that was it. We talked about rugby for 30 minutes and I was in.

'I was in tears when I first went out because the effort my parents had to make just to get the fare down to Cambridge had been immense, but it was wonderful. Dr Pratt was a most remarkable man and a great character.'

Cambridge was a whole new world to a young Scot from a totally different background who had scarcely set foot outside of Scotland but now found himself in a world of opulence and privilege. The learning process was sometimes a little hard, as when the rugby players were invited by the president, Windsor Lewis, to a 'port and nuts' evening. Robertson heard the invitation as 'pork and nuts' and, expecting a great meal, he had starved himself all day. 'I went along there and couldn't understand why they were just drinking, passing port and peanuts round. I was waiting for the roast pork and two veg with all the trimmings but nothing came. I remember thinking afterwards that I was in a different world and that somehow I had abandoned my social

Cambridge scrum-half Jacko Page in a match against the touring Fijians. Page won his Blue in 1968 when the Light Blues won a close contest by 9–6.

class and moved out of my own ken — none of this happened in Scotland. It seemed a different society.'

The rugby field, however, was familiar. Martin Green was the Cambridge skipper but because of severe problems with a knee injury he spent most of the time on the touch-line barking out orders. 'He was a very good coach and knew his rugby inside out. But it was a strange world — I had come from a democratic society in Scotland into this total dictatorship, but it was the most intensive rugby I had ever known and I loved it, it was the best two months of my life. We went out every single day except match days and I was playing some good rugby. We had an all-international back division because in those days, thanks to the Dr Pratts of this world, you didn't have to be a member of MENSA to get into the University. Tony Jorden and John Anthony were vying for the full-back spot; Jorden had already played international rugby, but Anthony kept him out. He later played for Newport for six years and had final Welsh trials — he was bloody fast coming into the line. Spencer and Smith were as good wings as you would see in international rugby at that time. One was in the Scotland team and the other in the England team. Chris Saville was one centre and Peter Price the other. Saville had played for the Barbarians while Price was as good as the England centres of the time. Jacko Page and Mansell Heslip were in contest for scrum-half. We also had some bloody good forwards, with Nick Martin in the second row and Charlie Hannaford, who went on to play for England at No 8, while Onyett at prop was very good. It was a super team and we played some great rugby in the run-up to the Varsity Match. We scored 30 points against Harlequins and Northampton and had some good wins.'

But this was to count for nothing on the day. Robertson maintains that skipper Martin Green had realised that one of his stand-off half's favourite tricks was to open the ball out when they won a scrum on their own five-yard line, and had warned him that while it might work against lesser teams, it wouldn't against Oxford. 'When it came to the Match he gave me very simple instructions. He said I could open it out wherever I liked and play off the cuff. What I didn't know was that he had told Heslip, the scrum-half, never to give me the ball. So I thought we were out to give the crowd one of the greatest matches at Twickenham. I was in charge of the backs and could do what I wanted. But Heslip never gave me the ball, not even when we were 50 metres from our own line. When the ball came out Heslip kicked to touch. Hannaford, at one stage, had to pick up from his own 22 and make his way up to the 10-metre line — I never got the ball in my own half. I had possession twice: first from a drop-goal attempt which hit the upright and the second time we scored a try in the corner, but I didn't touch it again. It was without question the dullest game of rugby I've been involved in. It was a crying shame, because of the skills we had in that team and the amount of ball we won that day, yet they kept it away from me the whole time. The backs spent a tedious 80 minutes while the forwards ground Oxford into the dust.'

However, there was one mitigating factor. Robertson had fractured a bone in his hand during the game against Harlequins and subsequently played with the aid of painkillers. It was said later that this was the reason why Heslip had been told not to give him the ball. Robertson refutes the suggestion because, he says, the doctor had told him that once he'd had the painkiller he could play flat out — no further damage could be done to the hand. Despite the disappointing nature of the game Robertson was overwhelmed by the occasion. Ken Scotland had told him that nothing was ever quite as important as that Match — even a Lions Test. For eight weeks the players lived in each others' pockets with only one match in mind. Scotland also claimed it was the most involved match he'd ever played in and that he felt more pleasure in winning the Varsity game than any other. 'I had had that in the back of my mind, and I remember when the final whistle went my initial reaction wasn't one of disgust that we'd actually beaten valium and mogadon in

*All Black scrum-half Chris Laidlaw had already made two
tours of the British Isles by the time he got to Oxford in
1968. He skippered the Dark Blues in 1969 when they beat
the Springboks.*

putting 40,000 people to sleep, it was one of sheer joy that we'd done it. I was only going to be
there one year, and this was my only chance. I felt absolutely ecstatic as the whistle went — it
wasn't until we came out of the dressing-room that the real truth struck home. All the way
through I was fantastically frustrated. I remember shouting at Heslip "Give me the bloody ball!" I
was up against Bob Phillips, who was a neat footballer, but I knew I could make breaks and I
knew right along the line we were better. We could have won that game spectacularly.'

The 1968 Varsity Match was a far more exciting affair. Cambridge led 6-0 at half-time from a
dropped goal and a penalty goal, Oxford drew level with two tries and then, at the very end of the
game, Roger Shackleton, the Cambridge stand-off half, raced through for the winning try. There
were many players of quality in both sides: Shackleton and his half-back partner, Jacko Page,
were both to play for England, as was Tony Jorden, the full-back, who subsequently became an
England selector. John Spencer, in the centre, was to captain England and to go on the successful
1971 Lions tour to New Zealand, and the other Cambridge centre was an especially formidable
recruit, Gerald Davies, who had already played seven times for Wales and who had been on the

1968 Lions tour to South Africa where he had played in three Tests against the Springboks. He was destined to be outstanding for the 1971 Lions in New Zealand as a wing threequarter and to gain a total of 46 Welsh caps. Davies was a small man, very light on his feet, with twinkling footwork whether jinking, side-stepping, swerving, accelerating or darting for the goal-line. He had all the attributes of a great threequarter, including sheer pace, and was a complete footballer. He and Spencer made a nicely contrasting pair of centres as Spencer was a big, tall, strapping player with a dashing outside break. In the Cambridge pack was Tony Rodgers, the lock, who subsequently became the University's coach.

Oxford had an outstanding newcomer of their own in 1968: Chris Laidlaw, the All Black scrum-half. By the time he arrived at Oxford, Laidlaw had already made two tours of the British Isles, with the All Blacks of 1963-64 and those of 1967, and had played in 17 Tests, including all four against the 1966 Lions in New Zealand. Such experience was to be of great benefit to Oxford rugby, especially when he captained the side in 1969, the year the Dark Blues defeated the Springboks.

Laidlaw was a solidly-built, chunky scrum-half with the strength and robustness to withstand opponents' spoiling. Like all New Zealand half-backs he was an extremely quick passer, and he had complete mastery of every type of pass. He was best known for his long spin pass but, if the occasion demanded, he could give the quickest of short passes, and the dive pass was also in his repertoire. He had the intelligence and the strength to force half-openings on which his loose forwards could feed, and his dummy could create clean breaches in the opposing defence. Had he been a little faster over the ground he might have saved the 1968 Varsity Match for Oxford, for he made a clever break up the touch-line only to be overhauled just short of the Cambridge line. His colleagues in that defeated Oxford side included two forwards who were to play for their countries and for the 1971 Lions in New Zealand. Lock Mike Roberts was to win eight Welsh caps between 1971 and 1979 and Peter Dixon was to play 22 times for England as a loose forward. Dixon was later to become the University's representative on the Rugby Football Union committee.

12
Oxford Beat the Odds

That Oxford won three consecutive Varsity Matches, in 1969, 1970 and 1971, and did so largely against the odds, was due in great measure to the presence of three outstanding captains, Chris Laidlaw, Peter Carroll and Owen Jones. Laidlaw in 1969 proved himself as clever a tactician and inspiring a leader as he was masterly in his scrum-half techniques. His first major contribution was to mastermind and to direct Oxford's defeat of the touring Springboks. This was the match which had to be transferred from Iffley Road to Twickenham because the police felt that Iffley Road was too open a ground to be protected from anti-apartheid demonstrations. In a heartening display of courage Oxford out-thought the Springboks and eventually won by two penalty goals to one. The man who kicked the University's penalty goals, full-back Mike Heal, had to wait until 1971 for his Blue at stand-off half. This victory temporarily silenced claims that the Universities were no longer strong enough to be accorded fixtures against the major touring teams.

In spite of this triumph Oxford were not favourites for the 1969 Varsity Match. Cambridge still had Tony Jorden at full-back, Gerald Davies and John Spencer in the centre and the experienced combination of Jacko Page and Roger Shackleton at half-back. In the pack Tony Rodgers had now been joined by Gerry Redmond who was to play at loose forward for England that season. He also had an experienced hooker in Phil Keith-Roach. Against this array of talent Laidlaw had only one man who was to play for his country — Peter Dixon, who was in his third year at loose forward. Yet, even though they were temporarily reduced to 12 men and a limping passenger, Oxford somehow managed to carry the day by 9-6. The scoring, three penalty goals to two, hides an afternoon of exciting thrust and counter-thrust. *Playfair Rugby Football Annual* reported 'a game of enormous movement, a high degree of skill among the players, and a fight-back against enormous odds by Oxford ... Seldom can a University side have risen to the heights on the day quite as Oxford did on this occasion.'

The following year, 1970, Cambridge were even stronger favourites. They were led by the great Gerald Davies, now on the right wing; they fielded Jacko Page and Roger Shackleton at half-back for the third year running; and in their pack they still had Phil Keith-Roach, Tony Rodgers and Gerry Redmond. Oxford had Peter Dixon, in his fourth year at loose forward, and had acquired a strong-running centre, Charles Kent, later capped for England. But the pundits made Cambridge likely winners.

Above: Tony Rodgers, who won three Blues for Cambridge in the 1960s and later became the University coach.

Below: The twinkling footwork of Gerald Davies in evidence for Cambridge University against the Fijians. This electrifying Welsh threequarter played in three Varsity Matches.

In my preview of this Varsity Match I wrote for the *Guardian* that 'ever since the early games of the term it has been clear that Cambridge this year possess a much greater share of talent than Oxford. Thoughts before today's match are therefore concerned with how Oxford can possibly win and how Cambridge can possibly lose. The psychological influences are probably more potent in the University Match than in most other games because of the tenseness of the occasion. As captain of Oxford, Peter Carroll certainly has an easier task in trying to inspire his men today than has Gerald Davies. There could be a chink in the Cambridge armour here: they might lose the psychological battle. But if you turn from possibilities to probabilities, it is difficult in the extreme to see logically how Cambridge can lose. Their superior forward play alone should be sufficient to ensure them of victory. But in addition they have the close understanding of Page and Shackleton at half-back, and they have a marked advantage in pace and skill in the three-quarter line. This could be Gerald Davies's match. Could it possibly be Peter Carroll's?'

In the event it was emphatically Carroll's Match. Carroll, who had played for New South Wales at home in Australia, came into the mature student category. At the age of nearly 30, he was in his third year as Oxford's full-back, although he had played much of his rugby at centre. One of Carroll's more inspired decisions was to play Stefan James, normally a loose forward, in the centre. It was James who scored Oxford's vital first try in their victory by a goal, a dropped goal and two tries to a penalty goal. *Playfair Rugby Football Annual* recorded: 'Davies, the Cambridge captain, who was expected to provide the thrust where it really mattered, needed the ball in order to perform, and this he rarely had with enough room or time in which to manoeuvre. Shackleton was blamed by Light Blue devotees for kicking too often, and this he did, without question but not, at times, without provocation, with the raiding forwards at his throat.' The 1970 Varsity Match, incidentally, provided another example of two brothers playing together — Peter Carroll's younger brother, Bruce, was Oxford's scrum-half. Peter, always a city gent even at Oxford, subsequently joined Bowring, sponsors of the Varsity Match from 1976.

In the summer of 1971 the two Universities put aside their traditional rivalry to combine for a tour of South America. Unfortunately seven players, plus the England international referee Johnny Johnson, who accompanied the touring party, contracted hepatitis during the tour. One of the sufferers was Phil Keith-Roach, who had been elected captain of Cambridge. During the term he did not feel up to captaining the side and, although he did eventually play in the Varsity Match, he handed over the captaincy to Redmond.

For the first time ever Oxford, in 1971, did not field a single player who was or who subsequently became an international. Cambridge, on the other hand, had three such players in their pack — Gerry Redmond of England at loose forward, Bob Wilkinson of England at lock and in the other lock position Mike Biggar, who was to win 24 caps for Scotland as a loose forward. Not surprisingly, Cambridge, who now had Chris Williams, a younger brother of the great J.P.R., in their centre, were favourites once again, and their forwards made a crushing start. Their tactics at this stage were to bombard the Oxford defence with high punts, several of which were fumbled, more than one by the Oxford captain, Owen Jones, who was now at full-back, after playing on the wing in his two previous Varsity Matches. Jones, an experienced Welshman from Ammanford who had already obtained a degree at Swansea University, refused to let these mistakes unsettle him. He showed his true worth as the game wore on, scoring a fine try near the end of the match. This was a good instance of a captain leading by example and of a team following their captain's lead. Just as Jones recovered his assurance, so did the whole Oxford side, and Cambridge were defeated 21–3. *Playfair* said of Oxford: 'If they were lacking in any virtues, it certainly was not in courage or in determination; and with plenty of those two, a lot can be accomplished.'

A soccer-writing colleague asked quite recently if a captain of a rugby team were really as important as he is made out to be. The answer is that, with the possible exception of cricket, no sportsman has, or should have, to make as many decisions as a rugby captain. And of course the cricket captain has a lot more time in which to work out what is the best course of action at any given point in a game. He has the time between overs and the time it takes the fast bowlers to stroll back to the start of their excessively long run-ups. A rugby captain can count only on the occasional stoppage for injury. It is often related that Australian cricket teams are chosen for their ability and that only after that selection is the choice of captain made. This system does not work in rugby. In modern rugby the first two choices should always be the goal-kicker and the captain. The captain should always be a man who will command respect, not primarily because of his ability as a player but because of the strength of his personality and his ability to relate to his team-mates. Oxford chose the right men for 1969, 1970 and 1971.

13
Cambridge to the Fore

It was splendidly appropriate that in their centenary year, 1972, Cambridge should not only win the Varsity Match but begin an unprecedented sequence of five consecutive victories. The programme for the 1972 game included some statistics which illustrated the great contribution Cambridge had made to rugby in their 100 years: 157 England internationals and 20 England captains; 66 Scottish internationals and ten Scotland captains; 38 Welsh internationals and 14 Welsh captains; 11 Irish internationals and five Irish captains; 49 Lions and four Lions captains.

By 1972 substitutes had been introduced but, at that stage of the development of the game, only in international matches, unluckily for Oxford in the Varsity Match. The Dark Blues lost one of their forwards shortly after half-time, when the score was 0-0, and Cambridge promptly scored a pushover try against Oxford's seven-man pack. On the other hand there have been many instances when the loss of a player or players has inspired the depleted side to rise to great heights — a notable example is Chris Laidlaw's team of 1969 — and in any case Bob Wilkinson dominated the line-outs for Cambridge throughout the match. Oxford had to play without their chosen captain, Tim Seymour, because of injury. The captaincy was taken over by Darryl Jones, a 30-year-old stand-off half, whose promotion is an extraordinary story. Having been a teacher at his old school, Neath Grammar School, he went up to Oxford on a post-graduate course. He played one game for the Greyhounds, but was then dropped and asked to coach the Oxford team. When the injury problems arose, Jones agreed to play in the University's penultimate match of the term, against Gloucester. His second game for Oxford was against Cambridge — and as captain. The attendance at Twickenham was only 26,400, the lowest thus far since the Second World War. Cambridge won by 16-6.

The attendance fell even further in 1973, when a crowd of 23,000 watched a match which was largely confined to punting by the half-backs of both sides. There was, however, an exciting finish as Oxford, 6-14 down with eight minutes to go, suddenly broke free from the pattern and started to fling the ball about. They scored six more points with a try and conversion by their scrum-half, Steve Lewis, but they could manage no more. Lewis, the son of the Welsh international referee Ernie Lewis, scored all Oxford's points with his try, the conversion and two penalty goals, and he did a lot of Oxford's punting as well. Cambridge had acquired a lively scrum-half from Millfield in Richard Harding, later capped by England, and in their centre was Alan Wordsworth, who

subsequently played at stand-off half for England. The third of Cambridge's string of five successive victories was a much more spectacular affair. Coached by Ian Robertson, the former Cambridge and Scotland stand-off half, Cambridge spent the term developing a quick-passing game and as a result lost only three of their 12 pre-Twickenham matches. Their attractive style of play was at least partly responsible for the rise in attendance at Twickenham to 30,000, and the spectators were not disappointed.

When Robertson went down from Cambridge he went to teach at Fettes College and coached rugby there for three years. He then went to London to work for the BBC in 1972 and, as he

Left: Her Majesty the Queen is introduced to the Cambridge team at Twickenham during their Centenary year. Fittingly, they beat Oxford 16–6 to begin a sequence of five consecutive victories.

A rare shot from the Twickenham dressing-rooms, after Cambridge had become the first holders of the Bowring Bowl by beating Oxford 15–0.

couldn't watch any Saturday rugby, he found himself going down to Cambridge to watch midweek games. Eventually John Howard, the skipper, asked him if he would coach the side. Bearing in mind his own experiences in 1967, Robertson laid down his terms. 'I said the only way I would coach was if we agreed to play 15-man running rugby whether we won or lost, that it was more important than the result. And it was agreed for the whole 13 years that I was involved that we ran the ball. Before we went out on the pitch my last words were always "throw the ball around for 80 minutes and enjoy it", and I never talked about winning or losing, because I felt we had an obligation to entertain the crowd. The Varsity Match had decreased in importance and from 1972 we tried to win it back. We were unlucky in some ways: Cambridge never had a great pack of forwards and so we didn't really have 13 wonderful, open matches. Most of the time Oxford, with a better pack, would try to keep it tight while we ran whatever we could. If you add up all the points over those years I think you'll find we scored quite a few.

'I didn't really know the boys in that first year but John Howard, the skipper, was a smashing chap. We also had Mark Rosser, a very good fly-half and a top-class footballer, and then Chris Williams, J.P.R.'s brother, in the centre. In the first year I went up three or four times to coach, then for several years I would go up twice a week to coach and watch as many midweek games as I could. My attitude was simply to try to play running rugby. So in two sessions, even though I never saw them play, I could at least show them how to improve. A lot of them didn't need to improve, they just needed confidence — after all they were 19-year-old kids playing against the likes of Leicester, Cardiff, Newport, London Scottish, Harlequins and Coventry. It was a hard fixture list and they were often overawed, so all I did was instil confidence in them, usually by running down the opposition.

'We just ran and ran and ran with the ball at all training sessions. I never did fitness work with them, it was all with a ball, getting the angles right so that they were running parallel to the touch-line. We had a very small number of moves, maybe seven or eight; really the aim was just to run it along the line. I've never been a great believer in having a catalogue of moves; I preferred the players to run and pass and to get that slick and sharp, and to work on how to create that half overlap. We were so much fitter than most teams in those days — real fitness has only come to most clubs in the mid-1980s. We won a lot of matches by running side to side twice, then with the third bit of possession we could literally stroll through.'

Robertson taught his Cambridge players to run bad possession — in fact in most cases it wasn't just bad, it was diabolical. He maintained that if the threequarters kept their alignment deep enough then they could even run ball delivered by a pack which had been pushed 15 yards back. He also worked on individual skills, but the main aim was, as he says, to get everyone running with the ball and to give them the confidence to run. 'The whole time I was coaching Cambridge winning was never that important to me. What I was trying to do was get young kids to enjoy their rugby and throw the ball around so that in the end they could beat Oxford, but it wasn't the end of the world if they didn't. As long as they left Cambridge at the end of three years better players than when they arrived that was the important thing. It was a change of emphasis. In 1967 the result was the only thing in the world that mattered to Martin Green: he would have been quite happy to win 1-0.'

However this style of rugby meant a lot of hard work for the forwards. Robertson felt that he had no expertise in this area so he brought in New Zealander Murray Meikle to drill the forwards. Meikle was a junior All Black international and a tremendous New Zealand forwards coach. They rucked everything, because they never had the physical strength to do otherwise. He taught them that and coached until 1980 when Tony Rodgers took over the role. 'It was a slightly unusual set-up at that time: all over Britain clubs had just one coach, and this extended even to the national teams. But right from the start I decided that I certainly wasn't good enough to train backs and forwards. I think we were the first to have separate coaches for forwards and backs — it was only in the mid-1980s that the national teams followed suit.

'It was huge fun and everybody enjoyed it. Unfortunately after the players left and went to club rugby I would meet many of them a year or so later and they would be thinking of giving up the game because the rugby they were playing was so boring.' Robertson did, however, have certain advantages over his club counterparts. The turnover of players at University is very fast so there just isn't time for strong factions to develop within the teams. Most of the players are there to win a Blue and wouldn't dream of shouting back at their coach for fear of not making the team. Every year Robertson would state his intention to coach running rugby to the new skipper, and every one accepted his philosophy. 'Of course, they were under pressure because we had established a tradition for it and had attracted kids like Rob Andrew and Huw Davies, who could have gone to either University, but we'd always thrown the ball around so it worked to our benefit.

'Our style transformed people like Steve Page, who was a left wing and had been a modest schoolboy player. When he played for our team we ran the ball out to his wing for 15 games prior to the Varsity Match. When he subsequently went up to Heriot's to play, he actually became one of the top try-scorers in Scottish rugby, yet he was of very modest ability. He couldn't beat a man, he just caught the ball and ran, but my theory was if you never give a ball to the wing because he's a poor player he'll remain a poor player, but if you keep feeding it out, however good he is, you'll get him at his absolute peak on that day.' Of course there had to be times when force of circumstance and injury severely tested this running rugby theory. Then Robertson would cut his cloth to suit. This didn't mean abandoning his style, but introducing miss-moves and using players whose ability was slightly below par as decoys. But the clear, defined style took some of the pressure off the coach: if everybody knew that style then all he had to do was to bring his players to a peak for the Varsity Match.

'I knew there would be mistakes but it was much more fun, and the players worked harder knowing there was a carrot at the end of it than they would have done if we had played nine-man rugby. I remember Mike Burton coming up with a Gloucester team who were unbeaten ten matches into the season. We put 36 points on them at Grange Road, simply running them ragged, and suddenly a lot of their forwards looked like old men. Afterwards they were very good with the lads and showed them how to scrummage. I asked them why they were doing that and their reply was "If we can teach them that, perhaps they won't mind staying down in the scrum like the rest of us instead of sprinting all over the field". It was Gloucester's biggest defeat that year, and we had eight nonentities in the pack, all of whom were sprinters. You hear people talk about the 1984 Aussies all being athletes — well, our forwards had been similarly trained since 1972, mainly because they couldn't win line-out ball. They couldn't hope to out-scrummage opposition who were five to ten stones heavier and six to eight years more mature, so we had to adopt that style of play.'

Inevitably over Robertson's 13-year tenure certain teams and individuals rate a special mention. Yet he is the first to admit that he made some great mistakes as coach and Alun Lewis was one of them. Lewis went to the Freshers' trial in 1974 and was soon pinging out 30-yard passes off either hand in any direction. But Robertson had already decided that his scrum-half would be Richard Harding, which prompted Lewis to play his rugby for Bedford. 'He went on to win the John Player Cup for them almost single-handedly and he turned out to be the best scrum-half I had seen in British rugby, and that probably includes Gareth Edwards. He had a phenomenal pass off either hand, faster than Catchpole or Hipwell and twice as long. Lewis had

Oxford full-back Hopkins tries in vain to stop Cambridge wing Greig scoring in the 1977 Match. But the astute kicking of Gareth Davies at fly-half eventually resulted in a 16–10 win for Oxford.

incredible wrists and his foot positioning was superb. He went out to join the 1977 Lions but was injured — he wasn't really a rugby fanatic and gave up soon after.'

However, Lewis did play in the 1975 Varsity Match. Robertson reckoned that this Cambridge side was superb by any standards. The back division was outstanding; at fly-half was Alan Wordsworth, who loved to let the ball out and who was eventually capped by England; on the right wing they had Michael O'Callaghan, an All Black international, and then there was Alastair Hignell. 'Hignell was another of my great mistakes. He had been an England Schools scrum-half, but now that Lewis was at scrum-half I told Hignell that he'd never be a scrum-half and put him at full-back. He ended up with about 15 caps there for England but he would probably have won a lot more at scrum-half. His reading of the game was superb, and he was probably the most natural footballer of any to have gone through Cambridge.

'We had a couple of steady centres in Roddy Grant and Jim Moyes. Neither was actually a centre — Roddy was a full-back and Jim was a wing — but because we had spent 15 matches spinning the ball along the line when they got to the Varsity Match they were completely *au fait* with what was going on. We had a half-decent pack and I reckoned we would break even up front, while all seven of our backs were light years ahead of Oxford.'

There was some betting on the 1975 game exceeding the biggest winning margin in the Varsity Match, which stood at 20 points. Cambridge had had some injuries in the run-up and some of their results were none too impressive. Robertson, who was going on his honeymoon after the game, put ten pounds on Cambridge to equal the winning margin at 25-1. 'In the last minute of the match, when Lewis went over for a try, the entire team turned to the BBC commentary box and put their hands in the air because they'd just paid for my honeymoon. That was a particularly satisfying victory!

'I think the most rewarding aspect of the University game is seeing players go on to play international rugby. No other players get the same opportunity to train day after day together and to build up for one match to get it right. We had real problems the following year because the front row of Boulding, Beringer and Vivian all got first-class honours. How can you coach a rugby team when you have a front row who are capable of thinking? Just imagine the challenge that presented to the rest of the guys! In 1977 we had Mathew Fosh, who was the best centre in England at the time. Again he was someone who went off to club rugby, was never the same again and retired in his early 20s. He could have had five years in the England team. He was 14½ stone, a beautiful passer of the ball and could make a break and side-step. I was lucky in that I had a string of teams in which there were a couple of internationals who could give confidence to all the 18-year-olds. The 1984 match, which we won 34-0, was a good one. It was the last for which I was able to spend a lot of time going to Cambridge to coach, and it was Rob Andrew's last year. There was a smashing back division; Richard Moon was at scrum-half; Andy Martin, who was really a full-back, was on one wing with Mark Bailey on the other, and in the centre were Simms and Clough with Gavin Hastings thundering in from full-back. Simms was almost as good as Mathew Fosh at giving and taking a pass, timing it and reading a situation.

'In those days Moon and Andrew were outstanding at club level; they had confidence, were young and didn't know any better. We had a smashing run-up and knew we were going to win. I think that was the greatest win. They played fabulous rugby and scored six tries. The Light Blues opened out the game in the first minute and Bailey, who had been injured and had played only once beforehand, had to run 80 yards in the opening minute. I don't think he did anything else for the rest of the match. Twenty years ago it would have been unheard of in a Varsity Match to run from your own goal-line in the first two minutes, but Andrew did it because we had done it for three years and eight weeks without thinking.'

The Varsity Match has had its ups and downs over the years, and Robertson realises that it can never be as important as it was in the early days, when it was considered to be virtually an extra national trial. But in recent years it has come out of the trough of the late 1960s and early 1970s, and he still believes it has a vital role to play in the fabric of British rugby. 'For a midweek club match to attract over 40,000 people, it has to be something more than just a social occasion. I still believe that the Match has an importance of its own, but I don't think it will ever go back to the old days. Most Universities have worked out that the best way to get a few internationals is to have post-graduate men in. I think that will help not only the image of the Match but also the other players in the sides.

'It should be treated as an important game in its own right, but also it should entertain the

Mathew Fosh, the Cambridge centre who Ian Robertson
rated as the best in England, clashes with Oxford wing
Eddie Quist-Arcton in the 1978 Match.

spectators and give everybody a good day out to maintain its traditional image. If it just became a dour struggle you wouldn't get the crowds and it would die; it was without question in serious danger of dying in the early 1970s but both Universities have taken positive steps. Sometimes we had a couple of boys wanting to come to Cambridge as post-graduates in positions where we already had good players, so I would send them to Oxford. Alan Jones is of the same view; he sends men to Oxford but also says "there's a couple of good props, would you like them to come to Cambridge?" He sees that the actual Match is more important than the winning. I think it has been great for the image of the game that Oxford now have these famous players. Over 40,000 people come to the games now and it seems to have re-established itself as the big occasion it once was.'

In 1974 Cambridge certainly had the right men to play 15-man rugby. They still had Harding at scrum-half and had recruited two internationals for the centre threequarter positions, Mick O'Callaghan, who had played on the wing for the All Blacks, and Peter Warfield, who had won three caps for England in 1973. Warfield was accompanied from Durham University to Cambridge by Gordon Wood, a talented wing threequarter.

This was the year Alastair Hignell arrived at Cambridge with his reputation as captain of England Schools and as an unusually gifted scrum-half. But within a week his rugby career was to undergo a remarkable change. 'I had been there only two days when I was put into a senior trial, which was quite an achievement. I played against a scrum-half from the Sixty Club, Alun Lewis, and there was another very good scrum-half called Joe Davies, who didn't get a Blue at scrum-half but eventually won one at centre. The three of us arrived at the same time and formed a great alliance, but we knew that Richard Harding was going to get the place in the team. However, I came through the senior trial and knew that I would play for the second team. The following week in the Freshers' trial Alun and Joe were scrum-halves. I was also invited along, and as there was a bit of uncertainty about the fitness of the full-back, Mark Hodgson, and fly-half Mark Rosser, they needed a goal-kicker. They asked me to play full-back — I had never played there before so I had one 20-minute session. I must have done reasonably well because three days later I was playing there against Cardiff. It was a fair old shock to the system but they just said, "You're there to take the goal-kicks and anything else is a bonus. Come into the line if you can". My role was reduced to its simplest so there was no pressure. I never really thought about the fact that Gerald Davies was playing. We actually drew 16-16 — and I loved it.'

Hignell soon realised that he had joined a team of very talented players. Harding was at scrum-half, Warfield in the centre and there were O'Callaghan, the All Black wing, and Gordon Wood. Then there was the inspiration of Ian Robertson as coach. 'He was a great coach at that level because all he said was, "You forwards get us the ball and we'll run and run". Wordsworth was a fantastic fly-half: if there was anything on he wanted to move it. We were all young and fit and alive to the situations, it was great. Of course, playing that kind of rugby dulled the need to want to play scrum-half.'

After only 12 first-class games as a full-back the 19-year-old freshman found himself in his first Varsity Match. Up until then he had taken everything in his stride but suddenly the enormity of the occasion began to dawn on him. Everywhere he went tutors and students were wishing him well for the big day. Hignell had played at Twickenham before with England Schools, but that was nothing compared to running out in front of over 30,000 spectators and millions of television viewers. He had a sudden attack of nerves, but being in such a good team and blessed with confidence Hignell was determined to enjoy the big match. He scored 12 points that day, which included a spectacular try. 'Robbo had had us doing a lot of complicated moves, one of which

Left: Alastair Hignell could not get into the Cambridge side in his usual position of scrum-half. So he was persuaded to play at full-back, and went on to score a record 46 points in his four appearances in the Varsity Match.

Oxford's D.S.M. MacDonald collars Cambridge centre A.R. Grant during the 1976 encounter. MacDonald's brother Dugald, who had played for the Springboks against the Lions in 1974, skippered the side.

actually worked, and I scored. When you do something like that in front of a big crowd you do feel special. We had some points on the board and were playing pretty well until the second half, when the referee, Mr Pattinson, seemed to take exception to the way our forwards played. They were continually penalised, and the Oxford fly-half, Nigel Quinnen, kept potting at goal, ending up with five penalties. He had one right near the end which shaved the underside of the bar and could have won the Match for them. In fact we were told, afterwards, that the referee had blown up about three minutes too early because his watches had been wrong.' In this his first Varsity Match Hignell scored 12 of his side's 16 points with two penalty goals, a conversion and a spectacular try. Cambridge persisted in their endeavours to play fluent, open rugby and their efforts delighted the crowd. The only disadvantage of their style of play was the frequency with which they gave away penalties, but they played much the better football. In the end justice was done and Cambridge won by a single point, 16-15.

Despite his success at full-back, Hignell saw the position as a temporary measure. He thought his chance of the scrum-half spot would materialise once Harding had gone down. Having already helped out at full-back and having earned a Blue, he felt sure his colleagues would allow him to play in his favourite position the following year. But he had reckoned without the intervention of the England selectors. 'I played all the second term at scrum-half in such fixtures as Moseley and Gloucester away, and I did reasonably well, receiving favourable comments in the press. I thought I'd done my bit by filling in at full-back, and I would be able to return to scrum-half. Then I went on tour to Japan with Cambridge as a full-back and number two scrum-half. While I was away I had a phone call to say that I'd been picked to tour Australia with England. I said, "Great! Who's the other scrum-half?", only to be told I was to go as a full-back. That was in the summer of 1975, so at the start of the next Varsity season Peter Warfield told me "You've been picked at full-back for England so you can play there for us, especially as we've got Alun Lewis".'

Lewis, who had of course left to play for Bedford when he could not get into the University side the previous year, was very much his own man. He never played for Wales, but he was flown out to New Zealand as a replacement for the 1977 Lions. He arrived at Auckland airport early in the morning after a flight of approaching 30 hours to be driven northwards, straight to a Lions practice at a club on the way to Whangarei, where the next match was to take place. He immediately astonished the New Zealand press and all the rest of us by throwing out the quickest and longest passes we had seen from the Lions on that tour. In his own way he was something of a genius — what the French would call *un original* — but, alas, he did not stay long enough in top-class rugby to do justice to his talents.

The line-up of Cambridge backs for the 1975 Match was much the same as the previous year except that O'Callaghan was now in his best position on the wing and Wordsworth returned at fly-half. Everyone it seemed was finding their true positions except Hignell, but he soon had other matters to worry about. 'I had been injured a few times that season and didn't play many games — I probably played only once in the four or five weeks leading up to the Varsity Match. But we were very confident going into the Match and won a lot of ball in the line-outs and scrums. Everything came right on the day — even with my bad ankle the kicks were flying over.' Hignell scored 19 points in all, five penalties and two conversions, but Quinnen once again kept Oxford in with a chance. He kicked three penalties and Cambridge were held 16-12 until the final 15 minutes, when they really cut loose and scored a further 18 points to give them a 34-12 victory and their biggest score in more than 100 years of the fixture. 'It is a funny game to look back on. We seemed to be in command: everything went well, even to the point late in the game when we were awarded a penalty. I should have run up and slotted it over, but Alun Lewis spotted that no one was watching him so he just tapped it to himself and went over for the try. Robbo had given us the confidence — he was superb at that.' Fittingly that final piece of quick-wittedness was responsible for coach Ian Robertson's 25-1 wedding present!

Oxford, meanwhile, had acquired the services of an exceptional player in No 8 Dugald MacDonald from Western Province, who had played in a Test for the Springboks against Willie John McBride's 1974 Lions in South Africa. He was a stocky, beavering player who had much to do with Oxford's resistance to a superior Cambridge side in the 1975 Varsity Match. He was to captain the University in 1976, which was an important year in the long-term future of the Varsity Match.

It was in 1976 that Bowring started their sponsorship of the Match so that Cambridge became the first holders of the Bowring Bowl as well as winners of the Varsity Match for the fifth consecutive year. They also levelled the series, at 41 wins each, for the first time since 1899.

Cambridge were captained at Twickenham, for the second successive year, by Canadian Angus Stewart, who brought into his pack at No 8 Eddie Butler, later captain of Wales. There were two brothers Lewis at half-back, while Oxford also had two brothers, the South African MacDonalds, one of whom, Donald, was to win seven caps for Scotland. Cambridge's clear-cut victory by 15-0 owed much to Alastair Hignell who, with three penalty goals and a conversion, took his points total for three Varsity Matches to 43. He was to kick another penalty goal the following year when he was captain.

Having played several times for England at full-back and with Alun Lewis well established in the Cambridge side, Hignell abandoned all thoughts of returning to the scrum-half position. Cambridge still had a very strong team but the 1976 match was something of an anti-climax. 'We expected to win and knew we were the better side so we didn't need to try anything fancy or elaborate. The year before had been a bit of a celebration but in 1976 we just went out and played

A Welsh captain in the making: Eddie Butler in the first of his three appearances for Cambridge in 1976.

Ian Greig, brother of cricketer Tony, followed up his try for Cambridge in 1977 with this touchdown the following year.

a percentage game. It was perhaps the least satisfying win of the lot.' Had Cambridge won in 1977, Hignell and Mick O'Callaghan would have equalled the feat of Carl Aarvold (1926-29) of playing in four winning Cambridge sides at Twickenham. But it was not to be — Oxford at last turned the tide with a 16-10 victory. Hignell was aware of the record but he also had other things on his mind. 'I had checked the statistics and knew that both myself and O'Callaghan were on course to equal Aarvold's record. We should have won the game, but I had spent most of the year injured and only played in the Varsity Match because Robbo persuaded me to. I had been injured in the first week in October when the grounds were still fairly hard. I have congenitally weak ankles and, having played cricket in the summer, I went straight on to play rugby for Bristol in September. I suppose, looking back, I didn't give myself the opportunity to get fit. Maybe with the right medical advice I would have been slapped into plaster and told just to keep the weight off it

but the doctors weren't sure what it was. It was a stress fracture type of injury — they told me to keep running on it but it actually got worse. I played in one match against Harlequins a couple of weeks before the Varsity Match and survived it, managing to plonk over a couple of goals. Robbo felt I was better value on the field than on the side-lines. I went along with him because I was desperate to play.

'It's funny being captain of the University and not playing, because for a whole term you're at every training session, every match, and there's all the off-the-field organisation. I had done the secretary's job two years before, and so was involved in the whole set-up. It's very difficult to concentrate on yourself: the best thing for me would have been to have gone away and got fit. But I wasn't fit, and played with cortisone in my foot to try to kill the pain. But Gareth Davies exposed me quite cleverly. I missed a few kicks while Tony Watkinson succeeded with his for

Oxford and we were stuffed. It was a very disappointing way to finish my Varsity career. I should never have played, but I suppose it was all due to the impetuosity of youth. In a way you gamble with yourself, you think that once you get out there you'll be OK. The Varsity Match means so much to those who play in it that it's difficult to explain to anyone outside.'

Gareth Davies, who was later to captain Wales and to play for his country on 21 occasions, had already played for Wales B and for the Barbarians. Moreover he had had experience of Twickenham, having represented the University of Wales Institute of Science and Technology in the Universities Athletic Union final. He subsequently made the 1980 Lions tour of South Africa where, in spite of being dogged by injury, he proved on the firm, dry grounds that he could be a most deceptive runner as well as a precise kicker.

Cambridge had acquired yet another exceptional scrum-half in John Robbie, formerly a successful captain of Trinity College, Dublin, who had already won five caps for Ireland. Altogether he was to play for Ireland on nine occasions and to play in a Test for the 1980 Lions in

Cambridge had a succession of brilliant scrum-halves in the 1970s including Irishman John Robbie, seen here playing against the All Blacks in 1978.

South Africa before emigrating to that country and becoming a travelling reserve for the Springboks. Robbie possessed the rare ability to take control of a match, and this he did when he captained Cambridge in 1978, passing accurately, kicking precisely and breaking with clever deception. Helped by having the bigger pack of forwards on his side, he contributed 17 points to the Light Blues' 25-7 victory with a try, two conversions and three penalty goals.

Robbie was succeeded as captain in 1979 by another skilful scrum-half, Ian Peck, who, uniquely, had captained both the rugby and cricket teams at the same time without winning a Blue in either sport. His half-back partner was Marcus Rose, soon to become England's full-back. Simon Halliday, later of England, was in the centre for Oxford, but it was their cunning forwards who gave the Dark Blues the opportunities to win the Varsity Match by 9-3. Their captain, Peter Enevoldson, was a skilled prop, and at No 8 they fielded Nick Mallett who later played for South Africa. The match was dominated by the punting of the two stand-off halves, and *Playfair* described it as 'a poor advertisement for the present state of the game at the two Universities.'

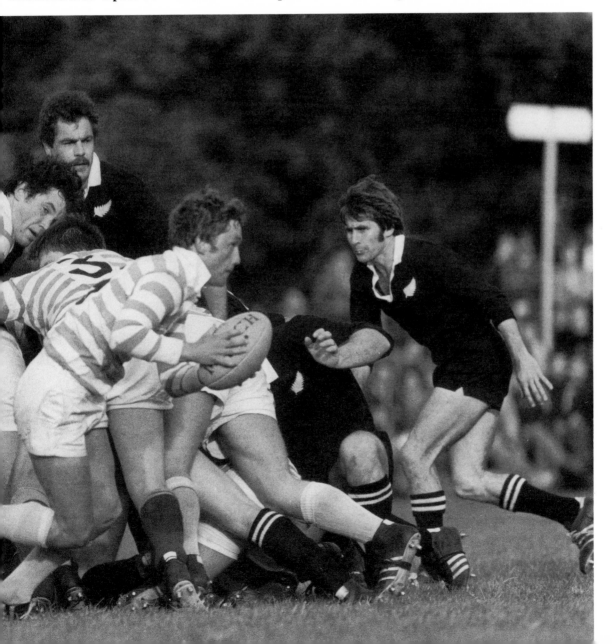

14
The 1980s: Riding High

No one could have guessed that when Cambridge won the 1980 Varsity Match by 13-9 they were embarking on a second run of five consecutive wins, a sequence which was to take them ahead of Oxford, in the number of wins achieved, for the first time since the series began more than 100 years earlier. Their preparations for the Varsity Match did not go according to plan, however. Ian Peck, elected captain for the second consecutive year, was injured two weeks before the game and had to hand over the captaincy to Marcus Rose, now established at full-back. The absence of Peck was a blow to Cambridge because he had been consolidating a half-back partnership with Huw Davies which had been forged on England's tour of Japan, Fiji and Tonga during the summer. Davies had to have his appendix taken out during the term and, although he recovered quickly, he was denied his only chance to play with Peck's deputy at scrum-half, John Cullen, by the cancellation, through snow, of the University's game against Northampton. Cambridge thus included a pair of half-backs who had never played together when they took the field at Twickenham.

Davies went on to play for England at stand-off half, centre and full-back, prompting any number of discussions about which was his true position. I have seen him play equally well in all three places. Before he went to Cambridge, he was at UWIST — during which period he also played for Cardiff — and I remember watching UWIST put 30 points or more over Loughborough in a UAU Championship match at Worcester. Davies was in the centre that day, and he carved out try after try for his right wing, Tony Swift, with a classic display of centre threequarter craft. In this company Davies looked a born centre: in his first Varsity Match he looked a born stand-off half.

By a strange quirk of fate Oxford likewise had to change their captain at the eleventh hour. When Nick Mallett was injured, the captaincy was given again to Peter Enevoldson who, believe it or not, was playing in his fifth Varsity Match, having already played 115 games for the University. Simon Halliday, not subsequently renowned for his place-kicking, kicked two of Oxford's three penalty goals.

Although the series of Varsity Matches began in 1872, the absence of official rugby combat during the two World Wars meant that the 1981 match was the 100th. Thus Cambridge had more to celebrate than the second leg of what was to be a five-match winning sequence. An extra reason to rejoice was that their 9-6 victory put them ahead of Oxford in wins and losses for the very first

*Two future England internationals oppose each other in the snow of 1981.
Cambridge fly-half Huw Davies eludes Oxford centre Simon Halliday.*

Cambridge full-back Marcus Rose clears the snow and the ball in the 1981 epic. Rose's three penalty goals gave his team a 9–6 victory in one of the most remarkable Varsity Matches ever.

time. The record now stood at 44 wins for Cambridge and 43 for Oxford, with 13 matches drawn. The celebratory centenary dinner was held at the Hilton Hotel, Park Lane, London and was attended by over 400 old Blues, more than 50 of them from overseas. The chair was taken most appropriately by the 83-year-old Lord Wakefield, whose gravelly wit was unimpaired — 'we will now have a break of ten minutes for you to shake the snake,' he announced at one stage — and the highlight was a maiden public speech by Prince Andrew, aged 21, who showed fortitude and a talent for succinct repartee in dismissing the mild barracking he received from the players.

The Varsity Match itself will be remembered largely for the three to four inches of snow which covered the Twickenham pitch as a result of an unexpected overnight blizzard. Both sides coped manfully with the difficult conditions, Cambridge adapting the more readily, but no one could score a try, the issue being decided by penalty goals: three to Cambridge by Marcus Rose and two to Oxford by Stuart Barnes. Huw Davies captained Cambridge and Nigel Roberts, from lock forward, led Oxford. Barnes, a little man with tremendous acceleration through the outside gap, was to play for England, and he was not the only valuable recruit at Oxford. Phil Crowe, a mature student in the centre, had already won six caps for Australia and Derek Wyatt, a 31-year-old on

John Cullen, the Light Blues' scrum-half, gets closer to the white carpet than most as he moves the ball from a scrum.

the left wing, had played for England against Scotland at Murrayfield in 1976. Wyatt had spent five years playing for Bedford and was in his fourth season for Bath when he decided to give up teaching and fund himself for a year at Oxford. In preparation for the rigours of Varsity rugby he went to see Bath's fitness specialist, Tom Hudson. 'I started training in May and didn't see a rugby ball until the first game of the season. He had me playing five-a-side soccer and squash, and swimming and weight-training. I had a programme, I regained my enthusiasm and went up to Oxford fitter than I had ever been in my life. I was treated as a fresher, nothing special, so I had to prove myself all over again — it was great.'

After years of first-class rugby he found the Oxford training regime a little narrow. It seemed that the revolution in coaching and fitness had passed Oxford by. Still, the team had a lot to offer and they beat London Scottish and Northampton and lost by only seven points to Australia. Oxford had every reason to feel confident as the Varsity Match approached. They had a back line which included Barnes, Halliday, Crowe and Millerchip and in the back row Tony Brooks and Richard Luddington. But as the day dawned they had a worse problem than Cambridge to contend with. 'All the players went out for a dinner the night before and woke up to find a small layer of snow on the ground, though it was nothing to what London had had,' recalls Wyatt. Alan Tayler, the treasurer, rang Twickenham, who said everything was fine. We took that to mean that the pitch was clear. We arrived at the ground late because we were held up in traffic, and the car-park seemed relatively clear because the cars had flattened the snow. But we were devastated when we got on to the ground. It was outrageous that it hadn't been cleared of snow, it was a total waste of 12 weeks' training. I was stunned, I put my foot in it and it came up past my ankle, but calling off the Match was never considered. The argument about the snow continues but the situation angered us beyond measure.'

The fact that the Centenary Dinner had been organised at the Hilton and would feature Prince Andrew must have been a prime factor in the decision not to postpone the Match — they couldn't really have a dinner without the game. So both teams took to the snow in what proved to be one of the most remarkable Varsity Matches ever. 'The quality was very high considering the conditions', says Wyatt. 'It was the most exciting game I've ever played in my life. I knew it would be my last top-level game and it was worth all the sweat. The snow didn't really make any difference to me — the footing was sound as the pitch was slightly frozen and it wasn't just mud underneath. The game was decided on penalties and Cambridge won 9-6, but really we lost the game as a result of one incident. A loose ball was kicked towards Andy Bibby's wing and I was loitering there. I picked it up and managed to run 50 or 60 yards before I was faced with two defenders. I hoisted a cross-kick and Marcus Rose caught it about five yards from his own line and was buried. We got the put-in from the ensuing scrum and could well at least have dropped a goal, but we lost the scrum and that was that.' More than 30,000 stand tickets had been sold in advance, and a crowd of 40,000 had been expected. In the event the snow disrupted road and rail transport, so that only 22,000 managed to get to Twickenham.

If anyone is still wondering when the rivalry between the England stand-off halves Stuart Barnes and Rob Andrew originated, the answer is in the 1982 Varsity Match. Andrew was one of three future England backs who won their Blues as freshmen that year, the others being Simon Smith on the right wing and Mark Bailey on the left. Andrew came to the attention of Cambridge in rather an unusual way. In his final term at Barnard Castle School he played in the Durham Under-19 schoolboy side along with Richard Cramb and Rory Underwood. In the summer before he went up to Cambridge he was introduced to John Kingston by Durham schoolmaster Nick Willings. Kingston, an old boy of Durham School, was Cambridge captain in 1982. He suggested

*After presenting Cambridge skipper Huw Davies with the
Bowring Bowl, Prince Andrew shakes hands with losing
captain Nigel Roberts. The Prince was later good-naturedly
pelted with snowballs by the students who managed to make
it to Twickenham for the Centenary game.*

that Andrew come down to Cambridge for pre-season training. After two weeks' training Cambridge went on tour to the North-east and Andrew went home to Yorkshire for the weekend. 'Cambridge were playing Durham City, West Hartlepool and a side called the Dolphins, a North Eastern invitation side. I had asked John if I could have a lift back to Cambridge with the team for the start of term. He agreed and invited me to come and watch the game against the Dolphins at Sunderland. I turned up about threequarters of an hour before the kick-off and the Dolphins were short of a fly-half. I had my kit with me and Nick Willings, who was involved with the team, asked me to play. I think we beat them 28-10 and I played pretty well, dropping a couple of goals from about 40 yards.'

All of this bode well for his career at Cambridge, but there were two other stand-off halves to be reckoned with, Martin Breddy and Nick Chesworth. Andrew's performance at Sunderland against Breddy helped him reach the second XV later in the term, but a first-team spot looked remote as the side were playing well with Chesworth at stand-off half. However, after a heavy defeat by Bedford the axe fell and Andrew found himself in the team facing Richmond. They won easily, Andrew collecting 13 points, and in the following game at Northampton he scored 21. He was on his way to winning a Blue as a freshman. 'We lost the next three games and they were starting to think about bringing Nick back, so I began to get a bit worried. But when the team was announced I was floating on cloud nine. From the moment I made the first team all I could think about was Twickenham and playing in front of 30,000 spectators and the television cameras. It's amazing what it does to you at that age. I was lucky in having John Cullen at scrum-half and Robin Boyd-Moss in the centre. Mark Bailey and Simon Smith on the wings also made things easier because I was told just to get the ball to the centres as quickly as possible, to tackle and support.

'The thing that really hit me at Twickenham was the noise as we went out. I was near the back and as soon as the skipper appeared at the tunnel there was a big eruption. It was deafening, almost frightening, and for a second on my way out I froze. I'll never forget it because I've never heard a noise like it. There's also a non-stop buzz throughout the whole game: it fires the adrenalin and I was just carried along. The first five minutes were played at a rocketing pace — I think we counter-attacked through Andy Hampel from a high kick — but the game gradually settled down.' It was Andrew's first major game and his introduction to the limelight. Attention was very much focused on Barnes, who had already established himself with Newport, Welsh Schoolboys and England Under-23s, but the Cambridge man proved his worth by kicking three penalties and dropping a goal in their 20-13 win.

Meanwhile Barnes failed narrowly with five place-kicks at goal, being successful only once. Oxford's most notable recruit in 1982 was Hugo MacNeill, who had already won nine caps for Ireland as a full-back and who was to make the 1983 Lions tour of New Zealand, playing in three Tests against the All Blacks. MacNeill captained Oxford at Twickenham in 1983 even though he was not fully fit because of a knee ligament injury. The most unusual newcomer in his side was centre Tim O'Brien, who had played in the previous two Varsity Matches for Cambridge, thus becoming the first man to gain rugby Blues at both Universities, and who went on to captain Oxford in 1984.

Mark Bailey captained Cambridge in 1983 and 1984 when they completed their second sequence of five consecutive victories in winning 20-9 and 32-6. He was helped by the arrival at Cambridge of even more budding international backs. In 1983 Kevin Simms, the England centre, moved straight into the University side after captaining England Schools earlier that same year. In 1984 Bailey was joined by Fran Clough, who was to play in the centre for England, and by Gavin Hastings, later the Scotland full-back. Moreover Richard Moon, the new scrum-half, had already played for England Under-23s.

This influx of talent to Cambridge made them hot favourites in both years, and they obliged their supporters with some splendid rugby at Twickenham. They scored two tries in 1983 and six in 1984, all of them from their backs. Against this, Oxford, who battled courageously against the odds, could manage only three penalty goals in 1983 and two penalty goals in 1984. It was in 1984 that Cambridge really let themselves go, and right from the start Andrew ran the ball from a defensive position in his own half of the field. The result of this enterprise was that Bailey sent Simms over for a try at the posts. Two more tries came quickly and, with Andrew converting all three, Cambridge led 18-0 with only a quarter of the game gone. This was not only Cambridge's

Cambridge stand-off half Rob Andrew threw caution to the wind in the opening 20 minutes of the 1984 Match. His promptings sparked some spectacular rugby which saw the Light Blues score six tries.

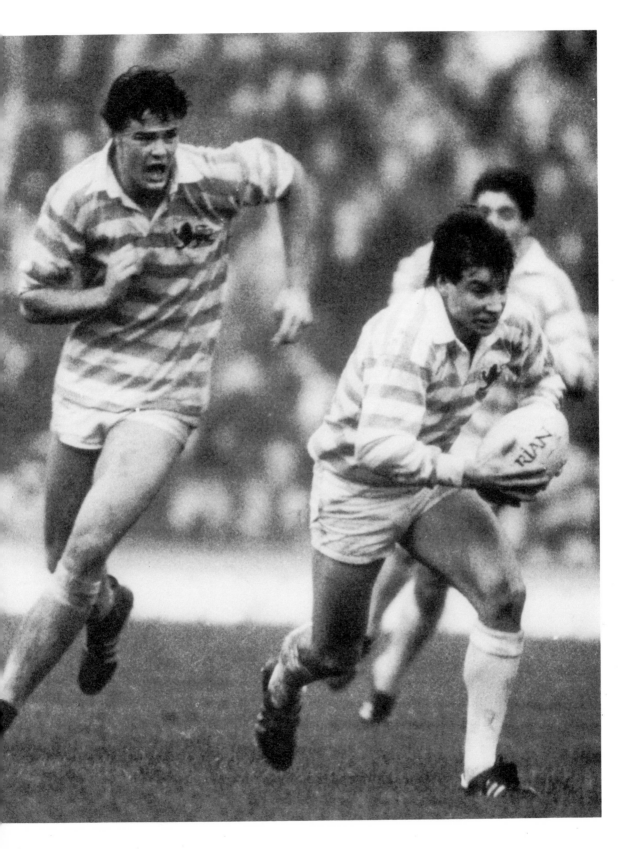

fifth consecutive victory in the Varsity Match, it was their tenth in 13 years. They were now well ahead in the series with 47 wins to Oxford's 43.

'We had an even stronger side in 1984', recalls Andrew. 'Fran Clough arrived and Kevin Simms had established himself. We still had Mark Bailey and Gavin Hastings was at full-back. We had had a very good term, and could sense that we were going to turn it on on the day. In the two previous matches we knew we were a good side but we were disappointed that we hadn't played as well as we had done in club games. That third year we really wanted to give it a go. Mark was captain and told us to be careful in the first 20 minutes. After the game he was quoted as having said that I disregarded everything he told me. It was just instinctive to me to run the ball in those opening minutes, but it seemed to set the standard for the rest of the game. Decisions like that either work or they don't. We scored a try from 70 yards but if we had been knocked down and put back to our own 22 then Bails might have said "hang on". But because we were successful everybody was lifted by the try and we knew we could do it again and again. From that moment we moved it whenever we could — it was fantastic.'

It seemed the following year that nothing could stop Cambridge winning for an unprecedented sixth season in succession, but in the event it was Oxford courage that triumphed. Captained by Neil MacDonald, a South African lock, the Dark Blues moved into an early 7-0 lead with a try from Coll MacDonald, another South African playing at No 8, and a penalty goal by Kennedy, the full-back, but they had to spend most of the second half defending desperately as Cambridge chipped away at their lead with two penalty goals from Hastings and with fierce assaults on the Oxford line. In the final moments Wyles, the Cambridge left wing, looked certain to score the winning try, only to be stopped by Oxford's fly-half, Johnson, and the two props, Willis and Dingemans, who had tackled ferociously throughout the game. Somehow Oxford held out, the score remained 7-6, and the Dark Blues had broken the Cambridge sequence.

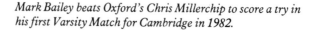

Mark Bailey beats Oxford's Chris Millerchip to score a try in his first Varsity Match for Cambridge in 1982.

Above: Cambridge centre Kevin Simms who, according to Ian Robertson, was 'almost as good as Mathew Fosh at giving and taking a pass, timing it and reading a situation'.

Below: Gavin Hastings powers past opposite number Hugo MacNeill on his way to another Cambridge try in the 1984 Match.

There were some interesting switches of allegiance for this match. Simon Roberts, who had been the Cambridge scrum-half in 1983, now appeared in the Oxford side and had much to do with the containing of his former team-mates in the second half. Nick Herrod, having won Blues in 1981, 1982 and 1983 as a prop for Oxford, moved in the opposite direction to join the Cambridge front row. There were also some significant positional changes because of injuries. Mark Bailey, the England wing, appeared at stand-off half for Cambridge and Steve Pearson, Oxford's scrum-half in 1983 and 1984, now played on the wing.

For Kevin Simms, who had figured prominently in two previous splendid wins and had gained England selection on the strength of his performances, defeat was a bitter pill to swallow. 'We started the game quite well and, with players of the calibre of Bailey, Hastings and Harriman, we were confident. Harriman had had a great season and as we knew that Fran Clough and I would be heavily marked we were looking to put him away. But he left the field injured early on, and that rather restricted our scope. Oxford blocked us out in midfield whenever we tried anything close in and we just didn't have that expansive option. I think it would have been a different game had Harriman stayed on: he would have loosened their defence and given Bailey time to adjust at fly-half, which he had been able to do in the Steele-Bodger's match. Having said that, we still had numerous opportunities in the second half, which was the most frustrating thing. It felt very strange walking off the field. We didn't feel anything for a long time afterwards and then about an hour later it hit us that we'd lost. It's not something I'd like to go through again.'

Oxford were reinforced in 1986 by the arrival of two internationals; Brendan Mullin, who had already played nine times as a centre for Ireland, and Bill Calcraft, the Wallaby loose forward. Cambridge had acquired Chris Oti, yet another dashing threequarter, and they had at full-back Mark Thomas, a son of Clem Thomas, a Blue in 1949. Thomas was to have been the Cambridge stand-off half the previous year, but a severe knee injury forced him out of the side. For once Oxford were favourites at Twickenham, but it was Cambridge who scored the first points when Thomas joined the threequarters and Oti went over for a try. This proved to be the only try of the match, the remaining points in Oxford's 15-10 victory coming from dropped goals and penalty goals. For much of the game Cambridge looked the more skilful side and, as they had the year before, Oxford owed much to their sheer doggedness.

There was some controversy, perhaps caused by envy, when Oxford acquired two more internationals from the Southern Hemisphere in 1987. David Kirk, the All Black scrum-half, who had won 17 caps and had captained his country to success in the final of the inaugural World Cup a few months earlier, arrived at Oxford as a Rhodes Scholar, and Bill Campbell, the tall Wallaby lock forward, who had played in 15 internationals for Australia, came up as a Kobe Steel Scholar. Since Oxford still had Calcraft, now captain, and Mullin, they were considered favourites to win the Varsity Match for a third consecutive year. In the event Oxford led 10-4 at the interval but Cambridge, playing much the more adventurous rugby, staged a fine rally and ran out winners by 15-10. Moreover Cambridge scored three tries to Oxford's one. The result gave special pleasure to Nick Herrod, the Cambridge prop. He had previously played in three Varsity Matches for Oxford and two for Cambridge, not once on the winning side!

Defeat in the Varsity Match brought a disappointing end to an incredible year for David Kirk. He was awarded the Rhodes Scholarship in 1985 but deferred it for a couple of years, which enabled him to captain the All Blacks and receive the inaugural World Cup in June 1987. But just one week before leaving New Zealand for Oxford he sustained a shoulder injury while playing for Auckland in a Ranfurly Shield match against Canterbury and this limited his ability to participate in the build-up to the Varsity Match. In fact he turned out just once for the University side prior

*Oxford's Stephen Pearson tackles Andrew Harriman in the
1985 encounter. The Light Blues began as strong favourites
but magnificent Oxford tackling resulted in a 7–6 victory
for the underdogs.*

World Cup-winning skipper David Kirk scored an early try
for Oxford in the 1987 Varsity Match but Cambridge staged
a fine late rally to take the game 15–10.

to Twickenham, in the game against Bedford, which was Kirk's first defeat of the year at any level of rugby. He had played against both Oxford and Cambridge while touring with the New Zealand Universities side in 1985 and knew something of the importance attached to the December meeting. The first thing that struck him was the crowded fixture list.

'Teams are expected to play twice a week, which is difficult when you have injuries and general unavailability of players. It's very difficult to keep the team together, functioning as a unit and playing to a pattern, you virtually lurch from match to match. Also a great deal was expected of the captain, who spent a long time organising rather than motivating the side on the field.' For someone who had played in so many Test matches and led his country to the greatest prize in rugby, the Varsity Match was not as important as it was to the players for whom running out at Twickenham represented the biggest day in their lives. But gradually the sense of the occasion began to rub off on the All Black. 'I guess like a lot of people I started to get caught up in the importance of the Match as it got closer and closer. I felt strongly that I wanted the team to play well — I wanted to win, obviously, but I wanted to win particularly for those for whom the Varsity Match would be the most important game ever. Naturally there was pressure on me to play, but I didn't find it too great a burden by any means. If I had felt I was unfit to play then I wouldn't have played, there's no question about it. Coming in at the last minute is disruptive and I certainly felt for Simon Taylor, who had played most of the term and was unable to win his Blue.'

Although Oxford began the game badly and Cambridge looked the more organised and determined of the teams, Kirk made a dream start by picking up an early try. A penalty stretched the lead to 7-0, but the scrum-half was far from happy. 'We weren't playing well enough to justify that lead, and you can't feel confident about winning a game unless you can dominate possession. We weren't doing that.' Kirk's doubts were to prove well-founded as Oti's two sparkling tries set up a Cambridge victory. Kirk, who had played in so many big matches, took the game in his stride and didn't find the pace too worrying. He enjoyed the crowd and the occasion but hated losing. 'We were good enough to win and we didn't perform. I felt sad for some of the young guys — it was their big match. In a sense they didn't seem to have taken on board the fact that the game wasn't going to be won by the Bill Calcrafts, Bill Campbells or Brendan Mullins, it needed to be won by them playing the game of their lives. Rugby is a team game, and unless the team performs no individual can perform. So we needed their best-ever efforts, we needed them to be jumping out of their skins. I think the presence of some of the older guys in a sense dampened that kind of build-up and perhaps more responsibility ought to have been put on their shoulders. Responsibility for winning the Match has to rest with the whole team, and especially with the younger guys. That's something we've learned from the build-up and we won't make the same mistake again. I'm looking forward to next season. I don't like losing and don't want to lose the next Varsity Match. I'm looking forward to being part of the team and giving them my best shot.'

Much has been made of the role played by Wallaby coach Alan Jones in the preparation of the Oxford teams. Jones took a post-graduate course at Worcester College after graduating in politics and education at Queensland University. In 1985, Derek Wyatt contacted him, seeking his advice on establishing a scholarship in Australia through Kobe Steel. The Wallaby coach came over at his own expense prior to the Varsity Match and was inveigled into doing some coaching with the Oxford team. Alan Tayler explains: 'Derek brought him to the Bowring lunch. It was something of a public relations job; that was the year, 1985, that we were trying to turn the tide and we saw it as a way of putting Cambridge's nose out of joint. At the lunch we unexpectedly announced that he was going to work with the team, which slightly upset the Cambridge complacency. The 1985 Oxford side was very successful, but limited, and I think he had a great input that year.'

Jones came the two following years, having the added incentive of the presence of Wallaby players Bill Calcraft and Bill Campbell in the Oxford line-up. In 1987, however, his motivation wasn't enough to win the day. David Kirk puts the Jones influence in perspective: 'He had a significant input in organising the team and preparing it for the Match, in terms of inspiring the germs of motivation. Realistically, in a week you can only have a limited influence and it would be an absolute mistake to expect him to come here and prepare the team to win the game. I think that if people believe that is possible it is greatly to our disadvantage. For the 1987 performance we were not prepared enough, but Alan Jones certainly helped in trying to make up some of the shortfall.'

15
Stanley's and Steele-Bodger's

The most public part of the preparation of the two sides for the Varsity Match is the staging every November of the game between Oxford and Major R.V. Stanley's XV at Iffley Road and that between Cambridge and M.R. Steele-Bodger's XV at Grange Road. These annual matches play a vital role in the preparations for the Varsity Match, but it is as well to remember that a great deal more goes on behind the scenes in the way of administration, organisation, coaching and so forth.

The name of Windsor Lewis comes immediately to mind because in his many years of involvement with rugby at Cambridge he did so much to help generations of undergraduates appreciate all aspects of the game. He won his Blue at stand-off half in 1926 and 1927 and played for Wales in 1926, 1927 and 1928. He was president of the CURUFC for more than 20 years through the 1950s and 1960s, and before that he was hon. treasurer. Oxford rugby meanwhile owes a great deal to Greig Barr who was hon. treasurer for 25 years from 1948 and followed this with ten years as president. He somehow managed to find time for rugby affairs between his duties as a Fellow, and later Rector, of Exeter College. As a player he was an enthusiastic Greyhound but never a Blue. In the old days there was C.N. Jackson, who was treasurer of the OURFC for 27 years from 1886 and who was largely responsible for the creation of the Iffley Road ground, which was first used in 1899. He was also treasurer of the athletics and soccer clubs at Oxford and treasurer of the Amateur Athletic Association from 1880 to 1910. He managed to do all this as well as being Bursar of Hertford.

Micky Steele-Bodger is a former Cambridge captain, chairman of England selectors and chairman of the International Board, to name but a few of the posts he has held in the game. His annual match at Cambridge was first played in 1948. By that time Steele-Bodger had left Cambridge to pursue his studies at Edinburgh University, and had already been capped by England. Windsor Lewis rang him to see if he would put a side together to play Cambridge, taking over the match usually played by Jenny Greenwood's XV. 'I think Jenny Greenwood's team had last played in 1938 but the fixture was degenerating into a social gathering', Steele-Bodger explains. 'As Greenwood got older he tended just to pick Old Blues who began to invite themselves back. It became a waste of time as far as a test was concerned. At the time I was asked to put together a side Cambridge were as strong as any team in the land, so it had to be the best. The half-backs in that first side were Bleddyn Williams and Haydn Tanner, so we started high. That

Oxford full-back Peter Carroll makes a break during the University's 1968 match against the all-star Major Stanley's XV at Iffley Road.

was the sort of quality we went for and have stuck to.' Steele-Bodger has been the sole selector of his team during its 40-year history, and the make-up and aim of the team is quite different to that of Stanley's. 'I try to equate, as best as I can, the Oxford team that Cambridge will play. So, if Oxford have a star player in a certain position I will try to select someone in that position with the same style of play. It doesn't always work, but in the last 26 years there have been 14 matches with just one score between the teams at the end. The objective is to improve the University side, not to indulge in a personal ego trip.' But there have been favourites over the years: people like Cliff Morgan, Tony Rodgers, Nick Martin and the great Andy Ripley have played in seven or eight games. Indeed, it was Ripley's appearance in the Steele-Bodger's game of 1971 that brought him to the notice of the England selectors and subsequently into the England team. 'It does become more difficult, particularly now we have leagues, and there may be a problem if the game falls between two league Saturdays. Generally, though, the players like to come. It's a nice ground, a good game to play in and there's a dinner afterwards, so we look after them and they seem to like it.' To mark 40 years of the Steele-Bodger game a special dinner was held in 1987 at Robinson College and of the 240 guests over half had actually played in the match. And just to prove that the standard has remained high, the team for the game that day included Paul Thorburn, Rob Andrew, Bob Norster and Andy Ripley.

Stanley's match at Oxford has been in existence much longer than Steele-Bodger's at Cambridge, and has continued even though Stanley himself died in 1957. Stanley represented the OURFC on the Rugby Football Union committee from 1907 to 1923, and became an England selector. Yet he was never a member of the University and, as far as anyone can establish, he never played rugby. Outside rugby he seems to have been best known as a musician, especially as an organist. It is said, though has not been substantiated, that Stanley first raised a side to play Oxford in the winter vacation of 1894. What is known is that the Stanley's fixture first appeared on the club's official list in 1914. That match never took place because of the outbreak of the First World War, so the first officially recorded Stanley's match was played in 1919. Stanley was the sole selector of his sides until the 1932 match, after which the Stanley Trust was set up to organise the annual occasion. His first team, that of 1919, included the two legendary forwards Wavell Wakefield and Tom Voyce. At the time of their selection for Stanley's neither of them had played for England, but Wakefield went on to win 31 England caps and Voyce 27.

Over the years many famous players have graced the Stanley's side, but as the demands on players increase, it becomes harder to put together a top-class Stanley's XV. That is something that Nigel Starmer-Smith knew all about. He kept up his connections with Oxford after he went down and was eventually asked by Alec Ramsay to take over as secretary of the Stanley's Trust. It appeared that the secretary's sole duty was to send out invitations to the Stanley's XV once the team had been picked, so he accepted. 'I learned my lesson very quickly', he recalls. 'I remember attending the dinner at which great names like Dan Drysdale, Vivian Jenkins and John Kendall-Carpenter sat round and selected a side. Once that was done, all I had to do was to get on and send out the invitations. Of course, on paper the best side in the British Isles was selected, featuring the likes of J.P.R. Williams, Gareth Edwards and Barry John, but half of them were unavailable. I went back to Alec and asked him what I should do. "This is where your discretion comes in", he told me. "We pick the team and you have to try to get as near to it as you can." Well, as the years passed and Oxford rugby waned, so the problem worsened.

'People had previously come because it was a Barbarians-type honour, but things were changing, and there was more pressure on players. That first year I think I ended up with about four or five of the original selection. It was very tempting, having organised a side, to go away the week before the game so that no one could contact me to cry off.' Despite the problems of late cry-offs, there were always the stalwarts who could be relied upon to turn out at short notice. People like Phil Blakeway, Gordon Sergeant, Gareth Davies and Andy Ripley saved the day on more than one occasion, but the man who played more times than anyone for Stanley's was the former Bristol and England flanker Dave Rollitt. As long as he was given enough time to drive from Bristol to Oxford, he could always be telephoned at the very last moment. In honour of his service to the team, he was eventually presented with a special tankard.

But Nigel's duties were not to end when the team was arranged. 'I soon found out that I was expected to be head cook and bottle-washer and I would end up driving myself mad. The fortnight prior to the match is crazy, people drop out, then you have to get the ties and organise the shirts and look after the plasters and the grease and introduce the side to one another and pay the expenses. It's a real nightmare. In recent years, though, the game has made a comeback and the crowds have returned. People say that the side is too strong, but once the calibre is allowed to drop you are never going to attract the top players and the crowds stop coming. It's difficult to get the right balance, but the match has to have a special status if it is to mean anything at all, and there have been some fabulous games.'

Former Blue Derek Wyatt was instrumental in raising the standing of the Stanley's match in the mid-1980s. One of the biggest problems in attracting a good crowd was the fact that in between the team being announced and the day of the match was likely to be eight to ten changes. So he took on the role of selector. 'My first priority was to find a sponsor which, thanks to Reg Clark, became Yamaichi, and that gave us some money to spend. Next we set about trying to entice one or two players from around the world who had an affinity with Oxford or who had mentioned that they might like to play. Oxford had some very good contacts abroad so it made sense to bring over Mark Loane when Phil Crowe was captain. Then we brought over John Robbie from Johannesburg and that was the start. It created some interest, and because we had a little money we brought in more people and gradually things picked up.' One of Stanley's major scoops was the inclusion of French centre Denis Charvet, who was unheard of in this country prior to the game. Journalist Peter Bills, who was writing a biography of Jean-Pierre Rives, suggested that they should bring the young centre over with Rives. There was a cry-off at the last minute and Charvet came over, delighting both the crowd and the assembled journalists with his performance. It brought the game massive publicity and the Stanley's match has become a major fixture once more.

16
The International Connection

One of the most fascinating aspects of the Varsity Match, which will have become apparent throughout this book, is the very large number of players from outside England who have contributed to it. At Cambridge this contribution has come to a great extent from Wales, Scotland and Ireland. One has only to think of Cliff Jones and Wilf Wooller playing together in midfield in the 1930s; of such Scots as Arthur Smith, Ken Scotland, Gordon Waddell and the Bruce Lockhart tribe and of Irishmen like Andrew Mulligan, David MacSweeney and Mike Gibson. While Oxford have, of course, had their famous Welshmen, Irishmen and Scots, they have tended to attract far more young men from South Africa, New Zealand and Australia than have Cambridge. This has been largely, though by no means entirely, due to the Rhodes Scholarships.

The name of Cecil Rhodes has become known to most people from their school history books. He was a major figure in southern Africa in the later years of the last century. After making his fortune in the diamond rush at Kimberley, he brought together several diamond companies to form De Beers Consolidated Mines in 1888. He became Prime Minister of Cape Colony in 1890, and Rhodesia, now Zimbabwe, was named after him. Rhodes was an Englishman, born at Bishop's Stortford, the son of the local vicar, and he went to Oriel College, Oxford. When he died in 1902, not yet 50 years old, he left most of his fortune to concerns in southern Africa, but some of it went to Oxford, where the Rhodes Scholarships were founded for 'colonials', Germans and Americans.

The first Rhodes Scholar to win a rugby Blue was W.W. Hoskin in 1905. He was a forward from St Andrew's College, Grahamstown, and he became captain in 1907. Since then there has been a steady flow of Rhodes Scholars from South Africa who have made their mark as rugby players. The Varsity Match has seen many Rhodes Scholars from other former colonies, mainly from Australia and New Zealand. The first American Rhodes Scholar to win a Blue was Donald Grant Herring, as long ago as 1909. There were, of course, rugby Blues from overseas before the founding of the Rhodes Scholarships. The first Australian Blue, for instance, was J. Allen, who played in the Cambridge sides of 1875 and 1876, and Oxford's first South African Blue and first New Zealand Blue both played in the Varsity Match of 1885. They were James Sutherland, from Pietermaritzburg, and John Hall, from Christchurch.

Some people argue that the presence of so many players from other countries in the Varsity

Matches over the years has done a disservice to rugby in England by keeping the home product out of the University sides. Such critics point to 1929, when only four Englishmen were included in the Oxford team. I would argue the reverse: that the different styles and the fresh thinking of men from outside England have greatly enhanced not only Oxbridge rugby but also English rugby in general. This has been especially true in the periods when the two Universities were among the strongest all-round clubs in the land. Conversely, the countries from which all these outsiders came to Oxford and Cambridge have benefited too. It must, for instance, have been a great comfort to the Welsh selectors of the 1930s to know that Cliff Jones and Wilf Wooller were playing and practising together day-in day-out at Cambridge. And Mike Gibson, who went on to play 69 times for Ireland, first came into the public eye when playing at stand-off half for Cambridge in the Varsity Match of 1963. Then there was Herbert Castens, the Oxford forward of 1886 from Port Elizabeth. At that time South African rugby was in its infancy — the South African Rugby Board was not founded until 1889 — and when Castens returned home he contributed a great deal of enthusiastic coaching and actually captained the Springboks in their first-ever international match, in 1891.

From the halcyon days of the 1950s the number of Rhodes Scholars winning rugby Blues certainly diminished in the 1970s and 1980s. This can be attributed to a number of factors, not least the change in the Universities' admissions policies. The continuing problems in South Africa have also reduced the number of students coming from there, and there has been a drift away from the Universities by students from New Zealand and Australia. According to OURFC hon. treasurer Alan Tayler, Britain's involvement with the Common Market has weakened the ties with Australasia. 'People who would naturally have come to England began to go to the USA instead. The major problem now is the whole question of overseas student fees. The Government insists on charging real fees which are massive sums of money. So for someone in Australia or New Zealand it is more difficult to come to Oxford than it is to go to the USA. However, there has been a slight resurgence in recent years. I think America was immensely attractive 20 years ago, but it is possibly less so now, and Europe is becoming more interesting again.'

This resurgence has also come about thanks to other scholarships being provided, the most recent being those of the Japanese company Kobe Steel. Although Oxford have long-established international links, in recent years they have been strengthened due to the efforts of one man, Reg Clark. Reg went to Japan in 1977 as the youngest member of the Oxford touring party. Alan Tayler recalls, 'He thought it was so wonderful that when he finished his undergraduate work he took a job with Kobe Steel. He worked for them for three years in Japan and played rugby for them. The president of the company is a rugby enthusiast and Reg decided to set up a kind of "Rhodes" scholarship for Kobe.' The company's major spheres of influence outside Japan are Australia and Europe, and the scholarship is open to Australians provided that they have an interest in Japan. So Bill Campbell, who came to Oxford on the scholarship, is due to spend three months with Kobe in Australia when he finishes at Oxford. 'I'm sure we will continue to have graduate students who play top-class rugby', says Alan Tayler. 'It is in their interests to come to Oxford to do graduate work — it benefits their career prospects and benefits the rugby club.'

Captains, of course, play a predominant role in the preparations for Varsity Matches as well as in the games themselves, and it is interesting to note that as long ago as 1884 an outside influence was exerted in the leadership of the teams. That year Oxford were captained by Grant Asher, from Loretto, and Cambridge by Milne, from Fettes. In 1891 the Scottish reign continued — both captains were from Fettes, Fleming for Oxford and Storey for Cambridge, and in 1900 both captains were Loretto men, Swanston for Oxford and Greenlees for Cambridge. Rowe Harding, in

One of the few Irish players who have captained Cambridge University, the incomparable Mike Gibson shows the Barbarians a clean pair of heels.

1927, was one of a long series of Welsh captains at Cambridge, among them Glyn Davies, Geoffrey Windsor Lewis, Roger Michaelson, Brian Rees and Gerald Davies. Ireland have produced fewer Cambridge captains than Wales, but the names of Mike Gibson, in 1965, and John Robbie, in 1978, readily spring to mind.

Oxford, not surprisingly, have had many captains from overseas: men like L.G. Brown from Australia in 1912; Denoon Duncan from South Africa in 1920; Trilby Freakes, another South African, in 1938; Ossie Newton-Thompson, South Africa, in 1946; Jika Travers from Australia in 1947; Nelles Vincent from South Africa in 1949; Paul Johnstone in 1954 and Roy Allaway in 1955, both South Africans; Springbok Tommy Bedford in 1966; All Black Chris Laidlaw in 1969; and three further Australians, Peter Carroll in 1970, Phil Crowe in 1982 and Bill Calcraft in 1987. While all these men have had an important influence on Oxbridge rugby, we should not forget the pioneering work achieved overseas by the Universities on tour. They have been particularly effective in places such as Japan and South America, whose rugby has benefited enormously from such stimulating visits. Just as in the early part of the century Oxford and Cambridge led the development of rugby in the British Isles, so later on they became trail-blazers in spreading the rugby message all over the world, a tradition which still exists today.

In the 1940s and 1950s the two Universities were in a unique position to tour abroad. Not only were their teams packed with top-class men playing the game at the highest level, but the student year lent itself perfectly to long tours. Before the advent of modern long-haul aircraft, foreign travel was necessarily undertaken by boat. This was a slow business, so rugby tours were measured in months as opposed to weeks. Only University sides, with their long vacations, could accommodate these tours on a regular basis, so the first glimpse many countries had of top-class rugby was when Oxford or Cambridge landed on their shores. One of the early pioneering trips was Oxford's tour to Japan in 1952. Although the Japanese had held rugby matches against teams from visiting navy ships, this was the first time they had entertained a major representative side and it was a major event. Oxford have maintained strong links with Japan ever since.

That first tour had some interesting origins. Alan Tayler explains: 'I think the connection was Emperor Hirohito's nephew who was up at Oxford before the War — I believe his widow is still president of the Japanese Rugby Union. Shiggy Konno was involved and Greig Barr managed the tour. It was a very interesting party of people and included Dudley Wood, the RFU secretary. They went part of the way by boat and I believe they also played a game in Hong Kong. They opened a new stand in 1952, and in September 1988 Oxford went back to open a second stand.' In between Oxford toured Japan in 1977 and a combined Oxford and Cambridge side went there in 1983.

The Japanese connection with the Universities is strong, particularly at Oxford, as is borne out by the scholarship funded by Kobe Steel and Yamaichi's sponsorship of the annual Stanley's match. So what is the attraction? According to Alan Tayler, the Japanese feel they have a great cultural bond with England. 'They have a particular view of England. The Japanese like to think that theirs is a similar country with similar traditions. They see Oxford and Cambridge as having great prestige, they like the links and seem to think they are worth cultivating, so we encourage it.'

The Universities have always made tours and, whether individually or jointly, they have spread the rugby message all over the world. There have been trips to North America and South America, and Cambridge have perhaps been a little more entrepreneurial in recent years with pioneering tours to South Korea and Taiwan.

17
Mutual Benefits

There are those who disapprove of sponsorship, and mainly on two grounds. First, they feel that the sponsor, as the provider of money, will have too great an influence on the event they support, and second, they worry about what will happen if the sponsor eventually withdraws his patronage. There need be no such worries about the sponsorship of the Varsity Match by Bowring, which began in 1976. The former chairman of Bowring, Gil Cooke, said recently: 'Our experience over 12 years has convinced us that our sponsorship of the Varsity Match has been of great benefit not only to Bowring but to the group internationally. We would hope to continue for our benefit and for that of the two Universities. We do think this sponsorship is a winner in every respect. It's here to stay. We can't contemplate not doing it. The whole exercise has been very cost-effective as far as publicity is concerned. I am convinced it has been good for the Universities, and for us it has been a substantial aid to recruitment, while getting us known commercially.'

When Bowring merged with Marsh & McLennan, the American firm, in 1980 to form the largest insurance and reinsurance broking business in the world, there were fears in some quarters that the Americans might not lend their support to the sponsorship of the Varsity Match. But Cooke quickly dispelled such thoughts. 'Marsh & McLennan are very much in favour of the sponsorship,' he has said. 'A growing number of Marsh & McLennan people want to be present at Twickenham. The fame of the Bowring Bowl has certainly reached their ears in America.' Bowring, in fact, have taken nearly 2,000 tickets at the Varsity Matches of recent years.

The involvement of Bowring in the Varsity Match came about because Tony Craigen, when he was appointed treasurer of the CURUFC in 1973, discovered that the income from the Varsity Match had halved in the ten years from 1963 to 1973. He decided to write to some Old Blues, among them Michael Melluish, a former captain of cricket at Cambridge and then a director of Singer and Friedlander, the merchant bankers, who were at that time part of the Bowring Group. By way of reply Melluish suggested the possibility of sponsorship by Bowring. Craigen's interest led to Melluish approaching Edgar Bowring, an old Cambridge man and then Bowring's chairman, and, after discussions between Bowring and the Rugby Football Union, Bowring agreed to sponsor the 1976 Varsity Match to the tune of £10,000, to be shared equally between the two Universities. Although the initial discussions took place between Bowring and the RFU, the company's agreement is with the rugby clubs of the two Universities. The terms do not specify the level of

1985: Gil Cooke, then Bowring's chairman, with 1985 captains Gavin Hastings (left), Cambridge and Neil MacDonald, Oxford.

Mr Edgar Bowring, chairman in 1976, meets the captains for that year, Dugald MacDonald on the right (Oxford) and Peter Warfield (Cambridge), who had to be replaced for the Match by A.A. Stewart.

The press conference that marked Bowring's announcement of their decision to sponsor the annual Varsity Match fixture.

Left to right: Philip Wroughton, now Bowring's chairman, 1987 captains Bill Calcraft (Oxford), Steve Kelly (Cambridge) and Gil Cooke.

sponsorship: Bowring are left to increase the sum as and when they think fit. In fact, in the first 11 years the amount of the sponsorship trebled to £30,000, with half that sum going to each University. The agreement is based on the principle of a three-year roll-over, which means that if Bowring ever wanted to withdraw their sponsorship, they would have to give the Universities three years' notice, an arrangement which would allow the Universities plenty of time to find a new backer.

Peter Bowring, a former chairman of the company, who was on the steering committee which formulated the terms of the original sponsorship agreement with the RFU, says the idea appealed to Bowring for three main reasons. First, the Varsity Match was a single event with which the company could become identified. Second, the Varsity Match was connected with the kind of young men Bowring would want to recruit into their firm. Third, the sponsorship of the Varsity Match would give Bowring the right kind of publicity. 'Sponsorship is not charity but a working agreement to the benefit of both parties', he says. Bowring are reaping the benefit of their sponsorship. The Bowring name is known considerably more widely than it was before, and the company's recruitment of high-calibre staff from the two Universities has gone on apace. So what have the two Universities gained? The benefits are to be seen mainly in the repairs, restoration, improvements and extensions that have been carried out on the grounds at Iffley Road and Grange Road. Oxford had particular cause to be grateful when the Bradford fire and the subsequent Safety of Sports Grounds Act obliged the OURFC to spend £39,000 on bringing the main stand up to the standards of the Act.

At Grange Road the stand has been re-roofed and given new seating, the pavilion has been extended with the Windsor Room and bar — named after Windsor Lewis, the former president of the club — and a bungalow has been built for the groundsman. There is a weight-training room, and further money has been spent on helping to finance tours. At Iffley Road the pavilion, the subject of a preservation order, has been renovated and extended with new plumbing, heating and lighting and with a proper club-room and bar, a medical room and a clock that works. Trees and shrubs have been planted, a new boundary fence has been erected, the playing surface has been improved and floodlights have been installed. And, like Cambridge, Oxford have used some of Bowring's money to help with the cost of pre-season tours.

For Public Relations Officer Carole Bowring, the Varsity Match is probably as important and nerve-wracking as it is for the players. In recent years she has had the task of organising the event on behalf of the sponsors and of liaising with Oxford, Cambridge and the Rugby Football Union to ensure that everything runs smoothly. And that one day takes many months of planning. 'I usually get the file out on 1 September. I have to start thinking of the advertising campaign in the national press, and the advertisements have to be designed and put in hand. I also make contact with the RFU to sort out things like ground advertising. Although much of the procedure remains the same, people change: there are different captains and occasionally administrators change too, and contact has to be established. I like to meet the captains and take them to lunch to tell them about the Company's preparations for the great event, such as the press luncheon. It also means that they have a contact with Bowring.' From mid-October regular press releases are sent out by the company giving information about the teams, their performances and any injury problems.

The next big date in the calendar is the Bowring press luncheon, at which all the media and officials as well as the two teams are present for the official announcement of the teams. It is held at the top of the Bowring building in London, overlooking the river. 'We feel it is very important for the players to see us in our City location', Carole explains, 'and also they get a chance to meet our chairman and directors and maybe some of them will eventually come into the firm. We have

*Exciting players like Cambridge and England wing Chris
Oti have brought the crowds back to the Varsity Match.*

television and radio there as well, so the media get the chance to talk to the players. We provide a coach for the teams and they train at Twickenham, one team on the way down before the lunch and the other on the way back afterwards.'

On the day of the Match itself, 25 coaches of Bowring staff and clients leave the City for Twickenham. For just over 300 senior executives, clients and prospective clients, there is lunch at Twickenham in the Rose Room. It is a frantic day for Carole Bowring; she has usually been there till late the previous evening making sure that everything is ready before returning at 9 o'clock on Tuesday morning. Pre-lunch drinks begin at 11.30 and at 12.30 sharp the guests sit down to a three-course meal plus wine and cheese. By 1.50 they are being ushered out to their seats. Many of the Bowring employees in their 30 offices around the country can't get to the game, but for them it is nevertheless a special day. Often lunches are arranged for the staff and clients in the offices and then they watch the game on television in the boardroom.

It is certainly a sponsorship that works both ways. As Gil Cooke says: 'The most excellent relationship that exists between all the parties concerned is the key to the whole thing.'

1986 Oxford skipper Simon Griffin clutches the most prized possession in Varsity rugby, the Bowring Bowl.

Nigel Starmer-Smith breaks away for Oxford in the historic 1966 Varsity Match. The game was notable for the inclusion of John Coker (on the Oxford left wing), who became the first black Blue.

The Russian Prince Alexander Obolensky, one of the many charismatic figures that have graced the Varsity Match over the years.

STATISTICS

Compiled by John Griffiths

Records are complete to the end of the 1987 Match.

MATCH RESULTS

Of the 106 matches played up to 1987-88, Cambridge won 48, Oxford won 45, and 13 of the matches were drawn.

1871-72 The Parks (Oxford)
Oxford won by 1G to 0

1872-73 Parker's Piece (Cambridge)
Cambridge won by 1G 2T to 0

1873-74 The Oval (London)
Drawn 1T each

1874-75 The Oval
Drawn Oxford 2T Cambridge 0
(Matches could only be won by a majority of goals at this date)

1875-76 The Oval
Oxford won by 1T to 0

1876-77 The Oval
Cambridge won by 1G 2T to 0

1877-78 The Oval
Oxford won by 2T to 0

1878-79 The Oval
Drawn no score

1879-80 The Oval
Cambridge won by 1G 1DG to 1DG

1880-81 Richardson's Field (Blackheath)
Drawn 1T each

1881-82 Richardson's Field
Oxford won by 2G 1T to 1G

1882-83 Richardson's Field
Oxford won by 1T to 0

1883-84 Rectory Field (Blackheath)
Oxford won by 3G 4T to 1G

1884-85 Rectory Field
Oxford won by 3G 1T to 1T

1885-86 Rectory Field
Cambridge won by 2T to 0

1886-87 Rectory Field
Cambridge won by 3T to 0

1887-88 Queen's Club (Kensington)
Cambridge won by 1DG 2T to 0

1888-89 Queen's Club
Cambridge won by 1G 2T to 0

1889-90 Queen's Club
Oxford won by 1G 1T to 0

1890-91 Queen's Club
Drawn each side scored 1G (5)

1891-92 Queen's Club
Cambridge won by 2T (4) to 0

1892-93 Queen's Club
Drawn no score

1893-94 Queen's Club
Oxford won by 1T (3) to 0

1894-95 Queen's Club
Drawn each side 1G (5)

1895-96 Queen's Club
Cambridge won by 1G (5) to 0

1896-97 Queen's Club
Oxford won by 1G 1DG (9) to 1G 1T (8)

1897-98 Queen's Club
Oxford won by 2T (6) to 0

1898-99 Queen's Club
Cambridge won by 1G 2T (11) to 0

1899-1900 Queen's Club
Cambridge won by 2G 4T (22) to 0

1900-01 Queen's Club
Oxford won by 2G (10) to 1G 1T (8)

1901-02 Queen's Club
Oxford won by 1G 1T (8) to 0

1902-03 Queen's Club
Drawn each side scored 1G 1T (8)

1903-04 Queen's Club
Oxford won by 3G 1T (18) to 2G 1T (13)

1904-05 Queen's Club
Cambridge won by 3G (15) to 2G (10)

1905-06 Queen's Club
Cambridge won by 3G (15) to 2G 1T (13)

1906-07 Queen's Club
Oxford won by 4T (12) to 1G 1T (8)

1907-08 Queen's Club
Oxford won by 1G 4T (17) to 0

1908-09 Queen's Club
Drawn each side scored 1G (5)

1909-10 Queen's Club
Oxford won by 4G 5T (35) to 1T (3)

1910-11 Queen's Club
Oxford won by 4G 1T (23) to 3G 1T (18)

1911-12 Queen's Club
Oxford won by 2G 3T (19) to 0

1912-13 Queen's Club
Cambridge won by 2G (10) to 1T (3)

1913-14 Queen's Club
Cambridge won by 1DG 3T (13) to 1T (13)

1919-20 Queen's Club
Cambridge won by 1DG 3T (13) to 1T (3)

1920-21 Queen's Club
Oxford won by 1G 4T (17) to 1G 3T (14)

1921-22 Twickenham
Oxford won by 1G 2T (11) to 1G (5)

1922-23 Twickenham
Cambridge won by 3G 2T (21) to 1G 1T (8)

1923-24 Twickenham
Oxford won by 3G 2T (21) to 1G 1PG 2T (14)

1924-25 Twickenham
Oxford won by 1G 2T (11) to 2T (6)

1925-26 Twickenham
Cambridge won by 3G 6T (33) to 1T (3)

1926-27 Twickenham
Cambridge won by 3G 5T (30) to 1G (5)

1927-28 Twickenham
Cambridge won by 2G 2PG 2T (22) to 1G 3T (14)

1928-29 Twickenham
Cambridge won by 1G 3T (14) to 1DG 1PG 1T (10)

1929-30 Twickenham
Oxford won by 1G 1DG (9) to 0

1930-31 Twickenham
Drawn Oxford 1PG (3); Cambridge 1T (3)

1931-32 Twickenham
Oxford won by 1DG 2T (10) to 1T (3)

1932-33 Twickenham
Oxford won by 1G 1T (8) to 1T (3)

1933-34 Twickenham
Oxford won by 1G (5) to 1T (3)

1934-35 Twickenham
Cambridge won by 2G 1DG 1PG 4T (29) to 1DG (4)

1935-36 Twickenham
Drawn no score

1936-37 Twickenham
Cambridge won by 2T (6) to 1G (5)

1937-38 Twickenham
Oxford won by 1G 4T (17) to 1DG (4)

1938-39 Twickenham
Cambridge won by 1G 1PG (8) to 2PG (6)

1945-46 Twickenham
Cambridge won by 1G 2T (11) to 1G 1PG (8)

1946-47 Twickenham
Oxford won by 1G 1DG 2T (15) to 1G (5)

1947-48 Twickenham
Cambridge won by 2PG (6) to 0

1948-49 Twickenham
Oxford won by 1G 1DG 2T (14) to 1G 1PG (8)

1949-50 Twickenham
Oxford won by 1T (3) to 0

1950-51 Twickenham
Oxford won by 1G 1PG (8) to 0

1951-52 Twickenham
Oxford won by 2G 1T (13) to 0

1952-53 Twickenham
Cambridge won by 1PG 1T (6) to 1G (5)

1953-54 Twickenham
Drawn Oxford 1PG 1T (6); Cambridge 2PG (6)

1954-55 Twickenham
Cambridge won by 1PG (3) to 0

1955-56 Twickenham
Oxford won by 1PG 2T (9) to 1G (5)

1956-57 Twickenham
Cambridge won by 1G 1DG 1PG 1T (14) to 2PG 1T (9)

1957-58 Twickenham
Oxford won by 1T (3) to 0

1958-59 Twickenham
Cambridge won by 1G 1PG 3T (17) to 1PG 1T (6)

1959-60 Twickenham
Oxford won by 3PG (9) to 1PG (3)

1960-61 Twickenham
Cambridge won by 2G 1T (13) to 0

1961-62 Twickenham
Cambridge won by 1DG 2T (9) to 1DG (3)

1962-63 Twickenham
Cambridge won by 1G 1PG 1DG 1T (14) to 0

1963-64 Twickenham
Cambridge won by 2G 1PG 2T (19) to 1G 1DG 1PG (11)

1964-65 Twickenham
Oxford won by 2G 1PG 2T (19) to 1PG 1GM (6)

1965-66 Twickenham
Drawn each side 1G (5)

1966-67 Twickenham
Oxford won by 1G 1T (8) to 1DG 1T (6)

1967-68 Twickenham
Cambridge won by 1PG 1T (6) to 0

1968-69 Twickenham
Cambridge won by 1DG 1PG 1T (9) to 2T (6)

1969-70 Twickenham
Oxford won by 3PG (9) to 2PG (6)

1970-71 Twickenham
Oxford won by 1G 1DG 2T (14) to 1PG (3)

1971-72 Twickenham
Oxford won by 3PG 3T (21) to 1PG (3)

1972-73 Twickenham
Cambridge won by 1G 1PG 1DG 1T (16) to 2PG (6)

1973-74 Twickenham
Cambridge won by 1DG 1PG 2T (14) to 1G 2PG (12)

1974-75 Twickenham
Cambridge won by 1G 2PG 1T (16) to 5PG (15)

1975-76 Twickenham
Cambridge won by 2G 1DG 5PG 1T (34) to 3PG 1DG (12)

1976-77 Twickenham
Cambridge won by 1G 3PG (15) to 0

1977-78 Twickenham
Oxford won by 4PG 1T (16) to 2PG 1T (10)

1978-79 Twickenham
Cambridge won by 2G 3PG 1T (25) to 1PG 1T (7)

1979-80 Twickenham
Oxford won by 2PG 1DG (9) to 1PG (3)

1980-81 Twickenham
Cambridge won by 3PG 1T (13) to 3PG (9)

1981-82 Twickenham
Cambridge won by 3PG (9) to 2PG (6)

1982-83 Twickenham
Cambridge won by 3PG 1DG 2T (20) to 1G 1PG 1T (13)

1983-84 Twickenham
Cambridge won by 4PG 2T (20) to 3PG (9)

1984-85 Twickenham
Cambridge won by 4G 2T (32) to 2PG (6)

1985-86 Twickenham
Oxford won by 1PG 1T (7) to 2PG (6)

1986-87 Twickenham
Oxford won by 3PG 2DG (15) to 1PG 1DG 1T (10)

1987-88 Twickenham
Cambridge won by 1DG 3T (15) to 2PG 1T (10)

* indicates captain

MATCH 1

10 February 1872, at The Parks, Oxford
Oxford won by 1G to 0

Oxford	
*W O Moberly	(Rugby · Balliol)
T S Pearson	(Rugby · Christ Church)
A T Michell	(Rugby · Oriel)
E A Deacon	(Marlborough · Exeter)
C K Francis	(Rugby · Brasenose)
K R Fletcher	(Rugby · New)
A S G Botfield	(Rugby · Brasenose)
C W L Bulpett	(Rugby · Trinity)
J W Gardner	(Rugby · Brasenose)
H W Peake	(Rugby · Corpus Christi)
H Brierly	(Rubgy · Wadham)
F G Cholmondeley	(Rugby · Christ Church)
F W Isherwood	(Rugby · Brasenose)
J Sayer	(Rugby · Christ Church)
E R Still	(Rugby · Brasenose)
A MacGregor	(Rugby · Corpus Christi)
J W Weston	(Rugby · University)
H B Carlyon	(Marlborough · Corpus Christi)
E M R Edgell	(Marlborough · Trinity)
W R B Fletcher	(Marlborough · Christ Church)

Try: Isherwood
Conversion: Isherwood

Cambridge	
H A Hamilton	(Wellington · Trinity)
J M Batten	(Haileybury · St John's)
R P Luscombe	(Marlborough · Clare)
*I C Lambert	(Rugby · Trinity)
C E Lyon	(Clifton · Trinity)
H Riley	(Rugby · Trinity)
G W Agnew	(Rugby · St John's)
R Baxter	(Rugby · Trinity)
J P Sisson	(Rugby · Trinity)
R Margerison	(Rugby · Trinity)
T Collin	(Rugby · Trinity)
R F Dudgeon	(Rugby · Trinity)
F M Hull	(Marlborough · Trinity)
E St J Morse	(Marlborough · St John's)
F F Back	(Marlborough · Christ's)
A Sprot	(Harrow · Trinity)
W Y Winthrop	(Wimbledon · Clare)
Hon M F Napier	(Wellington · Trinity)
J E Deakin	(Hereford C S · St John's)
A Macdonald	(Kingsbridge G S · Jesus)

MATCH 2

27 February 1873, at Parker's Piece, Cambridge
Cambridge won by 1G 2T to 0

Oxford		Cambridge	
A T Michell	(Rugby/Oriel)	W A Raikes	(Wellington/Trinity)
W H Game	(Sherborne/Oriel)	J M Batten	(Haileybury/St John's)
E A Deacon	(Marlborough/Exeter)	*H Riley	(Rugby/Trinity)
*W O Moberly	(Rugby/Balliol)	R P Luscombe	(Marlborough/Clare)
R W S Vidal	(Westminster/Christ Church)	G W Agnew	(Rugby/St John's)
W Brooks	(Rugby/Christ Church)	R Baxter	(Rugby/Trinity)
H Russell	(Haileybury/Keble)	A J Lushington	(Rugby/Jesus)
J E Lloyd	(Marlborough/Oriel)	R Margerison	(Rugby/Trinity)
A Sidgwick	(Rugby/Lincoln)	W Lewthwaite	(Rugby/Trinity)
W F Gooding	(Rugby/Christ Church)	E R Dalton	(Rugby/Trinity)
E C Fraser	(Blackheath Pty/Merton)	F M Hull	(Marlborough/Trinity)
C W Hamilton	(Royal H S/Balliol)	F F Back	(Marlborough/Christ's)
D Pearce	(Clifton/Trinity Hall)	H Rose	(Repton/Trinity)
G Podmore	(Marlborough/Keble)	G A Lewis	(Felsted/Trinity)

Tries: Luscombe, Lushington, Batten
Conversion: Luscombe

Oxford arrived for the match with only 13 players. They were given Pearce as a substitute, and Cambridge reduced their playing strength so that both sides had 14 men. There is also an account of this match in which 15 Cambridge men are listed: the 14 shown above, with F F Back as a threequarter, and another forward, T G Lushington, who has never appeared in a list of Blues.

MATCH 3

3 December 1873, at The Oval, Kennington, London
Drawn - each side scored 1T

Oxford		Cambridge	
W O Moberly	(Rugby/Balliol)	H A Hamilton	(Wellington/Trinity)
M J Brooks	(Rugby/Brasenose)	W G Michell	(Wellington/Trinity)
H Field	(Rugby/Wadham)	*J M Batten	(Haileybury/St John's)
W H Game	(Sherborne/Oriel)	A F Smith	(Wellington/Trinity)
G C Vecqueray	(Rugby/University)	R P Luscombe	(Marlborough/Clare)
A T Michell	(Rugby/Oriel)	H Riley	(Rugby/Trinity)
W H Bolton	(Rugby/Trinity)	G W Agnew	(Rugby/St John's)
W F Gooding	(Rugby/Christ Church)	J Bonham-Carter	(Rugby/Trinity)
H B Jupp	(Blackheath Pty/Magdalen)	R Baxter	(Rugby/Trinity)
C F Harrison	(Marlborough/University)	J M Chapman	(Marlborough/Trinity)
*E R Still	(Rugby/Brasenose)	W Lewthwaite	(Rugby/Trinity)
R F Brunskill	(Clifton/Trinity)	R Margerison	(Rugby/Trinity)
H Russell	(Haileybury/Keble)	F M Hull	(Marlborough/Trinity)
F G Cholmondeley	(Rugby/Christ Church)	H Wace	(Shrewsbury/St John's)
E M R Edgell	(Marlborough/Trinity)	J J Hornby	(Wellington/Trinity)
F S Baden-Powell	(Marlborough/Balliol)	A S Forbes	(Rugby/Caius)
W R B Fletcher	(Marlborough/Christ Church)	G A Lewis	(Felsted/Trinity)
R W Sheffield	(Blackheath Pty/St John's)	E R Dalton	(Rugby/Trinity)
E C Fraser	(Blackheath Pty/Merton)	D Pearce	(Clifton/Trinity Hall)
H Bourdillon	(Haileybury/Queen's)	W Fairbanks	(Clifton/Clare)

Try: Michell

Try: Batten

MATCH 4

12 December 1874, at The Oval, Kennington, London
Drawn — Oxford 2T Cambridge 0

Oxford		Cambridge	
W H Game	(Sherborne/Oriel)	A R Lewis	(Blackheath Pty/Corpus Christi)
F W Champneys	(Haileybury/St John's)	*J M Batten	(Haileybury/St John's)
D B Wilson	(Rugby/Balliol)	A Jameson	(London I C/Trinity)
R W Rucker	(Clifton/Brasenose)	W Fairbanks	(Clifton/Clare)
E H Nash	(Rugby/Trinity)		
*A T Michell	(Rugby/Oriel)	R P Luscombe	(Marlborough/Clare)
		J W Loxdale	(Wellington/Trinity Hall)
W H Bolton	(Rugby/Trinity)	H A Bull	(Rugby/Trinity)
R F Brunskill	(Clifton/Trinity)	E R Dalton	(Rugby/Trinity)
J H Bainbrigge	(Wellington/Oriel)	L T Williams	(Blackheath Pty/Trinity)
C W Crosse	(Rugby/Trinity)	R J Bealey	(Rugby/Trinity)
H D Bateson	(Rugby/Trinity)	A A Hopkins	(Rugby/Trinity)
G M Merivale	(Haileybury/New)	H Wace	(Shrewsbury/St John's)
H Russell	(Haileybury/Keble)	D B Roffey	(Jesus)
H Bourdillon	(Haileybury/Queen's)	A W Moore	(Rugby/Trinity)
E C Fraser	(Blackheath Pty/Merton)	D Pearce	(Clifton/Trinity Hall)
R W Sheffield	(Blackheath Pty/St John's)	E T Gurdon	(Haileybury/Trinity)
C F Harrison	(Marlborough/University)	C J C Touzel	(Wellington/St John's)
J E Lloyd	(Marlborough/Oriel)	A F Smith	(Wellington/Downing)
F H Lee	(Marlborough/Trinity)	W A Raikes	(Wellington/Trinity)
W R B Fletcher	(Marlborough/Christ Church)	J J Hornby	(Wellington/Trinity)

Tries: Fraser, Nash

Umpires: Mr F Stokes and Mr A G Guillemard

At this date, no match could be won unless a goal was scored.
Oxford did not field any threequarter backs.

MATCH 5

13 December 1875, at The Oval, Kennington, London
Oxford won by 1T to 0

Oxford		Cambridge	
F W Champneys	(Haileybury/St John's)	W G Michell	(Wellington/Trinity)
A H Heath	(Clifton/Brasenose)	A R Lewis	(Blackheath Pty/Corpus Christi)
E H Nash	(Rugby/Trinity)	W L T Dalton	(Rugby/Trinity)
J Forman	(Rugby/Oriel)	D B Roffey	(Jesus)
H Bourdillon	(Haileybury/Queen's)	L T Williams	(Blackheath Pty/Trinity)
E C Fraser	(Blackheath Pty/Merton)	G A Lewis	(Felsted/Trinity)
*W H Bolton	(Rugby/Trinity)	J Allen	(Clifton/St John's)
J James	(Rugby/New)	H H Child	(Rugby/Trinity)
H Russell	(Haileybury/Keble)	W H Blake	(Haileybury/Jesus)
H D Bateson	(Rugby/Trinity)	W J Darch	(Haileybury/Jesus)
T F Johnson	(Rugby/University)	*E T Gurdon	(Haileybury/Trinity)
A F Law	(Wellington/Oriel)	R Steward	(Haileybury/Jesus)
T W Wall	(Marlborough/Keble)	C M Agnew	(Rugby/Trinity)
F H Lee	(Marlborough/Trinity)	H A Bull	(Rugby/Trinity)
C F Harrison	(Marlborough/University)	C J C Touzel	(Wellington/St John's)

Try: Forman

Umpires: Mr F R Adams and Mr G L St Quintin

MATCH 6

11 December 1876, at The Oval, Kennington, London
Cambridge won by 1G 2T to 0

Oxford		Cambridge	
C C Atkinson	(Haileybury/Keble)	W G Michell	(Wellington/Trinity)
A C Sim	(Marlborough/New)	P H Clifford	(Dulwich/Christ's)
R W Rucker	(Clifton/Brasenose)	W L T Dalton	(Rugby/Trinity)
F W Champneys	(Haileybury/St. John's)	H A Williams	(St Paul's/St John's)
J Forman	(Rugby/Oriel)	R T Finch	(Sherborne/Pembroke)
H Bremridge	(Marlborough/St John's)	*E T Gurdon	(Haileybury/Trinity)
J H Bainbrigge	(Wellington/Oriel)	S R James	(Haileybury/Trinity)
C Phillips	(Rugby/Exeter)	R Steward	(Haileybury/Trinity)
M Macmillan	(Marlborough/Brasenose)	H H Child	(Rugby/Trinity)
J J Moubray	(Edinburgh Academy/St John's)	H R Clayton	(Rugby/Trinity)
*F H Lee	(Marlborough/Trinity)	C M Agnew	(Rugby/Trinity)
T W Wall	(Marlborough/Keble)	W L Agnew	(Rugby/St John's)
J James	(Rugby/New)	J Allen	(Clifton/St John's)
W H Cornish	(Rugby/Trinity)	C J C Touzel	(Wellington/St John's)
R B Gaisford	(Haileybury/St John's)	J J Hornby	(Wellington/Trinity)

Tries: Finch (2), Allen
Conversion: Michell

Umpires: Mr F R Adams and Mr L Stokes

MATCH 7

12 December 1877, at The Oval, Kennington, London
Oxford won by 2T to 0

Oxford		Cambridge	
J Ravenscroft	(Rugby/Exeter)	C E Jeffcock	(Cheltenham/Jesus)
A H Heath	(Clifton/Brasenose)	P H Clifford	(Dulwich/Christ's)
E T Hirst	(Rugby/Balliol)	G S Albright	(Grove House/Trinity)
P Springmann	(Craigmount/Balliol)	D Q Steel	(Uppingham/Trinity Hall)
A H Vecqueray	(Rugby/University)	R T Finch	(Sherborne/Pembroke)
A H Evans	(Clifton/Oriel)	J A Bevan	(Hereford CS/St John's)
*H D Bateson	(Rugby/Trinity)	*S R James	(Haileybury/Trinity)
J James	(Rugby/New)	H R Clayton	(Rugby/Trinity)
C Phillips	(Rugby/Exeter)	H H Browell	(Rugby/Trinity)
F H Lee	(Marlborough/Trinity)	C M Kennedy	(Rugby/Trinity)
H Bremridge	(Marlborough/St John's)	C Gurdon	(Haileybury/Jesus)
T W Wall	(Marlborough/Keble)	W L Agnew	(Rugby/St John's)
J J Moubray	(Edinburgh Academy/St John's)	C H Coates	(Christ's Coll Finchley/Trinity)
J H Bainbrigge	(Wellington/Oriel)	C P Wilson	(Marlborough/Trinity)
H Fowler	(Clifton/New)	P T Wrigley	(Clapham G S/St John's)

Tries: Fowler, Springmann

Umpires: Mr F R Adams and Mr L Stokes

MATCH 8

10 February 1879, at The Oval, Kennington, London
Drawn — no score

Oxford		Cambridge	
A H Heath	(Clifton/Brasenose)	C E W Boughton-Leigh	(Rugby/Trinity)
H A Tudor	(Sherborne/Keble)	P T Wrigley	(Clapham G S/St John's)
P Springmann	(Craigmount/Balliol)	P H Clifford	(Dulwich/Christ's)
E T Hirst	(Rugby/Balliol)	E Storey	(Fettes/Trinity)
A H Evans	(Clifton/Oriel)	R T Finch	(Sherborne/Pembroke)
A H Vecqueray	(Rugby/University)	H G Fuller	(Christ's Coll Finchley/Peterhouse)
*H Fowler	(Clifton/New)	H Y L Smith	(Wellington/Trinity)
C Phillips	(Rugby/Exeter)	C P Wilson	(Marlborough/Trinity)
A Back	(Christ's Hosp/Worcester)	C M Kennedy	(Rugby/Trinity)
G O Jacob	(Blackheath Pty/Oriel)	H H Browell	(Rugby/Trinity)
J J Moubray	(Edinburgh Academy/St John's)	*H R Clayton	(Rugby/Trinity)
G V Cox	(Clifton/Trinity)	W L Agnew	(Rugby/St John's)
J Ravenscroft	(Rugby/Exeter)	S E Jones	(Rugby/Trinity)
E P Branfoot	(Epsom/Balliol)	S R James	(Haileybury/Trinity)
M Shearman	(Merchant Taylors' London/St John's)	C H Coates	(Christ's Coll Finchley/Trinity)

Umpires: Mr F R Adams and Mr L Stokes

MATCH 9

25 February 1880, at The Oval, Kennington, London
Cambridge won by 1G 1DG to 1DG

Oxford		Cambridge	
N MacLachlan	(Loretto/Keble)	P T Wrigley	(Clapham G S/St John's)
A H Heath	(Clifton/Brasenose)	A S Taylor	(Merchant Taylors' London/Pembroke)
H A Tudor	(Sherborne/Keble)	J H Payne	(Manchester G S/St John's)
E T Hirst	(Rugby/Balliol)	E Storey	(Fettes/Trinity)
L Watkins	(Sherborne/Exeter)	E S Chapman	(Dulwich/St John's)
R L Knight	(Clifton/Corpus Christi)	*R T Finch	(Sherborne/Pembroke)
C F S Sanctuary	(Sherborne/Keble)	C H Coates	(Christ's Coll Finchley/Trinity)
A R Paterson	(Loretto/Trinity)	C H Golightly	(Wellington/Trinity Hall)
J G Walker	(Loretto/Trinity)	J J Gover	(Dulwich/Trinity)
H Vassall	(Marlborough/Hertford)	C P Wilson	(Marlborough/Trinity)
*C Phillips	(Rugby/Exeter)	H Y L Smith	(Wellington/Trinity)
E P Branfoot	(Epsom/Balliol)	J T Steele	(Wellington/Trinity Hall)
G O Jacob	(Blacheath Pty/Oriel)	R M Yetts	(Marlborough/Downing)
P A Newton	(Blackheath Pty/Brasenose)	F L Cox	(Haileybury/Trinity)
M Shearman	(Merchant Taylors' London/St John's)	H G Fuller	(Christ's Coll Finchley/Peterhouse)

Dropped Goal: MacLachlan

Try: Cox
Conversion: Smith
Dropped Goal: Finch

Umpires: Mr E T Gurdon and Mr L Stokes

MATCH 10

14 December 1880, at Richardson's Field, Blackheath, London
Drawn — each side scored 1T

Oxford		Cambridge	
N MacLachlan	(Loretto/Keble)	P T Wrigley	(Clapham G S/St John's)
J L Booker	(Rugby/Hertford)	A S Taylor	(Merchant Taylors' London/Pembroke)
A M Evanson	(Oundle/Jesus)	E Storey	(Fettes/Trinity)
H A Tudor	(Sherborne/Keble)	J A Bevan	(Hereford C S/St John's)
M B Peacock	(Wellington/Trinity)	E S Chapman	(Dulwich/St John's)
H Irwin	(St Columba's Dublin/Keble)	A R Don Wauchope	(Fettes/Trinity)
*P A Newton	(Blackheath Pty/Brasenose)	R M Yetts	(Marlborough/Downing)
W M Barwick	(Rugby/St John's)	*C P Wilson	(Marlborough/Trinity)
C F H Leslie	(Rugby/Oriel)	S Pater	(Haileybury/Trinity)
H Vassall	(Marlborough/Hertford)	J G Tait	(Edinburgh Academy/Peterhouse)
A R Paterson	(Loretto/Trinity)	E Rice	(Cheltenham/Jesus)
J G Walker	(Loretto/Trinity)	W M Macleod	(Fettes/Trinity)
A Walker	(Loretto/Trinity)	H Y L Smith	(Wellington/Trinity)
A O M Mackenzie	(Loretto/Trinity)	J T Steele	(Wellington/Trinity Hall)
C F S Sanctuary	(Sherborne/Keble)	H G Fuller	(Christ's Coll Finchley/Peterhouse)

Try: Tudor

Try: Smith

Umpires: Mr E T Gurdon and Mr L Stokes

MATCH 11

13 December 1881, at Richardson's Field, Blackheath, London
Oxford won by 2G 1T to 1G

Oxford		Cambridge	
H W Cave	(Rugby/Balliol)	H S Cooper	(Clifton/Christ's)
H A Tudor	(Sherborne/Keble)	A S Taylor	(Merchant Taylors' London/Pembroke)
C P Allen	(Rugby/University)	J W Dickson	(Tonbridge/Jesus)
A M Evanson	(Oundle/Jesus)	C E Chapman	(Stony Stratford/Sidney Sussex)
W R Richardson	(Manchester G S/Unattached)	J L Templer	(Dulwich/Caius)
A G Grant Asher	(Loretto/Brasenose)	A R Don Wauchope	(Fettes/Trinity)
E L Strong	(Edinburgh Academy/St John's)	*H Y L Smith	(Wellington/Trinity)
C F H Leslie	(Rugby/Oriel)	R Threlfall	(Clifton/Caius)
W M Barwick	(Rugby/St John's)	C J B Marriott	(Tonbridge/Clare)
A O M Mackenzie	(Loretto/Brasenose)	J Hammond	(Tonbridge/Trinity)
A R Paterson	(Loretto/Trinity)	R M Pattisson	(Tonbridge/Emmanuel)
J G Walker	(Loretto/Trinity)	E Rice	(Cheltenham/Jesus)
*H Vassall	(Marlborough/Hertford)	S Pater	(Haileybury/Trinity)
W M Tatham	(Marlborough/Brasenose)	R M Yetts	(Marlborough/Downing)
F W Hodgson	(Marlborough/Trinity)	H G Fuller	(Christ's Coll Finchley/Peterhouse)

Tries: Vassall, Evanson, Strong
Conversions: Walker (2)

Try: Don Wauchope
Conversion: Smith

Referee: Mr H H Taylor

191

*The 1881 Cambridge XV defeated by Harry Vassall's
innovative Oxford side. Left to right; on balcony: S. Pater,
C.J.B. Marriott; standing: J.W. Dickson, E. Rice,
R. Threlfall, R.M. Pattisson, J.L. Templer, C.E. Chapman;
seated: A.S. Taylor, H.G. Fuller, H.Y.L. Smith (captain),
A.R. Don Wauchope, R.M. Yetts; on ground: H.S. Cooper,
J. Hammond.*

MATCH 12

14 February 1883, at Richardson's Field, Blackheath, London
Oxford won by 1T to 0

Oxford		Cambridge	
H B Tristram	(Loretto / Hertford)	C H Sample	(Edinburgh Academy / Emmanuel)
C P Allen	(Rugby / University)	J F Gibbons	(St John's Wood / Caius)
G C Lindsay	(Loretto / Wadham)	C H Newman	(Monmouth / St John's)
C G Wade	(King's Parramatta / Merton)	C H Ware	(Hereford C S / Jesus)
A G Grant Asher	(Loretto / Brasenose)	J L Templer	(Dulwich / Caius)
A Rotherham	(Uppingham / Balliol)	E A Douglas	(St Peter's York / Christ's)
E J Moore	(Epsom / Christ Church)	H F Ransome	(Uppingham / Caius)
*H Vassall	(Marlborough / Hertford)	P M Lucas	(Haileybury / Jesus)
W M Tatham	(Marlborough / Brasenose)	C J B Marriott	(Tonbridge / Clare)
W H Squire	(Rugby / St John's)	C J B Milne	(Fettes / Pembroke)
G F Bradby	(Rugby / Balliol)	B C Burton	(Rugby / Trinity)
E D Court	(Rugby / New)	J G Tait	(Edinburgh Academy / Peterhouse)
R S Kindersley	(Clifton / Exeter)	R M Pattisson	(Tonbridge / Emmanuel)
C S Wooldridge	(Winchester / St John's)	W M Macleod	(Fettes / Trinity)
F J C Mackenzie	(Loretto / Keble)	*H G Fuller	(Christ's Coll Finchley / Peterhouse)

Try: Rotherham

Referee: Mr W N Bolton

MATCH 13

12 December 1883, at Rectory Field, Blackheath, London
Oxford won by 3G 4T to 1G

Oxford		Cambridge	
H B Tristram	(Loretto / Hertford)	C H Sample	(Edinburgh Academy / Emmanuel)
C P Allen	(Rugby / University)	E W Chilcott	(Sherborne / St John's)
G C Lindsay	(Loretto / Wadham)	G L Colbourne	(St John's Leatherhead / Corpus Christi)
C G Wade	(King's Parramatta / Merton)	E B Brutton	(Durham / Jesus)
A G Grant Asher	(Loretto / Brasenose)	E A Douglas	(St Peter's York / Christ's)
A Rotherham	(Uppingham / Balliol)	W B Salmon	(Hull ER Coll / Clare)
C W Berry	(Loretto / Brasenose)	*C J B Marriott	(Tonbridge / Clare)
F J C Mackenzie	(Loretto / Keble)	C J B Milne	(Fettes / Pembroke)
*W M Tatham	(Marlborough / Brasenose)	H F Ransome	(Uppingham / Caius)
R E Inglis	(Rugby / University)	R Threlfall	(Clifton / Caius)
E L Strong	(Edinburgh Academy / St John's)	B C Burton	(Rugby / Trinity)
R S Kindersley	(Clifton / Exeter)	J Lees	(Uppingham / Jesus)
E J Moore	(Epsom / Christ Church)	W P Richardson	(Clifton / Christ's)
W H Squire	(Rugby / St John's)	G B Guthrie	(RI Liverpool / Jesus)
E D Court	(Rugby / New)	H G Fuller	(Christ's Coll Finchley / Peterhouse)

Tries: Wade (3), Allen, Lindsay, Berry, Tatham
Conversions: Berry (3)

Try: Chilcott
Conversion: Salmon

Referee: Mr G R Hill

MATCH 14

10 December 1884, at Rectory Field, Blackheath, London
Oxford won by 3G 1T to 1T

Oxford		Cambridge	
H B Tristram	(Loretto / Hertford)	H F S Adams	(King William's IOM / Queens')
A S Blair	(Loretto / Brasenose)	J Le Fleming	(Tonbridge / Clare)
G C Lindsay	(Loretto / Wadham)	C H Sample	(Edinburgh Academy / Emmanuel)
C G Wade	(King's Parramatta / Merton)	C E Chapman	(Stony Stratford / Sidney Sussex)
*A G Grant Asher	(Loretto / Brasenose)	E A Douglas	(St Peter's York / Christ's)
A Rotherham	(Uppingham / Balliol)	H Neilson	(Merchiston / Clare)
A B Turner	(Marlborough / Keble)	L E Stevenson	(St Peter's York / Christ's)
H V Page	(Cheltenham / Wadham)	H F Ransome	(Uppingham / Caius)
R C M Kitto	(Loretto / Keble)	V C Le Fanu	(Haileybury / Trinity)
W H Squire	(Rugby / St John's)	*C J B Milne	(Fettes / Pembroke)
R E Inglis	(Rugby / University)	W J Plews	(Cheltenham / Trinity Hall)
P Coles	(Rugby / University)	H W Sample	(Edinburgh Academy / Peterhouse)
B A Cohen	(Rugby / Balliol)	E P Alexander	(Llandovery / Jesus)
C W Berry	(Loretto / Brasenose)	G L Jeffery	(St John's Wood / Caius)
A McNeill	(Loretto / Trinity)	F G Swayne	(KE VI Birmingham / Trinity)

Tries: Wade, Inglis, Blair, Lindsay   *Try*: Jeffery
Conversions: Berry (3)

Referee: Mr G R Hill

MATCH 15

16 December 1885, at Rectory Field, Blackheath, London
Cambridge won by 2T to 0

Oxford		Cambridge	
J G B Sutherland	(Fettes / Exeter)	H F S Adams	(King William's IOM / Queens')
*G C Lindsay	(Loretto / Wadham)	*E B Brutton	(Durham / Jesus)
J R Wordsworth	(TC Glenalmond / New)	J Le Fleming	(Tonbridge / Clare)
K J Key	(Clifton / Oriel)	M M Duncan	(Fettes / Clare)
E A Surtees	(Haileybury / Oriel)	M T Scott	(Craigmount / Jesus)
J D Hall	(Christ's Coll Christchurch / St John's)	W R M Leake	(Dulwich / Selwyn)
G F Bradby	(Rugby / Balliol)	V C Le Fanu	(Haileybury / Trinity)
R C M Kitto	(Loretto / Keble)	L E Stevenson	(St Peter's York / Christ's)
J D Boswell	(Loretto / Brasenose)	J H Dewhurst	(Mill Hill / Trinity)
C R Carter	(Cheltenham / Corpus Christi)	J A Shirer	(Clifton / Trinity)
P Coles	(Rugby / University)	G L Jeffery	(St John's Wood / Caius)
P H Blyth	(Loretto / Brasenose)	E P Alexander	(Llandovery / Jesus)
H V Page	(Cheltenham / Wadham)	F G Swayne	(KE VI Birmingham / Trinity)
F C Cousins	(Christ's Coll Finchley / Wadham)	F W J Goodhue	(Merchiston / Caius)
C R Cleveland	(Christ's Coll Finchley / Balliol)	W P Carpmael	(Christ's Coll Finchley / Jesus)

Tries: Brutton, Leake

Referee: Mr F I Currey

MATCH 16

15 December 1886, at Rectory Field, Blackheath, London
Cambridge won by 3T to 0

Oxford		Cambridge	
K J Key	(Clifton / Oriel)	W G Mitchell	(Bromsgrove / Caius)
M H Orr-Ewing	(Christ's Coll Finchley / Queen's)	M M Duncan	(Fettes / Clare)
P Christopherson	(Bedford G S / University)	*E B Brutton	(Durham / Jesus)
J D Hall	(Christ's Coll Christchurch / St John's)	J Le Fleming	(Tonbridge / Clare)
A P Koe	(Haileybury / University)	W R M Leake	(Dulwich / Selwyn)
L R Paterson	(Loretto / Keble)	M T Scott	(Craigmount / Jesus)
*P Coles	(Rugby / University)	V C Le Fanu	(Haileybury / Trinity)
R C M Kitto	(Loretto / Keble)	E P Alexander	(Llandovery / Jesus)
J D Boswell	(Loretto / Brasenose)	F W J Goodhue	(Merchiston / Caius)
P H Blyth	(Loretto / Brasenose)	A Methuen	(Fettes / Clare)
H H Castens	(Rugby / Brasenose)	A A Surtees	(Rugby / Trinity)
N F Henderson	(Dulwich / Magdalen)	A Robinson	(Cheltenham / Jesus)
R C M Harvey	(Marlborough / Keble)	W H Thomas	(Llandovery / Corpus Christi)
F C Cousins	(Christ's Coll Finchley / Wadham)	J H Dewhurst	(Mill Hill / Trinity)
C R Cleveland	(Christ's Coll Finchley / Balliol)	F G Swayne	(KE VI Birmingham / Trinity)

Tries: Le Fleming (2), Robinson

Referee: Mr G R Hill

MATCH 17

14 December 1887, at Queen's Club, Kensington, London
Cambridge won by 1DG 2T to 0

Oxford		Cambridge	
W Rashleigh	(Tonbridge / Brasenose)	E Bromet	(Richmond / Caius)
P Christopherson	(Bedford G S / University)	*M M Duncan	(Fettes / Clare)
C J N Fleming	(Fettes / Queen's)	P H Morrison	(Loretto / Caius)
J B Sayer	(Christ's Coll Finchley / Queen's)	F H R Alderson	(Durham / Clare)
W G Wilson	(St Peter's York / Worcester)	W R M Leake	(Dulwich / Selwyn)
L R Paterson	(Loretto / Keble)	M T Scott	(Craigmount / Jesus)
*R C M Kitto	(Loretto / Keble)	A Methuen	(Fettes / Clare)
H H Castens	(Rugby / Brasenose)	D L MacEwen	(Fettes / Trinity)
J M Glubb	(Bedford G S / Exeter)	W H Thomas	(Llandovery / Corpus Christi)
C C Bradford	(Clifton / Brasenose)	J W Cave	(Wellington / Trinity)
R O B Lane	(Marlborough / Trinity)	J W Fogg-Elliot	(Durham / Jesus)
J D Boswell	(Loretto / Brasenose)	F J L Ogilvy	(Fettes / Trinity)
E P Simpson	(Wellington / Magdalen)	A Robinson	(Cheltenham / Jesus)
D W Evans	(Llandovery / Jesus)	E H Wynne	(Bradford G S / Clare)
R T D Budworth	(Ch Coll Brecon / Magdalen)	W Bevan	(Wellington / Trinity)

Tries: Wynne, Duncan
Dropped Goal: Duncan

Referee: Mr G R Hill

MATCH 18

12 December 1888, at Queen's Club, Kensington, London
Cambridge won 1G 2T to 0

Oxford		Cambridge	
W Rashleigh	(Tonbridge/Brasenose)	E Bromet	(Richmond/Caius)
A K Lewis	(Christ's Hosp/Trinity)	P H Morrison	(Loretto/Caius)
C J N Fleming	(Fettes/Queen's)	F H R Alderson	(Durham/Clare)
*P Christopherson	(Bedford G S/University)	T Todd	(Fettes/Clare)
F Morgan	(Llandovery/Keble)	W M Scott	(Craigmount/Jesus)
R F C de Winton	(Marlborough/Exeter)	W Wotherspoon	(Fettes/Clare)
D W Evans	(Llandovery/Jesus)	F C Bree-Frink	(Sherborne/Peterhouse)
W T Grenfell	(Marlborough/Queen's)	*A Methuen	(Fettes/Clare)
J E Aldridge	(Malvern/Worcester)	J W Bowhill	(Fettes/Clare)
E H G North	(Blackheath Pty/Keble)	E C Langton	(Wellington/Trinity)
R S Hunter	(Fettes/New)	W N Mayne	(Bromsgrove/Jesus)
T Parker	(Durham/Brasenose)	J W Cave	(Wellington/Trinity)
J H G Wilson	(St Peter's York/Queen's)	S M J Woods	(Brighton Coll/Jesus)
R O B Lane	(Marlborough/Trinity)	A Trethewy	(Haileybury/Caius)
R T D Budworth	(Ch Coll Brecon/Magdalen)	P T Williams	(Christ's Coll Christchurch/Jesus)

Tries: Scott, Morrison, Alderson
Conversion: Scott

Referee: Mr G R Hill

MATCH 19

14 December 1889, at Queen's Club, Kensington, London
Oxford won by 1G 1T to 0

Oxford		Cambridge	
P C Cochran	(Loretto/Oriel)	G MacGregor	(Uppingham/Jesus)
C J N Fleming	(Fettes/Queen's)	C E Fitch	(Mill Hill/Jesus)
P R A Clauss	(Loretto/Keble)	R L Aston	(Tonbridge/Caius)
J S Longdon	(Ch Coll Brecon/Jesus)	*P H Morrison	(Loretto/Caius)
R F C de Winton	(Marlborough/Exeter)	W Wotherspoon	(Fettes/Clare)
R G T Coventry	(Hereford CS/Brasenose)	P H Illingworth	(London IC/Jesus)
A M Paterson	(Loretto/New)	J W Bowhill	(Fettes/Clare)
L J Percival	(Clifton/Trinity)	T W P Storey	(Fettes/Trinity Hall)
R S Hunter	(Fettes/New)	S M J Woods	(Brighton Coll/Jesus)
E H G North	(Blackheath Pty/Keble)	F C Bree-Frink	(Sherborne/Peterhouse)
*R O B Lane	(Marlborough/Trinity)	J Smith	(Cheltenham/Jesus)
W E Bromet	(Richmond/Wadham)	A L Jackson	(Marlborough/Clare)
R T D Budworth	(Ch Coll Brecon/Magdalen)	E C Langton	(Wellington/Trinity)
A R Kay	(Fettes/Oriel)	J C MacDonnell	(Armagh Royal/Pembroke)
J H G Wilson	(St Peter's York/Queen's)	P T Williams	(Christ's Coll Christchurch/Jesus)

Tries: de Winton, Percival
Conversion: Fleming

Referee: Mr G R Hill

MATCH 20

3 March 1891, at Queen's Club, Kensington, London
Drawn — each side scored 1G (3)

Oxford		Cambridge	
F I Cowlishaw	(Rugby/Brasenose)	G MacGregor	(Uppingham/Jesus)
*C J N Fleming	(Fettes/Queen's)	C A Hooper	(Clifton/Trinity)
P R A Clauss	(Loretto/Keble)	R L Aston	(Tonbridge/Caius)
W H Parkin	(Sedbergh/Brasenose)	P H Morrison	(Loretto/Trinity Hall)
R G T Coventry	(Hereford C S/Brasenose)	A Rotherham	(Uppingham/Trinity)
R F C de Winton	(Marlborough/Exeter)	P H Illingworth	(London IC/Jesus)
J H G Wilson	(St Peter's York/Queen's)	S M J Woods	(Brighton Coll/Jesus)
A R Kay	(Fettes/Oriel)	R Thompson	(Cheltenham/Pembroke)
E H G North	(Blackheath Pty/Keble)	C P Simpson	(Wellington/Trinity)
E Bonham-Carter	(Clifton/New)	H W T Patterson	(Wellington/Trinity Hall)
P R Cadell	(Haileybury/Balliol)	C B Nicholl	(Llandovery/Queens')
R W Hunt	(Dover Coll/Corpus Christi)	F C Bree-Frink	(Sherborne/Peterhouse)
A M Paterson	(Loretto/New)	W I Rowell	(Marlborough/Jesus)
S E Wilson	(Liverpool Coll/Trinity)	W H Thorman	(Richmond/Caius)
W Rice-Evans	(Craufurd Coll/Jesus)	*T W P Storey	(Fettes/Trinity Hall)

Try: Kay
Conversion: S E Wilson

Try: Simpson
Conversion: MacGregor

Refereee: Mr G R Hill

MATCH 21

16 December 1891, at Queen's Club, Kensington, London
Cambridge won by 2T (4) to 0

Oxford		Cambridge	
P C Cochran	(Loretto/Oriel)	C M Wells	(Dulwich/Trinity)
*P R A Clauss	(Loretto/Keble)	R Montgomery	(Queen's Belfast/Trinity)
J Conway-Rees	(Llandovery/Jesus)	W Neilson	(Merchiston/Clare)
F I Cowlishaw	(Rugby/Brasenose)	A B Fforde	(Bedford G S/Christ's)
W E Wilkinson	(Durham/Keble)	J C Orr	(Clifton/Trinity)
R G T Coventry	(Hereford C S/Brasenose)	A Rotherham	(Uppingham/Trinity)
L J Percival	(Clifton/Trinity)	*T W P Storey	(Fettes/Trinity Hall)
G H F Cookson	(Clifton/Lincoln)	E Mayfield	(Leys/Caius)
F O Poole	(Cheltenham/Keble)	C B Nicholl	(Llandovery/Queens')
W H Wakefield	(Charterhouse/New)	H Staunton	(Bromsgrove/Selwyn)
E Bonham-Carter	(Clifton/New)	B F Robinson	(Newton Abbot/Jesus)
A R Kay	(Fettes/Oriel)	W Cope	(Repton/Clare)
C D Baker	(Sherborne/Merton)	R N Douglas	(Dulwich/Selwyn)
E Selby	(Sedbergh/Queen's)	H J Craig	(Rugby/Trinity)
G M Carey	(Sherborne/Exeter)	A E Elliott	(Cheltenham/St John's)

Tries: Fforde, Neilson

Referee: Mr H L Ashmore

MATCH 22

14 December 1892, at Queen's Club, Kensington, London
Drawn — no score

Oxford		Cambridge	
L C Humfrey	(Ch Coll Brecon/Keble)	E Field	(Clifton/Trinity)
L Mortimer	(Clifton/Exeter)	D D Robertson	(Glasgow Academy/Christ's)
J Conway-Rees	(Llandovery/Jesus)	W Neilson	(Merchiston/Clare)
A Latter	(King's Canterbury/Trinity)	J J Gowans	(Harrow/Clare)
W P Donaldson	(Loretto/Brasenose)	T L Jackson	(Leys/St John's)
H M Taberer	(St Andrew's Grahamstown/Keble)	C M Wells	(Dulwich/Trinity)
*G H F Cookson	(Clifton/Lincoln)	T W P Storey	(Fettes/Trinity Hall)
F O Poole	(Cheltenham/Keble)	*C B Nicholl	(Llandovery/Queens')
J A Smith	(Loretto/Trinity)	D B Hill	(Heretaunga/Jesus)
G M Carey	(Sherborne/Exeter)	B F Robinson	(Newton Abbot/Jesus)
W B Stewart	(Loretto/Brasenose)	J C A Rigby	(Oundle/Caius)
A H Grant	(Fettes/Balliol)	J J Robinson	(Appleby G S/St John's)
A C Elwes	(Bedford G S/St John's)	W E Nelson	(Haileybury/Clare)
W H Wakefield	(Charterhouse/New)	H D Rendall	(Rugby/Trinity)
A H Colville	(Merchant Taylors' Crosby/Merton)	W E Tucker	(Trinity Coll Port Hope/Caius)

Referee: Mr H L Ashmore

MATCH 23

13 December 1893, at Queen's Club, Kensington, London
Oxford won by 1T (3) to 0

Oxford		Cambridge	
L C Humfrey	(Ch Coll Brecon/Keble)	E Field	(Clifton/Trinity)
W L Thomas	(Ch Coll Brecon/Keble)	L E Pilkington	(Clifton/King's)
*J Conway-Rees	(Llandovery/Jesus)	W G Druce	(Marlborough/Trinity)
E M Baker	(Denstone/Keble)	*W Neilson	(Merchiston/Clare)
H T S Gedge	(Loretto/Keble)	J J Gowans	(Harrow/Clare)
R H B Cattell	(TC Stratford/Exeter)	A H Greg	(Marlborough/Trinity)
W P Donaldson	(Loretto/Brasenose)	R O Schwarz	(St Paul's/Christ's)
C D Baker	(Sherborne/Merton)	H Laing	(Wellington/Trinity)
F O Poole	(Cheltenham/Keble)	H D Rendall	(Rugby/Trinity)
J A Smith	(Loretto/Trinity)	C B Nicholl	(Llandovery/Queens')
A C Elwes	(Bedford G S/St John's)	B F Robinson	(Newton Abbot/Jesus)
A H Colville	(Merchant Taylors' Crosby/Merton)	A F Todd	(Mill Hill/Caius)
D W Donaldson	(Loretto/New)	F Mitchell	(St Peter's York/Trinity)
E R Balfour	(Edinburgh Academy/University)	S E A Whiteway	(Sedbergh/Trinity)
R B Littlewood	(Merchant Taylors' London/Wadham)	W E Tucker	(Trinity Coll Port Hope/Caius)

Try: Cattell

Referee: Mr H L Ashmore

MATCH 24

12 December 1894, at Queen's Club, Kensington, London
Drawn — each side scored 1G (5)

Oxford		Cambridge	
G T Unwin	(Marlborough/Exeter)	E Field	(Clifton/Trinity)
A R Smith	(Loretto/Trinity)	H B J Taylor	(Newton Abbot/Jesus)
E M Baker	(Denstone/Keble)	W G Druce	(Marlborough/Trinity)
F A Leslie-Jones	(Bromsgrove/Lincoln)	W L Bunting	(Bromsgrove/Trinity Hall)
W L Thomas	(Ch Coll Brecon/Keble)	L E Pilkington	(Clifton/King's)
R S H Baiss	(Tonbridge/Brasenose)	S P Bell	(Uppingham/King's)
W P Donaldson	(Loretto/Brasenose)	P G Jacob	(Bedford G S/St John's)
*G M Carey	(Sherborne/Exeter)	R Griffith	(Clifton/Clare)
F O Poole	(Cheltenham/Keble)	S J Lawry	(Clifton/Trinity)
E R Balfour	(Edinburgh Academy/University)	F Mitchell	(St Peter's York/Caius)
J C Hartley	(Tonbridge/Brasenose)	W Falcon	(St Bees/St John's)
A G Gibson	(Haileybury/University)	A F Todd	(Mill Hill/Caius)
W J Carey	(Bedford G S/Hertford)	C Dixon	(Sherborne/Trinity Hall)
M A Robertson	(Loretto/Trinity)	L F Giblin	(Hutchin's Hobart/King's)
R C Mullins	(St Andrew's Grahamstown/Keble)	*W E Tucker	(Trinity Coll Port Hope/Caius)

Try: Thomas
Conversion: Donaldson

Try: Jacob
Conversion: Mitchell

Referee: Capt H D Lawrence

Lawrence refereed when Mr H L Ashmore, the nominated referee, was unable to officiate.

MATCH 25

11 December 1895, at Queen's Club, Kensington, London
Cambridge won by 1G (5) to 0

Oxford		Cambridge	
G T Unwin	(Marlborough/Exeter)	T J Thomas	(Ch Coll Brecon/Jesus)
H F Newton	(Heversham G S/Queen's)	H T Wallis	(Allhallows'/Jesus)
E M Baker	(Denstone/Keble)	W L Bunting	(Bromsgrove/Trinity Hall)
F A Leslie-Jones	(Bromsgrove/Lincoln)	O G Mackie	(Haileybury/Clare)
A R Smith	(Loretto/Trinity)	E A A Jones	(Hereford C S/St John's)
R S H Baiss	(Tonbridge/Brasenose)	S P Bell	(Uppingham/King's)
C L Donaldson	(Newton Abbot/Jesus)	P G Jacob	(Bedford G S/St John's)
J A Kitson	(Haileybury/Keble)	*F Mitchell	(St Peter's York/Caius)
J C Hartley	(Tonbridge/Brasenose)	F Jacob	(Sandwich/Caius)
W J Carey	(Bedford G S/Hertford)	A F Todd	(Mill Hill/Caius)
W J Thomson	(Loretto/Brasenose)	W Falcon	(St Bees/St John's)
*E R Balfour	(Edinburgh Academy/University)	L F Giblin	(Hutchin's Hobart/King's)
A G Gibson	(Haileybury/University)	S J Lawry	(Clifton/Trinity)
G L MacEwen	(Loretto/Merton)	W Mortimer	(Marlborough/Trinity)
A C Rayner-Wood	(St Paul's/Trinity)	R Griffith	(Clifton/Clare)

Try: Giblin
Conversion: Thomas

Referee: Mr H L Ashmore

9 December 1896, at Queen's Club, Kensington, London
Oxford won by 1G 1DG (9) to 1G 1T (8)

Oxford		Cambridge	
A R Smith	(Loretto/Trinity)	T J Thomas	(Ch Coll Brecon/Jesus)
G S A Jones	(Magdalen C S/Keble)	H T Wallis	(Allhallows'/Jesus)
E M Baker	(Denstone/Keble)	O G Mackie	(Haileybury/Clare)
*F A Leslie-Jones	(Bromsgrove/Lincoln)	W N Pilkington	(Clifton/Trinity)
H F Newton	(Heversham G S/Queen's)	H B J Taylor	(Newton Abbot/Jesus)
G T Unwin	(Marlborough/Exeter)	*S P Bell	(Uppingham/King's)
L M Crump	(Merchant Taylors' Crosby/Merton)	P G Jacob	(Bedford G S/St John's)
A O Dowson	(Rugby/New)	L F Giblin	(Hutchin's Hobart/King's)
C J Reid	(Haileybury/University)	T M W McGown	(Merchiston/Clare)
C Thomson	(Loretto/Trinity)	A J L Darby	(Cheltenham/Clare)
J C Hartley	(Tonbridge/Brasenose)	R A Brandram	(Blackheath Pty/Christ's)
W J Carey	(Bedford G S/Hertford)	W Mortimer	(Marlborough/Trinity)
A C Rayner-Wood	(St Paul's/Trinity)	F Jacob	(Sandwich/Caius)
W J Thomson	(Loretto/Brasenose)	A Balfour	(Watson's Coll/Caius)
M A Robertson	(Loretto/Trinity)	A F C C Luxmoore	(King's Canterbury/Jesus)

Try: Baker
Conversion: Crump
Dropped Goal: Unwin

Tries: Wallis (2)
Coneversion: Bell

Referee: Mr H L Ashmore

15 December 1897, at Queen's Club, Kensington, London
Oxford won by 2T (6) to 0

Oxford		Cambridge	
T Stone	(Marlborough/Trinity)	D Johnston	(Sedbergh/Trinity)
P L Nicholas	(Monmouth/Keble)	G M Bennett	(Birkenhead/Trinity Hall)
H F Newton	(Heversham G S/Queen's)	*O G Mackie	(Haileybury/Clare)
T A Nelson	(Edinburgh Academy/University)	R F Cumberlege	(Durham/Trinity)
*A R Smith	(Loretto/Trinity)	W N Pilkington	(Clifton/Trinity)
F H B Champain	(Cheltenham/Hertford)	F H Fasson	(Merchiston/Clare)
J W Stratton	(Cheltenham/Keble)	M A Black	(Rugby/Christ's)
C P Evers	(Rugby/Queen's)	A J L Darby	(Cheltenham/Clare)
C H Harper	(Blundell's/Exeter)	A S Pringle	(Edinburgh Academy/Trinity)
W J Carey	(Bedford G S/Hertford)	L B Hopper	(Haileybury/Caius)
C E Barry	(St Paul's/Trinity)	J A Campbell	(Fettes/Trinity)
H Alexander	(Uppingham/Corpus Christi)	R W Bell	(Durham/Jesus)
D Legge	(Haileybury/Trinity)	A Balfour	(Watson's/Caius)
J F A Swanston	(Loretto/Trinity)	A F C C Luxmoore	(King's Canterbury/Jesus)
L B Dunn	(Wellington/Worcester)	N C Fletcher	(Merchant Taylors' London/Queens')

Tries: Nicholas, Stratton

Referee: Mr G H Harnett

MATCH 28

14 December 1898, at Queen's Club, Kensington, London
Cambridge won by 1G 2T (11) to 0

Oxford		Cambridge	
T O Jones	(Llandovery/Keble)	H Rottenburg	(Loretto/King's)
P L Nicholas	(Monmouth/Keble)	G M Bennett	(Birkenhead/Trinity Hall)
L J J Orpen	(Cheltenham/Keble)	A Hacking	(Giggleswick/Christ's)
*T A Nelson	(Edinburgh Academy/University)	G F Collett	(Cheltenham/Pembroke)
J E Crabbie	(Edinburgh Academy/University)	F H Jones	(Bedford G S/Emmanuel)
F Kershaw	(Cheltenham/Trinity)	F H Fasson	(Merchiston/Clare)
F H B Champain	(Cheltenham/Hertford)	M A Black	(Rugby/Christ's)
C P Evers	(Rugby/Queen's)	J G Fordham	(St Paul's/Trinity)
C H Harper	(Blundell's/Exeter)	J Daniell	(Clifton/Emmanuel)
C E Barry	(St Paul's/Trinity)	J R C Greenlees	(Loretto/St John's)
W L Y Rogers	(Rugby/Trinity)	*A J L Darby	(Cheltenham/Clare)
J F A Swanston	(Loretto/Trinity)	R W Bell	(Durham/Jesus)
H Alexander	(Uppingham/Corpus Christi)	J A Campbell	(Fettes/Trinity)
W H Peat	(St Paul's/Trinity)	A S Pringle	(Edinburgh Academy/Trinity)
A J Chadwick	(Rossall/Corpus Christi)	N C Fletcher	(Merchant Taylors' London/Queens')

Tries: Fasson, Daniell, Bell
Conversion: Campbell

Referee: Mr G H Harnett

MATCH 29

13 December 1899, at Queen's Club, Kensington, London
Cambridge won by 2G 4T (22) to 0

Oxford		Cambridge	
W Grischotti	(Rugby/Brasenose)	J W Sagar	(Durham/Jesus)
J E Crabbie	(Edinburgh Academy/University)	T A Cock	(Marlborough/Trinity)
J Strand-Jones	(Lampeter/Jesus)	F H Jones	(Bedford G S/Emmanuel)
F M Luce	(Cheltenham/Magdalen)	E E Walker	(Bradford G S/Trinity)
P L Nicholas	(Monmouth/Keble)	H R Palmer	(Oundle/Trinity Hall)
F Kershaw	(Cheltenham/Trinity)	F H Fasson	(Merchiston/Clare)
F H B Champain	(Cheltenham/Hertford)	A Hacking	(Giggleswick/Christ's)
*C E Barry	(St Paul's/Trinity)	*J A Campbell	(Fettes/Trinity)
J F A Swanston	(Loretto/Trinity)	J R C Greenless	(Loretto/St John's)
A J Chadwick	(Rossall/Corpus Christi)	R W Bell	(Durham/Jesus)
T Couper	(Fettes/Worcester)	C T Scott	(Tonbridge/Sidney Sussex)
R C Grellet	(Bedford G S/Hertford)	G H Keeton	(Oakham/Emmanuel)
C E L Hammond	(Bedford G S/Hertford)	J Daniell	(Clifton/Emmanuel)
D D Dobson	(Cheltenham/Keble)	D R Bedell-Sivright	(Fettes/Trinity)
A G Cairns	(Watson's Coll/Trinity)	N C Fletcher	(Merchant Taylors' London/Queens')

Tries: Palmer (2), Cock (2), Jones, Bedell-Sivright
Conversions: Campbell, Jones

Referee: Mr G H Harnett

201

MATCH 30

12 December 1900, at Queen's Club, Kensington, London
Oxford won by 2G (10) to 1G 1T (8)

Oxford		Cambridge	
J Strand-Jones	(Lampeter / Jesus)	J W Sagar	(Durham / Jesus)
J E Crabbie	(Edinburgh Academy / University)	A E Hind	(Uppingham / Trinity Hall)
F M Luce	(Cheltenham / Magdalen)	E E Walker	(Bradford G S / Trinity)
H F Terry	(Uppingham / University)	F H Jones	(Bedford G S / Emmanuel)
J W F A Crawfurd	(Merchant Taylors' London / St John's)	S C Talbot	(Cheltenham / Caius)
F Kershaw	(Cheltenham / Trinity)	P Powell	(Dulwich / King's)
E J Walton	(St Peter's York / Queen's)	O V Payne	(Exeter / St John's)
A G Cairns	(Watson's Coll / Trinity)	T Drysdale	(St Paul's / Jesus)
R C Grellet	(Bedford G S / Hertford)	W Cobby	(Uppingham / Pembroke)
T Couper	(Fettes / Worcester)	J V Bedell-Sivright	(Fettes / Emmanuel)
S H Osborne	(Fettes / Hertford)	*J R C Greenlees	(Loretto / St John's)
D D Dobson	(Cheltenham / Keble)	J Daniell	(Clifton / Emmanuel)
W L Y Rogers	(Rugby / Trinity)	D R Bedell-Sivright	(Fettes / Trinity)
*J F A Swanston	(Loretto / Trinity)	G H Keeton	(Oakham / Emmanuel)
C E L Hammond	(Bedford G S / Hertford)	B C Hartley	(Dulwich / Jesus)

Tries: Walton, Crabbie
Conversions: Rogers (2)

Tries: Hind (2)
Conversion: Sagar

Referee: Mr G H Harnett

MATCH 31

11 December 1901, at Queen's Club, Kensington, London
Oxford won by 1G 1T (8) to 0

Oxford		Cambridge	
J Strand-Jones	(Lampeter / Jesus)	S Horsley	(Loretto / Clare)
*J E Crabbie	(Edinburgh Academy / University)	J Hearfield	(Dover Coll / Jesus)
H F Terry	(Uppingham / University)	E V Oulton	(Leys / Christ's)
J E Raphael	(Merchant Taylors' London / St John's)	A J Rae	(Cheltenham / Caius)
G S J F Eberle	(Clifton / Trinity)	A J R Roberts	(Mill Hill / Jesus)
E J Walton	(St Peter's York / Queen's)	A B Sanderson	(Rugby / Clare)
F Kershaw	(Cheltenham / Trinity)	R J Stone	(Dover Coll / Jesus)
S H Osborne	(Fettes / Hertford)	J R C Greenlees	(Loretto / St John's)
D D Dobson	(Cheltenham / Keble)	T Drysdale	(St Paul's / Jesus)
W B Odgers	(Sedbergh / Balliol)	*D R Bedell-Sivright	(Fettes / Trinity)
A J Swanzy	(Rugby / Univeristy)	A F Roberts	(Merchiston / Clare)
A G Cairns	(Watson's Coll / Trinity)	F W Odgers	(Sedbergh / Trinity)
R C Grellet	(Bedford G S / Hertford)	N Spicer	(Leys / Trinity Hall)
V H Cartwright	(Rugby / Corpus Christi)	T A Gibson	(Uppingham / Queens')
N Kennedy	(Rugby / Univeristy)	J V Bedell-Sivright	(Fettes / Emmanuel)

Tries: Crabbie (2)
Conversion: Strand-Jones

Referee: Mr G H Harnett

MATCH 32

13 December 1902, at Queen's Club, Kensington, London
Drawn — each side scored 1G 1T (8)

Oxford		Cambridge	
A D Sloane	(Blundell's/Merton)	S Horsley	(Loretto/Clare)
J R P Sandford	(Marlborough/Exeter)	J R Walkey	(Plymouth Coll/Christ's)
C D Fisher	(Campbell Belfast/St John's)	A J R Roberts	(Mill Hill/Jesus)
J E Raphael	(Merchant Taylors' London/St John's)	A H McNeill	(Loretto/Clare)
G S J F Eberle	(Clifton/Trinity)	C E Pumphrey	(Sedbergh/Christ's)
A M P Lyle	(Fettes/Trinity)	J S Pringle	(Merchiston/Clare)
A D Stoop	(Rugby/University)	H Mainprice	(Blundell's/Jesus)
S H Osborne	(Fettes/Hertford)	J V Bedell-Sivright	(Fettes/Emmanuel)
A J Swanzy	(Rugby/University)	T A Gibson	(Uppingham/Queens')
*R C Grellet	(Bedford G S/Hertford)	C J Newbold	(Uppingham/Caius)
R O Hutchison	(Rugby/Hertford)	*D R Bedell-Sivright	(Fettes/Trinity)
W B Odgers	(Sedbergh/Balliol)	N Spicer	(Leys/Trinity Hall)
G V Kyrke	(Marlborough/Lincoln)	W T C Cave	(Tonbridge/Caius)
C W Wordsworth	(Loretto/Queen's)	A F Roberts	(Merchiston/Clare)
V H Cartwright	(Rugby/Corpus Christi)	J B Waters	(Loretto/Pembroke)

Tries: Raphael, Eberle
Conversion: Wordsworth

Tries: Walkey (2)
Conversion: Spicer

Referee: Mr G H Harnett

MATCH 33

15 December 1903, at Queen's Club, Kensington, London
Oxford won by 3G 1T (18) to 2G 1T (13)

Oxford		Cambridge	
H Cheyne	(Edinburgh Academy/University)	*S Horsley	(Loretto/Clare)
R E S Gregson	(Rugby/Corpus Christi)	A H McNeill	(Loretto/Clare)
J R P Sandford	(Marlborough/Exeter)	L M MacLeod	(Fettes/Pembroke)
J E Raphael	(Merchant Taylors' London/St John's)	E D Evans	(UC Aberystwyth/St John's)
A A Lawrie	(Fettes/Trinity)	W T Ritchie	(Wanganui CS/St John's)
P Munro	(Leeds G S/Christ Church)	H Laxon	(King Henry VIII Coventry/Pembroke)
A D Stoop	(Rugby/University)	H Mainprice	(Blundell's/Jesus)
A M Robertson	(Rugby/University)	E C Hodges	(Haileybury/Trinity)
G V Kyrke	(Marlborough/Lincoln)	R O C Ward	(Clifton/Trinity)
C Bourns	(Merchant Taylors' London/St John's)	J B Waters	(Loretto/Pembroke)
E Fearenside	(Denstone/Queen's)	J Horsfall	(Tonbridge/Caius)
*V H Cartwright	(Rugby/Corpus Christi)	W T C Cave	(Tonbridge/Caius)
M R Dickson	(Marlborough/Merton)	C J Newbold	(Uppingham/Caius)
J C L Farquharson	(Dulwich/University)	H G Monteith	(Fettes/Pembroke)
J G Bussell	(St Edward's Oxford/Brasenose)	J V Bedell-Sivright	(Fettes/Emmanuel)

Tries: Raphael, Sandford, Gregson, Dickson
Conversions: Fearenside (3)

Tries: McNeill, Ritchie, Laxon
Conversions: MacLeod (2)

Referee: Mr T Williams

MATCH 34

13 December 1904, at Queen's Club, Kensington, London
Cambridge won by 3G (15) to 2G (10)

Oxford		Cambridge	
H Cheyne	(Edinburgh Academy / University)	H Lee	(Tettenhall Coll / St John's)
J V Nesbitt	(Rugby / Christ Church)	W T Ritchie	(Wanganui CS / St John's)
A E Wood	(Liverpool Coll / University)	L M MacLeod	(Fettes / Pembroke)
J E Raphael	(Merchant Taylors' London / St John's)	E D Evans	(UC Aberystwyth / St John's)
A M P Lyle	(Fettes / Trinity)	H F P Hearson	(Uppingham / King's)
*A D Stoop	(Rugby / University)	*H Mainprice	(Blundell's / Jesus)
P Munro	(Leeds G S / Christ Church)	H Laxon	(King Henry VIII Coventry / Pembroke)
B Cozens-Hardy	(Rugby / Trinity)	J B Waters	(Loretto / Pembroke)
V H Cartwright	(Rugby / Corpus Christi)	A Forman	(Loretto / Pembroke)
J V S Wilkinson	(Rugby / University)	W T C Cave	(Tonbridge / Caius)
R S Wix	(Marlborough / Brasenose)	J Horsfall	(Tonbridge / Caius)
E G Morris	(Bedford G S / Hertford)	E C Hodges	(Haileybury / Trinity)
J G Bussell	(St Edward's Oxford / Brasenose)	H G Monteith	(Fettes / Pembroke)
W D Kennedy	(Glenalmond / University)	E L Chambers	(Bedford G S / Emmanuel)
W W Hoskin	(St Andrew's Grahamstown / Trinity)	B G Harris	(Cheltenham / Pembroke)

Tries: Stoop, Raphael
Conversions: Nesbitt (2)

Tries: MacLeod, Hearson, Cave
Conversions: Hearson (3)

Referee: Mr J C Findlay

MATCH 35

12 December 1905, at Queen's Club, Kensington, London
Cambridge won by 3G (15) to 2G 1T (13)

Oxford		Cambridge	
D B Davies	(Lampeter / Jesus)	J G Scoular	(St Bees / St John's)
A A Lawrie	(Fettes / Trinity)	G G Koop	(Tonbridge / Caius)
L Parker	(Marlborough / Christ Church)	*L M MacLeod	(Fettes / Pembroke)
N W Milton	(Marlborough / University)	K G MacLeod	(Fettes / Pembroke)
J V Nesbitt	(Rugby / Christ Church)	J Burt-Marshall	(Fettes / Clare)
*P Munro	(Leeds G S / Christ Church)	H Mainprice	(Blundell's / Jesus)
A M P Lyle	(Fettes / Trinity)	T G Pitt	(Sutton Valence G S / Emmanuel)
R S Wix	(Marlborough / Brasenose)	R B Gibbins	(Sedbergh / King's)
B Cozens-Hardy	(Rugby / Trinity)	J W Alexander	(Merchiston / Clare)
N R F G Howe-Browne	(Diocesan Rondebosch / Oriel)	A Forman	(Loretto / Pembroke)
N T White	(Marlborough / Trinity)	W C Currie	(Fettes / Trinity)
H A Hodges	(Sedbergh / Trinity)	H G Monteith	(Fettes / Pembroke)
W W Hoskin	(St Andrew's Grahamstown / Trinity)	E C Hodges	(Haileybury / Trinity)
C J Gardner	(St Andrew's Grahamstown / Trinity)	B G Harris	(Cheltenham / Pembroke)
A A Hoadley	(Diocesan G S King Williamstown / Keble)	R McCosh	(Fettes / Trinity)

Tries: Parker, Nesbitt, Lawrie
Conversions: Nesbitt (2)

Tries: L M MacLeod , Burt-Marshall (2)
Conversions: L M MacLeod (3)

Referee: Mr J I Gillespie

MATCH 36

11 December 1906, at Queen's Club, Kensington, London
Oxford won by 4T (12) to 1G 1T (8)

Oxford		Cambridge	
D B Davies	(Lampeter / Jesus)	J G Scoular	(St Bees / St John's)
N W Milton	(Marlborough / University)	K G MacLeod	(Fettes / Pembroke)
H H Vassall	(Bedford G S / Keble)	*H F P Hearson	(Uppingham / King's)
F E Steinthal	(Bradford G S / Trinity)	W M Penny	(Mill Hill / Jesus)
T B Batchelor	(Rugby / University)	T G Pitt	(Sutton Valence G S / Emmanuel)
R H Williamson	(St Andrew's Grahamstown / Trinity)	J V Young	(Eastbourne / Emmanuel)
W K Flemmer	(St Andrew's Grahamstown / Trinity)	T A Godby	(Loretto / Magdalene)
R S Wix	(Marlborough / Brasenose)	B G Harris	(Cheltenham / Pembroke)
N T White	(Marlborough / Trinity)	R McCosh	(Fettes / Trinity)
H A Hodges	(Sedbergh / Trinity)	W G Lely	(Fettes / Emmanuel)
*B Cozens-Hardy	(Rugby / Trinity)	J W Alexander	(Merchiston / Clare)
N R F G Howe-Browne	(Diocesan Rondebosch / Oriel)	A E Evans	(Llandovery / St John's)
W W Hoskin	(St Andrew's Grahamstown / Trinity)	R B Gibbins	(Sedbergh / King's)
C J Gardner	(St Andrew's Grahamstown / Trinity)	J E Mellor	(Leys / Jesus)
A A Hoadley	(Diocesan G S King Williamstown / Keble)	J van Schalkwijk	(Victoria Stellenbosch / Caius)

Tries: Wix, Steinthal, Milton, Vassall

Tries: MacLeod, Hearson
Conversion: MacLeod

Referee: Mr F W Marsh

MATCH 37

10 December 1907, at Queen's Club, Kensington, London
Oxford won by 1G 4T (17) to 0

Oxford		Cambridge	
D B Davies	(Lampeter / Jesus)	R C C Campbell	(Edinburgh Academy / King's)
N W Milton	(Marlborough / University)	V H M Coates	(Haileybury / Caius)
H H Vassall	(Bedford G S / Keble)	F C Pyman	(Leys / Caius)
F N Tarr	(Uppingham / University)	*K G MacLeod	(Fettes / Pembroke)
H Martin	(Edinburgh Academy / Balliol)	C C G Wright	(Tonbridge / Pembroke)
G Cunningham	(Fettes / Magdalen)	B H Holloway	(Leys / Jesus)
R H Williamson	(St Andrew's Grahamstown / Trinity)	T A Godby	(Loretto / Magdalene)
A Howard	(Haileybury / Christ Church)	W G Lely	(Fettes / Emmanuel)
R S Wix	(Marlborough / Brasenose)	W D C L Purves	(Fettes / Trinity)
S N Cronje	(St Andrew's Grahamstown / Trinity)	R McCosh	(Fettes / Trinity)
H A Hodges	(Sedbergh / Trinity)	F C T Tudsbery	(Dulwich / King's)
H E Latham	(Sedbergh / Trinity)	G V Carey	(Eastbourne / Caius)
G D Roberts	(Rugby / St John's)	A E Evans	(Llandovery / St John's)
*W W Hoskin	(St Andrew's Grahamstown / Trinity)	R S Kennedy	(Tonbridge / Christ's)
L C Blencowe	(St Edward's Oxford / Queen's)	G M Chapman	(Waitaki H S / Caius)

Tries: Martin (3), Milton, Vassall
Conversion: Roberts

Referee: Mr G Evans

There are some sources which credit both Martin and Milton with two tries.

MATCH 38

12 December 1908, at Queen's Club, Kensington, London
Drawn — each side scored 1G (5)

Oxford		Cambridge	
T Sloan	(Glasgow Academy/Christ Church)	M L Atkinson	(Fettes/Emmanuel)
C M Gilray	(Otago H S/University)	C C G Wright	(Tonbridge/Pembroke)
H H Vassall	(Bedford G S/Keble)	F C Pyman	(Leys/Caius)
F N Tarr	(Uppingham/University)	K G MacLeod	(Fettes/Pembroke)
H Martin	(Edinburgh Academy/Balliol)	J S Jones	(Clifton/Pembroke)
G Cunningham	(Fettes/Magdalen)	A H Ashcroft	(Birkenhead/Caius)
R H Williamson	(St Andrew's Grahamstown/Trinity)	J F Sutherland	(Glenalmond/Caius)
G D Roberts	(Rugby/St John's)	W D C L Purves	(Fettes/Trinity)
R Lloyd	(Llandovery/Keble)	*W G Lely	(Fettes/Emmanuel)
P R Diggle	(Marlborough/University)	R Fraser	(Merchiston/Pembroke)
F H Turner	(Sedbergh/Trinity)	G V Carey	(Eastbourne/Caius)
*H A Hodges	(Sedbergh/Trinity)	H J S Morton	(Uppingham/Pembroke)
L C Blencowe	(St Edward's Oxford/Queen's)	F C T Tudsbery	(Dulwich/King's)
S N Cronje	(St Andrew's Grahamstown/Trinity)	J V Fiddian	(Leys/Emmanuel)
R H M Hands	(Diocesan Rondebosch/University)	G M Chapman	(Waitaki H S/Caius)

Try: Martin
Conversion: Cunningham

Try: Pyman
Conversion: MacLeod

Referee: Mr J C Findlay

MATCH 39

11 December 1909, at Queen's Club, Kensington, London
Oxford won by 4G 5T (35) to 1T (3)

Oxford		Cambridge	
F G Buchanan	(Kelvinside Academy/Trinity)	M L Atkinson	(Fettes/Emmanuel)
R W Poulton	(Rugby/Balliol)	B R Lewis	(Swansea G S/Trinity Hall)
F N Tarr	(Uppingham/University)	J A Scholfield	(Sedbergh/Caius)
C M Gilray	(Otago H S/University)	B H Holloway	(Leys/Jesus)
H Martin	(Edinburgh Academy/Balliol)	J S Jones	(Clifton/Pembroke)
*G Cunningham	(Fettes/Magdalen)	A H Ashcroft	(Birkenhead/Caius)
A L H Gotley	(Tonbridge/Brasenose)	C W Boyd	(Carlisle G S/St Catharine's)
F H Turner	(Sedbergh/Trinity)	R Fraser	(Merchiston/Pembroke)
R W Evers	(Rugby/Queen's)	L H T Storey	(Mill Hill/Caius)
T Allen	(Cheltenham/Trinity)	J V Fiddian	(Leys/Emmanuel)
R O Lagden	(Marlborough/Oriel)	*W D C L Purves	(Fettes/Trinity)
P R Diggle	(Marlborough/University)	G M Chapman	(Waitaki H S/Caius)
D G Herring	(Princetown Univ/Merton)	R S Kennedy	(Tonbridge/Christ's)
R H M Hands	(Diocesan Rondebosch/University)	C L H Marburg	(Merchiston/Pembroke)
R Honey	(Diocesan Rondebosch/University)	E P Reynolds	(Clifton/Caius)

Tries: Poulton (5), Martin (4)
Conversions: Cunningham (2), Lagden (2)

Try: Purves

Referee: Mr F C Potter-Irwin

MATCH 40

13 December 1910, at Queen's Club, Kensington, London
Oxford won by 4G 1T (23) to 3G 1T (18)

Oxford		Cambridge	
H F Sampson	(St Andrew's Grahamstown/Trinity)	C Pinkham	(Leys/Caius)
W P Geen	(Haileybury/University)	B R Lewis	(Swansea G S/Trinity Hall)
R W Poulton	(Rugby/Balliol)	J A Scholfield	(Sedbergh/Caius)
F G Buchanan	(Kelvinside/Trinity)	E McCosh	(Fettes/Clare)
W C Allen	(Merchant Taylors' London/Lincoln)	A B Ovens	(Fettes/Clare)
F H Knott	(Tonbridge/Brasenose)	J H Bruce Lockhart	(Sedbergh/Jesus)
W I Cheesman	(Merchant Taylors' London/Wadham)	B S Cumberlege	(Durham/Emmanuel)
H S Sharp	(Rugby/University)	B T C Sawyer	(Tonbridge/Pembroke)
H Bullock	(Sydney Univ/New)	A E Kitching	(Oundle/Jesus)
*F H Turner	(Sedbergh/Trinity)	*R Fraser	(Merchiston/Pembroke)
R O Lagden	(Marlborough/Oriel)	F T Mann	(Malvern/Pembroke)
D M Bain	(Edinburgh Academy/Trinity)	P C B Blair	(Fettes/King's)
L G Brown	(Brisbane G S/Balliol)	J E Greenwood	(Dulwich/King's)
P A M Hands	(Diocesan Rondebosch/University)	L A McAfee	(Merchiston/Pembroke)
R Honey	(Diocesan Rondebosch/University)	C L H Marburg	(Merchiston/Pembroke)

Tries: Geen (3), Poulton (2)   *Tries*: Ovens (2), Lewis (2)
Conversions: Turner (4)   *Conversions*: Bruce Lockhart (3)

Referee: Mr J D Dallas

MATCH 41

12 December 1911, at Queen's Club, Kensington, London
Oxford won by 2G 3T (19) to 0

Oxford		Cambridge	
H F Sampson	(St Andrew's Grahamstown/Trinity)	L L Pienaar	(S African Coll Cape Town/King's)
W P Geen	(Haileybury/University)	A B Ovens	(Fettes/Clare)
*R W Poulton	(Rugby/Balliol)	C Thorne	(Haileybury/Clare)
A J Dingle	(Durham/Keble)	C N Lowe	(Dulwich/Pembroke)
S S L Steyn	(Diocesan Rondebosch/University)	B R Lewis	(Swansea G S/Trinity Hall)
F H Knott	(Tonbridge/Brasenose)	J G Will	(Merchant Taylors' London/Downing)
W I Cheesman	(Merchant Taylors' London/Wadham)	B S Cumberlege	(Durham/Emmanuel)
R O Lagden	(Marlborough/Oriel)	A W Symington	(Fettes/Clare)
L G Brown	(Brisbane G S/Balliol)	A H Wilson	(Merchiston/Pembroke)
H S Sharp	(Rugby/University)	W C Neild	(Uppingham/Clare)
D G Donald	(Dulwich/University)	J E Greenwood	(Dulwich/King's)
A Gilmour	(Edinburgh Academy/Trinity)	*A E Kitching	(Oundle/Jesus)
H Bullock	(Sydney Univ/New)	P C B Blair	(Fettes/King's)
D M Bain	(Edinburgh Academy/Trinity)	T G Fowler	(Eastbourne/Caius)
W E Thomas	(S African Coll Cape Town/Brasenose)	C M Ure	(Merchiston/Pembroke)

Tries: Poulton, Steyn, Bullock (2), Dingle
Conversions: Lagden (2)

Referee: Mr F C Potter-Irwin

MATCH 42

10 December 1912, at Queen's Club, Kensington, London
Cambridge won by 2G (10) to 1T (3)

Oxford		Cambridge	
W M Dickson	(Diocesan Rondebosch/University)	W M Wallace	(Edinburgh Academy/King's)
W P Geen	(Haileybury/University)	C N Lowe	(Dulwich/Pembroke)
K C M Hands	(Diocesan Rondebosch/University)	P Middlemass	(Christ's Hosp/Pembroke)
N Reid	(Diocesan Rondebosch/Oriel)	W H B Baxter	(Merchiston/Pembroke)
S S L Steyn	(Diocesan Rondebosch/University)	J G Will	(Merchant Taylors' London/Downing)
F H Knott	(Tonbridge/Brasenose)	H W Thomas	(Monmouth/King's)
L R Broster	(St Andrew's Grahamstown/Trinity)	B S Cumberlege	(Durham/Emmanuel)
E F Boyd	(Rugby/University)	A H Wilson	(Merchiston/Pembroke)
J G Monteath	(Edinburgh Academy/University)	W C Neild	(Uppingham/Clare)
D G Donald	(Dulwich/University)	*J E Greenwood	(Dulwich/King's)
D M Bain	(Edinburgh Academy/Trinity)	P C B Blair	(Fettes/King's)
*L G Brown	(Brisbane G S/Balliol)	T G Fowler	(Eastbourne/Caius)
H B Moore	(Uppingham/Brasenose)	A F Maynard	(Durham/Emmanuel)
F W Thomson	(Edinburgh Academy/University)	A W Symington	(Fettes/Clare)
W E Thomas	(S African Coll Cape Town/Brasenose)	E C Benthall	(Eton/King's)

Try: Brown

Tries: Symington, Blair
Conversions: Greenwood (2)

Referee: Mr J D Dallas

MATCH 43

9 December 1913, at Queen's Club, Kensington, London
Cambridge won by 1DG 3T (13) to 1T (3)

Oxford		Cambridge	
N Reid	(Diocesan Rondebosch/Oriel)	W M Wallace	(Edinburgh Academy/King's)
G B Crole	(Edinburgh Academy/University)	C N Lowe	(Dulwich/Pembroke)
O Jenkins	(Aberystwyth Univ/Jesus)	D I de Villiers	(Stellenbosch Univ/Trinity Hall)
E G Loudoun-Shand	(Dulwich/University)	W H B Baxter	(Merchiston/Pembroke)
E A Southee	(Sydney H S/St John's)	J G Will	(Merchant Taylors' London/Downing)
A C Williamson	(Fettes/Brasenose)	J M C Lewis	(Bridgend G S/St Catharine's)
F H Knott	(Tonbridge/Brasenose)	*B S Cumberlege	(Durham/Emmanuel)
F W Thomson	(Edinburgh Academy/University)	A W Symington	(Fettes/Clare)
L P B Merriam	(St Paul's/University)	W D Doherty	(Dulwich/King's)
H J V Rees	(Ch Coll Brecon/Exeter)	A F Maynard	(Durham/Emmanuel)
I A Clarke	(Aberdeen G S/Christ Church)	P C B Blair	(Fettes/King's)
*D M Bain	(Edinburgh Academy/Trinity)	J E Greenwood	(Dulwich/King's)
H B Moore	(Uppingham/Brasenose)	A H Wilson	(Merchiston/Pembroke)
D G Donald	(Dulwich/University)	R Juckes	(King's Canterbury/Pembroke)
J M Moresby-White	(Diocesan Rondebosch/New)	C A Vincent	(Uppingham/Pembroke)

Try:-Southee

Tries: Maynard, Lewis, Lowe
Drop Goal: Lewis

Referee: Mr F C Potter-Irwin

MATCH 44

9 December 1919, at Queen's Club, Kensington, London
Cambridge won by 1DG 1PG (7) to 1G (5)

Oxford		Cambridge	
V R Price	(Bishop's Stortford / Magdalen)	C F K Watson	(Bradford G S / Peterhouse)
G B Crole	(Edinburgh Academy / University)	K R J Saxon	(Nelson Coll / Emmanuel)
O Jenkins	(Aberystwyth Univ / Jesus)	A R Trubshaw	(Uppingham / Clare)
*E G Loudoun-Shand	(Dulwich / University)	A M Smallwood	(R G S Newcastle / Caius)
G F Wood	(King's Canterbury / Trinity)	G E C Wood	(Cheltenham / Pembroke)
E Campbell	(Edinburgh Academy / Oriel)	J M C Lewis	(Bridgend G S / St Catharine's)
F A Waldock	(Uppingham / Hertford)	A B S Young	(Fettes / St John's)
D D Duncan	(S A Coll / University)	*J E Greenwood	(Dulwich / King's)
H F Waldock	(Uppingham / Hertford)	W C D Considine	(Merchiston / Caius)
J M Moresby-White	(Diocesan Rondebosch / New)	P A Batty	(Mill Hill / Caius)
C H Evans	(Tonbridge / Brasenose)	G S Conway	(Fettes / Caius)
D G Francis	(Aberystwyth Univ / Jesus)	W R F Collis	(Rugby / Trinity)
W T Havard	(Aberystwyth Univ / Jesus)	K P Smith	(Haileybury / Caius)
R G Sharp	(Rugby / University)	D Orr-Ewing	(Royal Navy / King's)
V H Neser	(S A Coll / Brasenose)	R Cove-Smith	(Merchant Taylors' London / Caius)

Try: Crole
Conversion: Havard

Penalty Goal: Lewis
Dropped Goal: Smallwood

Referee: Mr F C Potter-Irwin

MATCH 45

7 December 1920, at Queen's Club, Kensington, London
Oxford won by 1G 4T (17) to 1G 3T (14)

Oxford		Cambridge	
H H Forsayth	(King's Parramatta / Exeter)	C F K Watson	(Bradford G S / Peterhouse)
B L Jacot	(K E Aston / St John's)	R H Hamilton-Wickes	(Wellington / Pembroke)
V R Price	(Bishop's Stortford / Magdalen)	H W C Craigmile	(Uppingham / King's)
E F van der Riet	(St Andrew's Grahamstown / Trinity)	S Cook	(Crypt / St Catharine's)
H B Simpson	(Kingswood / Oriel)	D D B Cook	(Merchiston / Pembroke)
V H Neser	(S A Coll / Brasenose)	J P Maclay	(Fettes / Trinity)
E Campbell	(Edinburgh Academy / Oriel)	A B S Young	(Fettes / St John's)
J A B Davies	(St Bees / Queen's)	P A Batty	(Mill Hill / Caius)
C H Evans	(Tonbridge / Brasenose)	W R F Collis	(Rugby / Trinity)
*D D Duncan	(S A Coll / University)	*G S Conway	(Fettes / Caius)
R H B Bettington	(King's Parramatta / New)	A Carnegie-Brown	(Trent / St John's)
J E Maxwell-Hyslop	(Wellington / Balliol)	R Cove-Smith	(Merchant Taylors' / Caius)
H F Waldock	(Uppingham / Hertford)	J L H Miller	(Fettes / Pembroke)
B G Scholefield	(Westminster / Christ Church)	T E Morel	(Leys / Jesus)
H L Price	(Bishop's Stortford / Corpus Christi)	H K P Smith	(Haileybury / Caius)

Tries: Jacot (3), Simpson, Neser
Conversion: Bettington

Tries: S Cook (2), D D B Cook, Cove-Smith
Conversion: Conway

Referee: Mr S H Crawford

MATCH 46
8 December 1921, at Twickenham
Oxford won by 1G 2T (11) to 1G (5)

Oxford		Cambridge	
H H Forsayth	(King's Parramatta/Exeter)	F A Gardiner	(Loretto/Pembroke)
I J Pitman	(Eton/Christ Church)	E R H Seddon	(Uppingham/Clare)
V R Price	(Bishop's Stortford/Magdalen)	R H Hamilton-Wickes	(Wellington/Pembroke)
A M David	(Dulwich/Trinity)	S Cook	(Crypt/St Catharine's)
E F van der Riet	(St Andrew's Grahamstown/Trinity)	D D B Cook	(Merchiston/Pembroke)
T Lawton	(Queensland Univ/New)	H B Style	(Marlborough/Pembroke)
*E Campbell	(Edinburgh Academy/Oriel)	K R J Saxon	(Nelson Coll/Emmanuel)
A W L Rowe	(Brisbane G S/Brasenose)	*R Cove-Smith	(Merchant Taylors'/Caius)
C A Siepmann	(Clifton/Keble)	G S Conway	(Fettes/Caius)
J C Chambers	(Downside/Balliol)	A Carnegie-Brown	(Trent/St John's)
J W Robertson	(Merchiston/Balliol)	W W Wakefield	(Sedbergh/Pembroke)
H P Marshall	(Haileybury/Oriel)	D J MacMyn	(Fettes/Pembroke)
B G Scholefield	(Westminster/Christ Church)	R R Stokes	(Downside/Trinity)
J E Maxwell-Hyslop	(Wellington/Balliol)	T R K Jones	(Sutton Valence G S/Sidney Sussex)
H L Price	(Bishop's Stortford/Corpus Christi)	D C D Ryder	(Sherborne/Pembroke)

Tries: Pitman (2), David
Conversion: Lawton

Try: Wakefield
Conversion: Conway

Referee: Mr J C Sturrock

MATCH 47
12 December 1922, at Twickenham
Cambridge wom by 3G 2T (21) to 1G 1T (8)

Oxford		Cambridge	
T Lawton	(Queensland Univ/New)	R K Melluish	(Merchant Taylors'/Caius)
G G Aitken	(Victoria Univ/St John's)	R H Hamilton-Wickes	(Wellington/Pembroke)
A M David	(Dulwich/Trinity)	D P Evans	(Tonbridge/Pembroke)
G P S Macpherson	(Fettes/Oriel)	F A Gardiner	(Loretto/Pembroke)
A C Wallace	(Sydney G S/New)	W G B Mackenzie	(Fettes/Peterhouse)
H J Kittermaster	(Rugby/University)	T E S Francis	(Tonbridge/Pembroke)
G J German	(Rugby/Magdalen)	A T Young	(Tonbridge/Caius)
D G Fildes	(Clifton/Balliol)	D C Cumming	(Giggleswick/Caius)
A Shacksnovis	(Cape Town Univ/Oriel)	D M W Maxwell	(Merchiston/Clare)
C R Wordsworth	(Marlborough/Balliol)	A S Cohen	(Perse/Jesus)
A D Grant	(Winchester/Brasenose)	J B White	(Glasgow Academy/Corpus Christi)
G E MacDonald	(Rhodes Univ/New)	W E Tucker	(Sherborne/Caius)
H B L Wake	(Marlborough/Keble)	D J MacMyn	(Fettes/Pembroke)
R H B Bettington	(King's Parramatta/New)	*W W Wakefield	(Sedbergh/Pembroke)
*J E Maxwell-Hyslop	(Wellington/Balliol)	T E Morel	(Leys/Jesus)

Tries: Kittermaster (2)
Conversion: Bettington

Tries: Hamilton-Wickes (3), Young, Cohen
Conversion: Cohen (3)

Referee: Mr T H Vile

MATCH 48

11 December 1923, at Twickenham
Oxford won by 3G 2T (21) to 1G 1PG 2T (14)

Oxford		Cambridge	
H W F Franklin	(Christ's Hosp/Christ Church)	D N Rocyn-Jones	(Leys/Downing)
I S Smith	(Winchester/Brasenose)	*R H Hamilton-Wickes	(Wellington/Pembroke)
H P Jacob	(Cranleigh/Christ Church)	F A Gardiner	(Loretto/Pembroke)
G P S Macpherson	(Fettes/Oriel)	J H Bordass	(RGS Newcastle/Caius)
A C Wallace	(Sydney G S/New)	Sir T G Devitt	(Sherborne/Corpus Christi)
T Lawton	(Queensland Univ/New)	T E S Francis	(Tonbridge/Pembroke)
M W Humphrey	(Rhodes Univ/University)	A T Young	(Tonbridge/Caius)
C R Wordsworth	(Marlborough/Balliol)	D J MacMyn	(Fettes/Pembroke)
A Shacksnovis	(Cape Town Univ/Oriel)	W E Tucker	(Sherborne/Caius)
R J Hillard	(St Paul's/Christ Church)	D C Ryder	(Sherborne/Pembroke)
G E B Abell	(Marlborough/Corpus Christi)	D C Cumming	(Giggleswick/Caius)
Hon B Pleydell-Bouverie	(Harrow/Magdalen)	W I Jones	(Llanelli G S/Caius)
A C Valentine	(Pennsylvania Univ/Balliol)	R H W Lowry	(Ch Coll NZ/Jesus)
T P Theron	(St Andrew's Grahamstown/Trinity)	W B Scott	(Fettes/Pembroke)
C Dalby	(Rugby/Balliol)	C S Barlow	(Clifton/Caius)

Tries: Smith (2), Lawton, Macpherson (2)
Conversions: Lawton (3)

Tries: Hamilton-Wickes, Devitt, Scott
Conversion: Francis
Penalty Goal: Francis

Referee: Mr A E Freethy

MATCH 49

9 December 1924, at Twickenham
Oxford won by 1G 2T (11) to 2T (6)

Oxford		Cambridge	
R L Raymond	(Sydney GS/New)	P S Douty	(Sedbergh/Pembroke)
A C Wallace	(Sydney GS/New)	W R Harding	(Gowerton GS/Pembroke)
G G Aitken	(Victoria Univ/St John's)	B R Turnbull	(Downside/Christ's)
G P S Macpherson	(Fettes/Oriel)	J H Bordass	(RGS Newcastle/Caius)
H P Jacob	(Cranleigh/Christ Church)	Sir T G Devitt	(Sherborne/Corpus Christi)
H J Kittermaster	(Rugby/University)	T E S Francis	(Tonbridge/Pembroke)
W I N Strong	(Eastbourne/Brasenose)	*A T Young	(Tonbridge/Caius)
*C R Wordsworth	(Marlborough/Balliol)	R G B Howell	(Eastbourne/Caius)
R J Hillard	(St Paul's/Christ Church)	W I Jones	(Llanelli GS/Caius)
G E B Abell	(Marlborough/Corpus Christi)	C S Barlow	(Clifton/Caius)
A C Valentine	(Pennsylvania Univ/Balliol)	D C Cumming	(Giggleswick/Caius)
A de H Boyd	(Rugby/Trinity)	W B Scott	(Fettes/Pembroke)
W N Roughead	(Rugby/Oriel)	W R Skinner	(Winchester/Trinity Hall)
W V Berkley	(Fettes/Hertford)	D J MacMyn	(Fettes/Pembroke)
V G Wesche	(King's Parramatta/New)	W E Tucker	(Sherborne/Caius)

Tries: Jacob (2), Wallace
Conversion: Berkley

Tries: Devitt (2)

Referee: Mr T H Vile

211

MATCH 50

10 December 1925, at Twickenham
Cambridge won by 3G 6T (33) to 1T (3)

Oxford		Cambridge	
D Drysdale	(Heriot's/Brasenose)	B R Turnbull	(Downside/Christ's)
C E W C Mackintosh	(Eastbourne/University)	W R Harding	(Gowerton GS/Pembroke)
A C Wallace	(Sydney GS/New)	C D Aarvold	(Durham/Emmanuel)
J V Richardson	(Uppingham/Brasenose)	T E S Francis	(Tonbridge/Pembroke)
*H P Jacob	(Cranleigh/Christ Church)	Sir T G Devitt	(Sherborne/Corpus Christi)
J A Nunn	(Sherborne/New)	C C Bishop	(UCS/Christ's)
W I N Strong	(Eastbourne/Brasenose)	W H Sobey	(Mill Hill/St John's)
G E B Abell	(Marlborough/Corpus Christi)	E Gibson	(Uppingham/Trinity)
A C Valentine	(Pennsylvania Univ/Balliol)	R M Barlow	(Clifton/Caius)
W V Berkley	(Fettes/Hertford)	*W E Tucker	(Sherborne/Caius)
W N Roughead	(Rugby/Oriel)	G A C Hamilton	(Haileybury/Caius)
D G Fildes	(Clifton/Balliol)	G Morpeth	(Durham/St John's)
D F Landale	(Eton/Balliol)	A D Allen	(Clifton/Caius)
B W Preston	(Rugby/New)	W I Jones	(Llanelli GS/Caius)
L S Seccombe	(Felsted/Pembroke)	C S Barlow	(Clifton/Caius)

Try: Mackintosh

Tries: Devitt (3), Aarvold, Tucker, Bishop, Francis, Gibson, R M Barlow
Conversions: C S Barlow (3)

Referee: Mr A E Freethy

MATCH 51

14 December 1926, at Twickenham
Cambridge won by 3G 5T (30) to 1G (5)

Oxford		Cambridge	
F F Spragg	(Merchant Taylors'/Pembroke)	C D Aarvold	(Durham/Emmanuel)
E G Taylor	(Loretto/Trinity)	W J Taylor	(Epsom/Trinity)
R M Byers	(Campbell Belfast/Trinity)	A F Hamilton-Smythe	(Haileybury/Trinity)
H A Caccia	(Eton/Trinity)	W G Morgan	(Ch Coll Brecon/St Catharine's)
M A McCanlis	(Cranleigh/St Edmund Hall)	W R Harding	(Gowerton GS/Pembroke)
J A Nunn	(Sherborne/New)	W H Lewis	(Ch Coll Brecon/Pembroke)
N L MacDonald	(Loretto/Trinity)	W H Sobey	(Mill Hill/St John's)
*G E B Abell	(Marlborough/Corpus Christi)	*C S Barlow	(Clifton/Caius)
D F Landale	(Eton/Balliol)	E Gibson	(Uppingham/Trinity)
W V Berkley	(Fettes/Hertfor)	A D Allen	(Clifton/Caius)
W N Roughead	(Rugby/Oriel)	G A C Hamilton	(Haileybury/Caius)
A F Heppenstall	(Dulwich/Wadham)	G A McIlwaine	(St Andrew's Grahamstown/Selwyn)
T W Gubb	(St Andrew's Grahamstown/University)	J J E Smith	(Loretto/Trinity)
J H F Edmiston	(Haileybury/Brasenose)	A G Williams	(Christian Bros/Caius)
D J W Dryburgh	(Uppingham/Oriel)	G B Coghlan	(Rugby/Clare)

Try: Landale
Conversion: Berkley

Tries: Hamilton-Smythe (2), Lewis, Allen, Taylor (2), Harding, Barlow
Conversions: Barlow (3)

Referee: Mr T H Vile

MATCH 52

13 December 1927, at Twickenham
Cambridge won by 2G 2PG 2T (22) to 1G 3T (14)

Oxford

M A McCanlis	(Cranleigh/St Edmund Hall)
W E Lusty	(St John's Leatherhead/University)
E A Sweatman	(Rugby/Brasenose)
J W G Hume	(Mill Hill/Merton)
*E G Taylor	(Loretto/Trinity)
A L Novis	(Epsom/Brasenose)
J P W Mallalieu	(Cheltenham/Trinity)
L L J Davies	(Ch Coll Brecon/Keble)
T W Gubb	(St Andrew's Grahamstown/University)
A F Heppenstall	(Dulwich/Wadham)
J H F Edmiston	(Haileybury/Brasenose)
J M Bannerman	(Glasgow HS/Balliol)
C H Gibson	(King's Canterbury/Trinity)
A N Goold	(Wellington/Pembroke)
K de J Hofmeyr	(Cape Town Univ/University)

Tries: Novis, Heppenstall, Hume, Sweatman
Conversion: Heppenstall

Cambridge

J Roberts	(Cardiff HS/St Catharine's)
C D Aarvold	(Durham/Emmanuel)
H M Bowcott	(Cardiff HS/St Catharine's)
W G Morgan	(Ch Coll Brecon/St Catharine's)
*W R Harding	(Gowerton GS/Pembroke)
W H Lewis	(Ch Coll Brecon/Pembroke)
J D Campbell	(Fettes/Clare)
A D Allen	(Clifton/Caius)
G B Coghlan	(Rugby/Clare)
G A McIlwaine	(St Andrew's Grahamstown/Selwyn)
A G Williams	(Christian Bros/Caius)
P T Cooper	(Marlborough/Caius)
J S Synge	(St Columba's Dublin/Clare)
J M Scott	(Fettes/Clare)
F H Waters	(Loretto/Pembroke)

Tries: Scott (2), Aarvold, Harding
Conversions: Lewis, Waters
Penalty Goals: Scott, Waters

Referee: Mr A E Freethy

MATCH 53

11 December 1928, at Twickenham
Cambridge won by 1G 3T (14) to 1DG 1PG 1T (10)

Oxford

J A Adamson	(Durham/Keble)
*E G Taylor	(Loretto/Trinity)
J W G Hume	(Mill Hill/Merton)
H H Turcan	(Rugby/Trinity)
N M S Macpherson	(Fettes/Trinity)
W Roberts	(Cardiff HS/Brasenose)
E T Benson	(Blundell's/Merton)
T W Gubb	(St Andrew's Grahamstown/University)
S J Hofmeyr	(Cape Town Univ/University)
A E C Prescott	(Marlborough/Christ Church)
J M Bannerman	(Glasgow HS/Balliol)
M J B Molohan	(Cheltenham/Trinity)
D S Troup	(Uppingham/St John's)
P C Hordern	(Brighton/Wadham)
A G Cridlan	(Uppingham/Worcester)

Try: Macpherson
Penalty Goal: Adamson
Dropped Goal: Adamson

Cambridge

J Roberts	(Cardiff HS/St Catharine's)
R W Smeddle	(Durham/St Catharine's)
*C D Aarvold	(Durham/Emmanuel)
W G Morgan	(Ch Coll Brecon/St Catharine's)
F M Heywood	(Haileybury/Caius)
H M Bowcott	(Cardiff HS/St Catharine's)
C E M Wiggins	(Mill Hill/Trinity)
G B Coghlan	(Rugby/Clare)
G A McIlwaine	(St Andrew's Grahamstown/Selwyn)
P T Cooper	(Marlborough/Caius)
F H Waters	(Loretto/Pembroke)
D Crichton-Miller	(Fettes/Pembroke)
J J A Embleton	(St Paul's/Caius)
A M Dixon	(Dulwich/Clare)
P W P Brook	(Whitgift/Emmanuel)

Tries: Smeddle (3), Aarvold
Conversion: Waters

Referee: Mr T H Vile

MATCH 54

10 December 1929, at Twickenham
Oxford won by 1G 1DG (9) to 0

Oxford		Cambridge	
J A Adamson	(Durham / Keble)	J G Askew	(Durham / Emmanuel)
T W King	(Uppingham / Trinity)	R W Smeddle	(Durham / St Catharine's)
M Robson	(Heriot's / Balliol)	G C A Adams	(Radley / Pembroke)
W P Rousseau	(Cape Town Univ / Brasenose)	*W G Morgan	(Ch Coll Brecon / St Catharine's)
C F Cardale	(Durham / St Edmund Hall)	H E Carris	(Mill Hill / St John's)
W Roberts	(Cardiff HS / Brasenose)	J A Tallent	(Sherborne / Clare)
J H Russell	(Cape Town Univ / University)	W D B Hopkins	(Llandovery / St Catharine's)
*T W Gubb	(St Andrew's Grahamstown / University)	F H Waters	(Loretto / Pembroke)
S J Hofmeyr	(Cape Town Univ / University)	J J A Embleton	(St Paul's / Caius)
W A H Druitt	(Edinburgh Academy / Oriel)	P W P Brook	(Whitgift / Emmanuel)
B H Black	(St Andrew's Grahamstown / Brasenose)	S M Saunders-Jacobs	(Uppingham / Trinity)
W E Henley	(Otago Univ / New)	C L Ashford	(Blundell's / Caius)
J V d'A Rowley	(St Andrew's Grahamstown / Trinity)	A W Walker	(Oundle / Clare)
P D Howard	(Mill Hill / Wadham)	G M Greenwood	(Rugby / Christ's)
A G Cridlan	(Uppingham / Worcester)	D M Marr	(Fettes / Caius)

Try: Robson
Conversion: Black
Dropped Goal: Robson

Referee: Mr A E Freethy

MATCH 55

9 December 1930, at Twickenham
Drawn — Oxford 1PG (3) Cambridge 1T (3)

Oxford		Cambridge	
H Rees	(St Andrew's Grahamstown / University)	J G Askew	(Durham / Emmanuel)
P C Minns	(Auckland Univ / Balliol)	R W Smeddle	(Durham / St Catharine's)
P C Alexander	(St Andrew's Grahamstown / Trinity)	L H Collison	(Mill Hill / St John's)
V G J Jenkins	(Llandovery / Jesus)	J A Tallent	(Sherborne / Clare)
C F Cardale	(Durham / St Edmund Hall)	C C Tanner	(Cheltenham / Pembroke)
W Roberts	(Cardiff HS / Brasenose)	J H L Phillips	(Weymouth / Trinity Hall)
N K Lamport	(Sydney Univ / Balliol)	F W Simpson	(Merchant Taylors' Crosby / Trinity Hall)
*S J Hofmeyr	(Cape Town Univ / University)	*J J A Embleton	(St Paul's / Caius)
W A H Druitt	(Edinburgh Academy / Oriel)	P W P Brook	(Whitgift / Emmanuel)
R R MacGibbon	(Fettes / Corpus Christi)	G M Greenwood	(Rugby / Christ's)
W E Henley	(Otago Univ / New)	D M Marr	(Loretto / Caius)
D H Swayne	(Bromsgrove / Worcester)	A W Walker	(Oundle / Clare)
P D Howard	(Mill Hill / Wadham)	A R Ramsay	(Harrow / Trinity Hall)
G V Shillito	(Taunton / Wadham)	G E Valentine	(Bishop's Stortford / St Catharine's)
A G Cridlan	(Uppingham / Worcester)	C H Williams	(Bedford / Jesus)

Penalty Goal: Henley

Try: Tallent

Referee: Mr R W Jeffares

MATCH 56

8 December 1931, at Twickenham
Oxford won by 1DG 2T (10) to 1T (3)

Oxford		Cambridge	
J A Adamson	(Durham/Keble)	*J G Askew	(Durham/Emmanuel)
F L Hovde	(Minnesota Univ/Brasenose)	R W Smeddle	(Durham/St Catharine's)
S G Osler	(Cape Town Univ/New)	J A Tallent	(Sherborne/Clare)
V G J Jenkins	(Llandovery/Jesus)	J I Rees	(Swansea HS/St John's)
P C Minns	(Auckland Univ/Balliol)	G H Bailey	(Spalding/St John's)
*W Roberts	(Cardiff HS/Brasenose)	W T Anderson	(Durham/St John's)
N K Lamport	(Sydney Univ/Balliol)	F W Simpson	(Merchant Taylors' Crosby/Trinity Hall)
K W J Jones	(Monmouth/Jesus)	D M Marr	(Fettes/Caius)
E S Nicholson	(Marlborough/Wadham)	P W P Brook	(Whitgift/Emmanuel)
W A H Druitt	(Edinburgh Academy/Oriel)	J G Watherston	(Sedbergh/Corpus Christi)
R R MacGibbon	(Fettes/Corpus Christi)	H B L Johnstone	(Ch Coll NZ/St Catharine's)
W E Henley	(Otago Univ/New)	W H Leather	(Sedbergh/King's)
D H Swayne	(Bromsgrove/Worcester)	W J Leather	(Sedbergh/Clare)
T L Tanner	(Clifton/Trinity)	R B Jones	(Uppingham/Clare)
F D Russell Roberts	(Rugby/New)	W O H Collins	(Tonbridge/St Catharine's)

Tries: Minns, Hovde
Dropped Goal: Roberts

Try: Smeddle

Referee: Mr A E Freethy

MATCH 57

6 December 1932, at Twickenham
Oxford won by 1G 1T (8) to 1T (3)

Oxford		Cambridge	
H G Owen-Smith	(Diocesan Rondebosch/Magdalen)	G W Parker	(Crypt/Selwyn)
P C Minns	(Auckland Univ/Balliol)	W G S Johnston	(Tonbridge/Clare)
H D B Lorraine	(Glenalmond/Christ Church)	J H L Phillips	(Weymouth/Trinity Hall)
V G J Jenkins	(Llandovery/Jesus)	J I Rees	(Swansea HS/St John's)
S L Waide	(Sedbergh/Brasenose)	K C Fyfe	(Oundle/Caius)
K L T Jackson	(Rugby/Trinity)	W T Anderson	(Durham/St John's)
*N K Lamport	(Sydney Univ/Balliol)	E B Pope	(Uppingham/Clare)
C A L Richards	(Clifton/Brasenose)	*D M Marr	(Fettes/Caius)
E S Nicholson	(Marlborough/Wadham)	R B Jones	(Uppingham/Clare)
M F Peacock	(Wellington/Brasenose)	W H Leather	(Sedbergh/King's)
K W J Jones	(Monmouth/Jesus)	C R B Birdwood	(Brighton/Sidney Sussex)
A E S Charles	(Sherborne/Worcester)	G S Waller	(Oundle/Queens')
R E Prescott	(Marlborough/Trinity)	W J Leather	(Sedbergh/Clare)
J B Bowers	(Cheltenham/Trinity)	J L P Reid	(Fettes/Jesus)
H M Kelly	(Sedbergh/Exeter)	G E Delafield	(St Paul's/Jesus)

Tries: Minns (2)
Conversion: Jenkins

Try: Reid

Referee: Mr A E Freethy

215

MATCH 58

12 December 1933, at Twickenham
Oxford won by 1G (5) to 1T (3)

Oxford		Cambridge	
H G Owen-Smith	(Diocesan Rondebosch / Magdalen)	G W Parker	(Crypt / Selwyn)
A L Warr	(Bromsgrove / Brasenose)	W G S Johnston	(Tonbridge / Clare)
*H D B Lorraine	(Glenalmond / Christ Church)	W Wooller	(Rydal / Christ's)
P Cranmer	(St Edward's Oxford / Christ Church)	R C S Dick	(Sherborne / Clare)
G R Rees-Jones	(Ipswich / University)	K C Fyfe	(Oundle / Caius)
K L T Jackson	(Rugby / Trinity)	C W Jones	(Llandovery / Clare)
J M S McShane	(Sydney Univ / New)	J E Bowcott	(Cardiff HS / St Catharine's)
M F Peacock	(Wellington / Brasenose)	*R B Jones	(Uppingham / Clare)
E S Nicholson	(Marlborough / Wadham)	W J Leather	(Sedbergh / Clare)
J H Pienaar	(Stellenbosch Univ / Worcester)	J H Bowman	(Sherborne / Trinity Hall)
M O Wray	(St George's Harpenden / Wadham)	J R C Lord	(Oundle / Christ's)
E G S Mather	(Uppingham / Balliol)	A M Rees	(Llandovery / St Catharine's)
R C S Low	(Rugby / Balliol)	R O Murray	(Loretto / St John's)
K C Burrow	(Ch Coll Brecon / Balliol)	C D Laborde	(Harrow / St Catharine's)
E L Phillips	(Eltham / St Edmund Hall)	J M Griffith	(Brighton / Trinity Hall)

Try: Nicholson
Conversion: Jackson

Try: Dick

Referee: Mr M A Allan

MATCH 59

11 December 1934, at Twickenham
Cambridge won by 2G 1DG 1PG 4T (29) to 1DG (4)

Oxford		Cambridge	
C F Grieve	(Ampleforth / Christ Church)	G W Parker	(Crypt / Selwyn)
A L Warr	(Bromsgrove / Brasenose)	W G S Johnston	(Tonbridge / Clare)
*H D B Lorraine	(Glenalmond / Christ Church)	P L Candler	(Sherborne / Pembroke)
P Cranmer	(St Edward's Oxford / Christ Church)	W Wooller	(Rydal / Christ's)
G R Rees-Jones	(Ipswich / University)	K C Fyfe	(Oundle / Caius)
A Bush	(Heversham GS / Queen's)	C W Jones	(Llandovery / Clare)
J C Guy	(Radley / Wadham)	O C Browning	(Harrow / Clare)
N F McGrath	(Stonyhurst / University)	*W J Leather	(Sedbergh / Clare)
E S Nicholson	(Marlborough / Wadham)	J H Bowman	(Sherborne / Trinity Hall)
J H Pienaar	(Stellenbosch Univ / Worcester)	J R C Lord	(Oundle / Christ's)
M O Wray	(St George's Harpenden / Wadham)	A M Rees	(Llandovery / St Catharine's)
J B Bowers	(Cheltenham / Trinity)	C D Laborde	(Harrow / St Catharine's)
M M Cooper	(Massey Agric Coll / University)	R O Murray	(Loretto / St John's)
C T Bloxham	(KE VI Nuneaton / Oriel)	G A Brathwaite	(Diocesan Grahamstown / Emmanuel)
A I James	(Ampleforth / Queen's)	H P Dinwiddy	(Radley / Pembroke)

Dropped Goal: Bush

Tries: Fyfe (3), Johnston, Jones, Rees
Conversions: Parker (2)
Penalty Goal: Parker
Dropped Goal: Wooller

Referee: Mr M A Allan

216

MATCH 60

10 December 1935, at Twickenham
Drawn — no score

Oxford		Cambridge	
J L Stuart-Watson	(Loretto / Brasenose)	G W Parker	(Crypt / Selwyn)
A Obolensky	(Trent / Brasenose)	J R Rawlence	(Wellington / Pembroke)
M M Walford	(Rugby / Trinity)	J R Stewart	(Fettes / Pembroke)
R F Harding	(Tonbridge / Brasenose)	W Wooller	(Rydal / Christ's)
G R Rees-Jones	(Ipswich / University)	*K C Fyfe	(Oundle / Clare)
C F Grieve	(Ampleforth / Christ Church)	C W Jones	(Llandovery / Clare)
J M S McShane	(Sydney Univ / New)	J D Low	(Dover / Jesus)
J H Pienaar	(Stellenbosch Univ / Worcester)	C D Laborde	(Harrow / St Catharine's)
N F McGrath	(Stonyhurst / University)	J R C Lord	(Oundle / Christ's)
J A Brett	(Durham / St Edmund Hall)	H P Dinwiddy	(Radley / Pembroke)
P C W Disney	(Cheltenham / Brasenose)	J S Young	(Dulwich / St Catharine's)
G A Reid	(Uppingham / University)	K G Irving	(Glenalmond / Jesus)
*M M Cooper	(Massey Agric Coll / University)	W B Young	(City of London / St Catharine's)
C T Bloxham	(KE VI Nuneaton / Oriel)	W M Inglis	(Rugby / Clare)
H M Hughes	(St David's Lampeter / University)	F W Cocks	(Haileybury / St Catharine's)

Referee: Mr C H Gadney

MATCH 61

8 December 1936, at Twickenham
Cambridge won by 2T (6) to 1G (5)

Oxford		Cambridge	
H D Freakes	(Rhodes Univ / Magdalen)	K D Downes	(Rydal / Christ's)
W N Renwick	(Loretto / University)	J R Rawlence	(Wellington / Pembroke)
M M Walford	(Rugby / Trinity)	J G S Forrest	(Strathallan / St Catharine's)
E L Button	(Trent / Balliol)	W H Roden	(Uppingham / Downing)
H R G Percy	(Uppingham / Brasenose)	J A MacDonald	(Blundell's / Clare)
C F Grieve	(Ampleforth / Christ Church)	T A Kemp	(Denstone / St Catharine's)
P Cooke	(St Edward's Oxford / Trinity)	J D Low	(Dover / Jesus)
J A Brett	(Durham / St Edmund Hall)	T R Parry	(Llandovery / Clare)
N F McGrath	(Stonyhurst / University)	C W Wilton	(Fettes / Caius)
G D Roos	(Stellenbosch Univ / University)	W O Chadwick	(Tonbridge / St John's)
G A Reid	(Uppingham / University)	D A Campbell	(King's Parramatta / Jesus)
R M Marshall	(Giggleswick / Oriel)	F M N Heath	(Clifton / Caius)
*M M Cooper	(Massey Agric Coll / University)	W B Young	(City of London / St Catharine's)
C T Bloxham	(KE VI Nuneaton / Oriel)	W M Inglis	(Rugby / Clare)
H M Hughes	(St David's Lampeter / University)	*C D Laborde	(Harrow / St Catharine's)

Try: Renwick
Conversion: Brett

Tries: MacDonald, Wilton

Referee: Mr C H Gadney

217

MATCH 62

7 December 1937, at Twickenham
Oxford won by 1G 4T (17) to 1DG (4)

Oxford		Cambridge	
F M M Forster	(Wellington / Trinity)	K D Downes	(Rydal / Christ's)
A Obolensky	(Trent / Brasenose)	E D E Reed	(Harrow / Fitzwilliam)
M M Walford	(Rugby / Trinity)	J G S Forrest	(Strathallan / St Catharine's)
H D Freakes	(Rhodes Univ / Magdalen)	W H Roden	(Uppingham / Downing)
W N Renwick	(Loretto / University)	J A MacDonald	(Blundell's / Clare)
I H Watts	(Sutton Valence GS / St Peter's Hall)	R B Bruce Lockhart	(Edinburgh Academy / Corpus Christi)
P Cooke	(St Edward's Oxford / Trinity)	*J D Low	(Dover / Jesus)
*J A Brett	(Durham / St Edmund Hall)	W O Chadwick	(Tonbridge / St John's)
R A Cooper	(Brighton / St Edmund Hall)	W B Young	(City of London / St Catharine's)
D G G Coles	(Clifton / Trinity)	F M N Heath	(Clifton / Caius)
R M Marshall	(Giggleswick / Trinity)	T R Parry	(Llandovery / Clare)
R G P Almond	(Loretto / Hertford)	P J C Bateman-Champain	(Cheltenham / Caius)
H H Pennington	(Upholland GS / St Edmund Hall)	E L A Folker	(Eastbourne / Queens')
C T Bloxham	(KE VI Nuneaton / Oriel)	C L Newton-Thompson	(Diocesan Coll / St John's)
P K Mayhew	(Haileybury / Christ Church)	P A R Lindsay	(Harrow / Clare)

Tries: Renwick, Bloxham, Mayhew (2), Cooke
Conversion: Brett

Dropped Goal: Bruce-Lockhart

Referee: Mr C H Gadney

MATCH 63

6 December 1938, at Twickenham
Cambridge won by 1G 1PG (8) to 2PG (6)

Oxford		Cambridge	
*H D Freakes	(Rhodes Univ / Magdalen)	K I Geddes	(Loretto / Caius)
H R G Percy	(Uppingham / Brasenose)	J C Swanson	(Fettes / Clare)
R E Luyt	(Diocesan Coll / Trinity)	R B Bruce Lockhart	(Edinburgh Academy / Corpus Christi)
T J Cowen	(St Bees / Trinity)	K D Downes	(Rydal / Christ's)
G Hollis	(St Edward's Oxford / Christ Church)	J G S Forrest	(Strathallan / St Catharine's)
I H Watts	(Sutton Valence GS / St Peter's Hall)	P Sherrard	(Stowe / Magdalene)
T R Thomas	(Llandovery / Hertford)	J Parsons	(Rydal / St Catharine's)
W M Jackson	(Sedbergh / University)	J H Steeds	(St Edward's Oxford / St Catharine's)
H Muller	(Pretoria Univ / University)	*W O Chadwick	(Tonbridge / St John's)
D G G Coles	(Clifton / Trinity)	F J Leishman	(Oundle / Corpus Christi)
P C Phillips	(St Edward's Oxford / University)	C L Newton-Thompson	(Diocesan Coll / St John's)
S Pether	(Magdalen Oxford / St Peter's Hall)	P A R Lindsay	(Harrow / Clare)
H H Pennington	(Upholland GS / St Edmund Hall)	T R Parry	(Llandovery / Clare)
R M Marshall	(Giggleswick / Trinity)	M Dods	(Rugby / King's)
I W Sutherland	(Merchant Taylors' Crosby / Magdalen)	T R Juckes	(Marlborough / Pembroke)

Penalty Goals: Watts (2)

Try: Bruce Lockhart
Conversion: Geddes
Penalty Goal: Geddes

Referee: Mr C H Gadney

MATCH 64

12 December 1945, at Twickenham
Cambridge won by 1G 2T (11) to 1G 1PG (8)

Oxford		Cambridge	
D H Sampson	(St Andrew's Grahamstown / Trinity)	T C K Marr	(Loretto / Trinity Hall)
*J K Pearce	(Uppingham / Brasenose)	J Fairgrieve	(Haileybury / Gonville-Caius)
A M Stobie	(Clifton / Brasenose)	L Bruce Lockhart	(Sedbergh / St John's)
J M Lennox-Cook	(KCS Wimbledon / Trinity)	H M Kimberley	(Christ's Coll NZ / Emmanuel)
J E Ramsden	(Eton / Trinity)	A W Scott	(Sedbergh / St John's)
T W Cuff	(City of Bath / Balliol)	T K M Kirby	(Arnold / Queens')
J O Newton-Thompson	(Diocesan Rondebosch / Trinity)	G S Lowden	(Strathallan / St John's)
W H J Summerskill	(Harrow / Christ Church)	J Thomas	(St David's Lampeter / Selwyn)
A B Harcourt	(St Charles' Natal / Brasenose)	A P Henderson	(Taunton / Pembroke)
M P Tahany	(Wyggeston GS / Jesus)	A V Owen	(Cotton / Christ's)
B W Cole	(Dulwich / Brasenose)	S Fox	(Hymer's / St Catharine's)
M A Sutton	(Ampleforth / Worcester)	J F Bance	(Radley / Clare)
C D Williams	(Cardiff TC / Merton)	G B R Oswald	(Loretto / Trinity Hall)
P B C Moore	(Cheltenham / Brasenose)	*E Bole	(Wycliffe / Magdalene)
J R C McGlashan	(Fettes / Christ Church)	M R Steele-Bodger	(Rugby / Gonville-Caius)

Try: Newton-Thompson
Conversion: McGlashan
Penalty Goal: McGlashan

Tries: Fairgrieve, Bole, Fox
Conversion: Kirby

Referee: Mr C H Gadney

MATCH 65

10 December 1946, at Twickenham
Oxford won by 1G 1DG 2T (15) to 1G (5)

Oxford		Cambridge	
S C Newman	(CBC SA / Exeter)	B T G Cangley	(Felsted / Trinity Hall)
D W Swarbrick	(Kingswood / Merton)	M F Turner	(Whitgift / St Catharine's)
J H Bevan	(Hawarden / Jesus)	K A N Spray	(Oundle / Trinity Hall)
R M Cooper	(Douai / St John's)	H M Kimberley	(Ch Coll NZ / Emmanuel)
D J W Bridge	(King's Peterborough / Hertford)	E J H Williams	(Bromsgrove / Emmanuel)
M P Donnelly	(New Plymouth HS / Worcester)	L Bruce Lockhart	(Sedbergh / St John's)
*J O Newton-Thompson	(Diocesan Coll / Trinity)	H J H Gatford	(Oundle / Trinity Hall)
A B Harcourt	(St Charles' / Brasenose)	H H Campbell	(Oundle / Magdalene)
C G Gilthorpe	(Chesterfield / Brasenose)	A P Henderson	(Taunton / Pembroke)
G L Cawkwell	(King's Coll NZ / Christ Church)	T S McRoberts	(Banbridge Acad / Trinity Hall)
G A Wilson	(Oundle / Brasenose)	J M Hunter	(Fettes / Clare)
M A Sutton	(Ampleforth / Worcester)	S V Perry	(K George V Southport / Trinity)
A J van Ryneveld	(Diocesan Coll / Trinity)	W G Davies	(Wrekin / Pembroke)
P B C Moore	(Cheltenham / Brasenose)	E Bole	(Wycliffe / Magdalene)
B H Travers	(Sydney Univ / New)	*M R Steele-Bodger	(Rugby / Caius)

Tries: Swarbrick (2), Cooper
Conversion: Newman
Dropped Goal: Donnelly

Try: Steele-Bodger
Conversion: Bruce Lockhart

Referee: Mr N H Lambert

MATCH 66

29 November 1947, at Twickenham
Cambridge won by 2PG (6) to 0

Oxford		Cambridge	
S C Newman	(CBC SA / Exeter)	R H Lloyd-Davies	(Ammanford GS / Trinity Hall)
N L Ilett	(Christ's Hosp / Brasenose)	J B Raine	(Uppingham / Clare)
C B van Ryneveld	(Diocesan Coll / University)	K A N Spray	(Oundle / Trinity Hall)
D W Swarbrick	(Kingswood / Merton)	H M Kimberley	(Ch Coll NZ / Emmanuel)
D J W Bridge	(King's Peterborough / Hertford)	W B Holmes	(St George's Buenos Aires / Queens')
A Stewart	(Mt Albert GS / University)	W N White	(Leys / Trinity Hall)
J H Galbraith	(Edinburgh Academy / Balliol)	A F Dorward	(Sedbergh / St John's)
E C C Wynter	(Lewes / St Edmund Hall)	P J de A Moore	(Oundle / Magdalene)
C G Gilthorpe	(Chesterfield / Brasenose)	A P Henderson	(Taunton / Pembroke)
W D K Stobie	(Clifton / Brasenose)	T S McRoberts	(Banbridge Acad / Trinity Hall)
G L Cawkwell	(King's Coll NZ / Christ Church)	S V Perry	(K George V Southport / Trinity)
P W Kininmonth	(Sedbergh / Brasenose)	J A Gwilliam	(Monmouth / Trinity)
A J van Ryneveld	(Diocesan Coll / Trinity)	W G Davies	(Wrekin / Pembroke)
R D Gill	(Dulwich / Brasenose)	*E Bole	(Wycliffe / Magdalene)
*B H Travers	(Sydney Univ / New)	H H Mills	(Marling / St Catharine's)

Penalty Goals: Lloyd-Davies (2)

Referee: Mr C H Gadney

MATCH 67

7 December 1948, at Twickenham
Oxford won by 1G 1DG 2T (14) to 1G 1PG (8)

Oxford		Cambridge	
A Stewart	(Mt Albert GS / University)	W B Holmes	(St George's Buenos Aires / Queens')
D W Swarbrick	(Kingswood / Merton)	A W Scott	(Sedbergh / St John's)
L B Cannell	(Northampton GS / Lincoln)	J V Smith	(Marling / St Catharine's)
C B van Ryneveld	(Diocesan Coll / University)	*H M Kimberley	(Ch Coll NZ / Emmanuel)
D J W Bridge	(King's Peterborough / Hertford)	L G Gloag	(Oundle / Trinity)
M B Hofmeyr	(Pretoria Univ / Worcester)	G Davies	(Pontypridd CS / St Catharine's)
R Green	(Denstone / Keble)	A F Dorward	(Sedbergh / St John's)
J M Kendall-Carpenter	(Truro / Exeter)	P J de A Moore	(Oundle / Magdalene)
H J Meadows	(Crypt / Pembroke)	R V Thompson	(Worksop / Christ's)
C T M Wilson	(Campbell Belfast / University)	T S McRoberts	(Banbridge Acad / Trinity Hall)
*G A Wilson	(Oundle / Brasenose)	A M James	(Sutton Valence / Clare)
A N Vincent	(Diocesan Coll / Trinity)	J A Gwilliam	(Monmouth / Trinity)
A J van Ryneveld	(Diocesan Coll / Trinity)	W G Jenkins	(Port Talbot / Pembroke)
P W Kininmonth	(Sedbergh / Brasenose)	A P de Nobriga	(Tonbridge / St John's)
R D Gill	(Dulwich / Brasenose)	H H Mills	(Marling / St Catharine's)

Tries: Gill, C B van Ryneveld (2)
Conversion: Stewart
Dropped Goal: Hofmeyr

Try: Davies
Conversion: Holmes
Penalty Goal: Holmes

Referee: Mr A S Bean

MATCH 68

6 December 1949, at Twickenham
Oxford won by 1T (3) to 0

Oxford		Cambridge	
M B Hofmeyr	(Pretoria Univ/Worcester)	J C Davies	(Bromsgrove/Downing)
I J Botting	(Ch Coll NZ/Worcester)	I S Gloag	(Oundle/Trinity)
L B Cannell	(Northampton GS/Lincoln)	J V Smith	(Marling/St Catharine's)
B Boobbyer	(Uppingham/Brasenose)	J M Williams	(Rugby/Clare)
P J Langley	(Ipswich/Queen's)	B M Jones	(St Edward's Oxford/Fitzwilliam)
C B van Ryneveld	(Diocesan Coll/University)	G Davies	(Pontypridd CS/St Catharine's)
R Green	(Denstone/Keble)	*A F Dorward	(Sedbergh/St John's)
J M Kendall-Carpenter	(Truro/Exeter)	H Willis	(Heaton Moor/Downing)
W J Hefer	(Grey Inst/University)	R V Thompson	(Worksop/Christ's)
D A Emms	(Tonbridge/Brasenose)	G P Vaughan	(Lucton/St John's)
G N Gent	(Clifton/University)	A M James	(Sutton Valence/Clare)
*A N Vincent	(Diocesan Coll/Trinity)	J M Jenkins	(Oundle/Clare)
A B Curtis	(Eastbourne/Trinity)	R C C Thomas	(Blundell's/St John's)
G C Rittson-Thomas	(Sherborne/Trinity)	P D Young	(Clifton/Pembroke)
H D Small	(Dundee HS SA/St John's)	G A B Covell	(Harrow/St Catharine's)

Try: Gent

Referee: Mr A S Bean

MATCH 69

5 December 1950, at Twickenham
Oxford won by 1G 1PG (8) to 0

Oxford		Cambridge	
D J Lewis	(Plumtree/Exeter)	M J M Thompson	(St Bees/Downing)
I J Botting	(Ch Coll NZ/Worcester)	J V Smith	(Marling/St Catharine's)
L B Cannell	(Northampton GS/Lincoln)	E W Marsden	(Sedbergh/St John's)
B Boobbyer	(Uppingham/Brasenose)	P B Reeve	(RGS Newcastle/Emmanuel)
C E Winn	(KCS Wimbledon/Exeter)	I S Gloag	(Oundle/Trinity)
M B Hofmeyr	(Pretoria Univ/Worcester)	*G Davies	(Pontypridd CS/St Catharine's)
R Green	(Denstone/Keble)	J K Shepherd	(Wyggeston/Pembroke)
D A Emms	(Tonbridge/Brasenose)	H Willis	(Heaton Moor/Downing)
W J Hefer	(Grey Inst/University)	H D Doherty	(Rugby/Pembroke)
C J L Griffith	(St Andrew's Grahamstown/Trinity)	C C U Williams	(Wycliffe/Downing)
M Walker	(Bryanston/University)	R H King	(Merchant Taylors'/Pembroke)
G L Bullard	(Blundell's/Balliol)	C Barrow	(Uppingham/Clare)
G C Rittson-Thomas	(Sherborne/Trinity)	N E Williams	(Tiffin/Fitzwilliam)
*J M Kendall-Carpenter	(Truro/Exeter)	T R Marshall	(Bedford/Pembroke)
H D Small	(Dundee HS SA/St John's)	G M D Archer	(Stonyhurst/Pembroke)

Try: Emms
Conversion: Hofmeyr
Penalty Goal: Hofmeyr

Referee: Mr T Jones

MATCH 70

11 December 1951, at Twickenham
Oxford won by 2G 1T (13) to 0

Oxford		Cambridge	
C J Saunders	(Hilton Coll/Christ Church)	T U Wells	(King's Coll NZ/King's)
A H Cooper	(Bradford GS/Queen's)	G A J Bevan	(Dame Allan's/Downing)
I D F Coutts	(Dulwich/Lincoln)	K J Dalgleish	(Fettes/St Catharine's)
B Boobbyer	(Uppingham/Brasenose)	P B Reeve	(RGS Newcastle/Emmanuel)
T J Brewer	(Newport HS/Jesus)	D G H Jones	(Denstone/Selwyn)
D G S Baker	(Merchant Taylors'/Lincoln)	R M Bartlett	(Stowe/Trinity)
K M Spence	(Loretto/Brasenose)	R B Harrison	(Eastbourne/Trinity)
B E Thomson	(Glenalmond/Keble)	H Willis	(Heaton Moor/Downing)
N A H Creese	(Blundell's/Brasenose)	F R Beringer	(Methodist Belfast/St Catharine's)
C J L Griffith	(St Andrew's Grahamstown/Trinity)	M J O Massey	(Oundle/St John's)
E J Wimperis	(Uppingham/Brasenose)	*J M Jenkins	(Oundle/Clare)
M Walker	(Bryanston/University)	V H Leadbetter	(Kettering GS/St Catharine's)
*G L Bullard	(Blundell's/Balliol)	B J C Woodall	(Oundle/Magdalene)
D E Davies	(KE GS Five Ways/Wadham)	P J F Wheeler	(Rugby/Magdalene)
H A Wydell	(Merchant Taylors'/St Edmund Hall)	G M D Archer	(Stonyhurst/Pembroke)

Tries: Bullard, Wydell, Brewer
Conversions: Bullard (2)

Referee: Dr P F Cooper

MATCH 71

9 December 1952, at Twickenham
Cambridge won by 1PG 1T (6) to 1G (5)

Oxford		Cambridge	
D A B Robinson	(Hilton Coll SA/Trinity)	P M Davies	(Llandovery/Trinity Hall)
D J Skipper	(Watford GS/Brasenose)	D G H Jones	(Denstone/Selwyn)
P G A Johnstone	(Hilton Coll SA/St John's)	K J Dalgleish	(Fettes/St Catharine's)
J M Jenkin	(Kelly Coll/Trinity)	J Roberts	(Mill Hill/Christ's)
D Pollard	(QE GS Wakefield/St Edmund Hall)	*I S Gloag	(Oundle/Trinity)
D G S Baker	(Merchant Taylors'/Lincoln)	H P Morgan	(Wycliffe/St John's)
*K M Spence	(Loretto/Brasenose)	T C Pearson	(Oundle/Clare)
C J L Griffith	(St Andrew's Grahamstown/Trinity)	M J O Massey	(Oundle/St John's)
G C Hoyer-Millar	(Harrow/Lincoln)	F R Beringer	(Methodist Belfast/St Catharine's)
B E Thomson	(Glenalmond/Keble)	D G Massey	(King's Macclesfield/Christ's)
A W Ramsay	(Mill Hill/Brasenose)	I D S Beer	(Whitgift/St Catharine's)
D E Wood	(Luton GS/St Edmund Hall)	V H Leadbetter	(Kettering GS/St Catharine's)
E A J Fergusson	(Rugby/Oriel)	O P Woodroffe	(Sherborne/Trinity Hall)
A W Boyce	(Kingswood Coll/St Edmund Hall)	P H Ryan	(Harrow/Caius)
J H Henderson	(Michaelhouse/Brasenose)	P J F Wheeler	(Rugby/Magdalene)

Try: Pollard
Conversion: Robinson

Try: Jones
Penalty Goal: Davies

Referee: Mr W C W Murdoch

MATCH 72

8 December 1953, at Twickenham
Drawn — Oxford 1PG 1T (6) Cambridge 2PG (6)

Oxford		Cambridge	
D A B Robinson	(Hilton Coll / Trinity)	P M Davies	(Llandovery / Trinity Hall)
J C Baggaley	(QE GS Wakefield / Keble)	H B Griffiths	(Llandovery / Christ's)
T J Fallon	(Belmont Abbey / Worcester)	K J Dalgleish	(Fettes / St Catharine's)
H B Birrell	(St Andrew's Grahamstown / Lincoln)	D R W Silk	(Christ's Hosp / Sidney Sussex)
P G A Johnstone	(Hilton Coll / St John's)	J Roberts	(Mill Hill / Christ's)
R R Winn	(Dauntsey's / Exeter)	H P Morgan	(Wycliffe / St John's)
L P MacLachlan	(Plumtree / Exeter)	T C Pearson	(Oundle / Clare)
J J Steel	(St Andrew's NZ / New)	M J O Massey	(Oundle / St John's)
R C P Allaway	(Durban HS / University)	R K G MacEwen	(Bristol GS / St Catharine's)
J P Fellows-Smith	(Durban HS / Brasenose)	D G Massey	(King's Macclesfield / Christ's)
A W Boyce	(Kingswood / St Edmund Hall)	*P J F Wheeler	(Rugby / Magdalene)
L W Bryer	(Gray Coll SA / University)	J P K Asquith	(Purley / Pembroke)
E A J Fergusson	(Rugby / Oriel)	I D S Beer	(Whitgift / St Catharine's)
*A W Ramsay	(Mill Hill / Brasenose)	J W Clements	(Cranleigh / Trinity Hall)
D E Wood	(Luton GS / St Edmund Hall)	P H Ryan	(Harrow / Caius)

Try: Johnstone
Penalty Goal: Robinson

Penalty Goals: Davies (2)

Referee: Dr P F Cooper

MATCH 73

7 December 1954, at Twickenham
Cambridge won by 1PG (3) to 0

Oxford		Cambridge	
M J K Smith	(Stamford / St Edmund Hall)	P M Davies	(Llandovery / Trinity Hall)
J C Baggaley	(QE GS Wakefield / Keble)	A R Smith	(Glasgow Univ / Caius)
W M Butcher	(Michaelhouse / Worcester)	A F Barter	(Christ's Hosp / Sidney Sussex)
R Leslie	(Wellingborough GS / St Peter's Hall)	D R W Silk	(Christ's Hospital / Sidney Sussex)
W Lawrence	(Magdalen Oxford / Wadham)	J Roberts	(Mill Hill / Christ's)
*P G A Johnstone	(Hilton Coll / St John's)	T McClung	(Sedbergh / Emmanuel)
S C Coles	(Magdalen Oxford / Magdalen)	R H Umbers	(Sedbergh / Queens')
P W Watson	(Blundell's / Trinity)	N C G Raffle	(King's Canterbury / Emmanuel)
R C P Allaway	(Durban HS / University)	R K G MacEwen	(Bristol GS / St Catharine's)
J P Fellows-Smith	(Durban HS / Brasenose)	W J Downey	(Sedbergh / Emmanuel)
V W Jones	(Dartmouth US / Brasenose)	D Jagger	(Leeds Univ / Christ's)
J D Currie	(Bristol GS / Wadham)	R W D Marques	(Tonbridge / Queens')
J S Abbott	(St Bart's Newbury / Trinity)	J W Clements	(Cranleigh / Trinity Hall)
R A Plumbridge	(St Andrew's Grahamstown / Trinity)	*I D S Beer	(Whitgift / St Catharine's)
P G D Robbins	(Bishop Vesey's GS / St Edmund Hall)	A J Herbert	(Marling / St Catharine's)

Penalty Goal: Davies

Referee: Mr I David

MATCH 74

6 December 1955, at Twickenham
Oxford won by 1PG 2T (9) to 1G (5)

Oxford		Cambridge	
J A Prodger	(Merchant Taylors' / Worcester)	J G G Hetherington	(Churcher's / Peterhouse)
J C Walker	(Edinburgh Academy / Worcester)	A R Smith	(Glasgow Univ / Caius)
I L Reeler	(Plumtree / University)	A F Barter	(Cardiff HS / Emmanuel)
T J Fallon	(Belmont Abbey / Worcester)	J T Hodgson	(Blackpool GS / St Catharine's)
M G Allison	(King's Peterborough / Brasenose)	M E Kershaw	(St Peter's York / Emmanuel)
M J K Smith	(Stamford / St Edmund Hall)	T B Richards	(Neath GS / Jesus)
D O Brace	(Gowerton GS / University)	A A Mulligan	(Gresham's Holt / Magdalene)
P W Watson	(Blundell's / Trinity)	W J Downey	(Sedbergh / Emmanuel)
*R C P Allaway	(Durban HS / University)	N C G Raffle	(King's Canterbury / Emmanuel)
J P Rigby	(Stonyhurst / Lincoln)	D N Tarsh	(Clifton / Clare)
J D Currie	(Bristol GS / Wadham)	W R Evans	(Cowbridge GS / Christ's)
J S Abbott	(St Bart's Newbury / Trinity)	R W D Marques	(Tonbridge / Queens')
R H Davies	(KCS Wimbledon / New)	*J W Clements	(Cranleigh / Trinity Hall)
R A Plumbridge	(St Andrew's Grahamstown / Trinity)	M R M Evans	(Wrekin / Queens')
P G D Robbins	(Bishop Vesey's GS / St Edmund Hall)	A J Herbert	(Marling / St Catharine's)

Tries: Walker, Reeler
Penalty Goal: Currie

Try: Kershaw
Conversion: Hetherington

Referee: Mr I David

MATCH 75

11 December 1956, at Twickenham
Cambridge won by 1G 1DG 1PG 1T (14) to 2PG 1T (9)

Oxford		Cambridge	
R W Wilson	(Warwick / Brasenose)	D E S Millard	(Diocesan Coll / St Catharine's)
J L Booth	(Nottingham HS / St John's)	A R Smith	(Glasgow Univ / Caius)
M S Phillips	(Arnold / Trinity)	G W Lewis	(Leys / Trinity Hall)
I L Reeler	(Plumtree / University)	A F Barter	(Cardiff HS / Emmanuel)
W S Lawrence	(Magdalen Oxford / Wadham)	J L F Allan	(Rugby / St John's)
*D O Brace	(Gowerton GS / University)	J P Horrocks-Taylor	(Heath GS / St John's)
S C Coles	(Magdalen Oxford / Magdalen)	A A Mulligan	(Gresham's Holt / Magdalene)
L T Lombard	(Kingswood SA / St Edmund Hall)	J A Turner	(Rydal / Clare)
A H M Hoare	(King's Canterbury / Trinity)	W M Patterson	(Stowe / Queens')
J P Rigby	(Stonyhurst / Lincoln)	W J Downey	(Sedbergh / Emmanuel)
J D Currie	(Bristol GS / Wadham)	R W D Marques	(Tonbridge / Queens')
H R Moore	(Kingswood / Brasenose)	B R Loveday	(Beckenham / Downing)
R H Davies	(KCS Wimbledon / New)	J F Wainwright	(KE VI Birmingham / Selwyn)
R A Plumbridge	(St Andrew's Grahamstown / Trinity)	R P Boggon	(Oundle / Clare)
P G D Robbins	(Bishop Vesey's GS / St Edmund Hall)	*A J Herbert	(Marling / St Catharine's)

Try: Robbins
Penalty Goals: Currie, Reeler

Tries: Barter, Horrocks-Taylor
Conversion: Horrocks-Taylor
Dropped Goal: Horrocks-Taylor
Penalty Goal: Horrocks-Taylor

Referee: Mr K S John

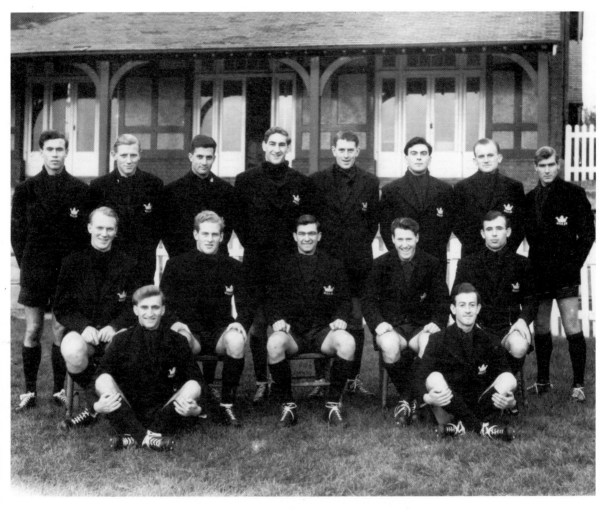

The victorious Oxford XV of 1955. Left to right; standing: J.C. Walker, N.J.K. Smith, I.L. Reeler, J.S. Abbott, J.D. Currie, J.P. Rigby, R.H. Davies, M.G. Allison; seated: R.A. Plumbridge, P.W. Watson, R.C.P. Allaway (captain), T.J. Fallon, P.G.D. Robbins; on ground: D.O. Brace, J.A. Prodger.

MATCH 76

10 December 1957, at Twickenham
Oxford won by 1T (3) to 0

Oxford		Cambridge	
J S M Scott	(Radley/Corpus Christi)	A Prosser-Harries	(Llanelli GS/Jesus)
A J Diamond	(Cape Town Univ/University)	A R Smith	(Glasgow Univ/Caius)
L D Watts	(Bristol GS/Wadham)	G W Lewis	(Leys/Trinity Hall)
M S Phillips	(Arnold/Trinity)	M J Hartley	(Giggleswick/Clare)
J R C Young	(Bishop Vesey's GS/St Edmund Hall)	R J N Leonard	(Sherborne/Trinity Hall)
B A G Weston	(City of Bath/St Peter's Hall)	J P Horrocks-Taylor	(Heath GS/St John's)
S C Coles	(Magdalen Oxford/Magdalen)	A A Mulligan	(Gresham's Holt/Magdalene)
L T Lombard	(Kingswood SA/St Edmund Hall)	*W J Downey	(Sedbergh/Emmanuel)
A H M Hoare	(King's Canterbury/Trinity)	J R Hockey	(Bedford/Christ's)
D Jesson	(W Hartlepool GS/St Edmund Hall)	J G Vaux	(Marlborough/Clare)
J D Currie	(Bristol GS/Wadham)	R W D Marques	(Tonbridge/Queens')
M W Swan	(Fettes/University)	B R Loveday	(Beckenham/Downing)
R H Davies	(KCS Wimbledon/New)	D A MacSweeney	(Rockwell/Christ's)
S H Wilcock	(Kirkham GS/St Peter's Hall)	K R F Bearne	(Rydal/Clare)
*P G D Robbins	(Bishop Vesey's GS/St Edmund Hall)	R R F Scott	(Michaelhouse/Trinity)

Try: Coles

Referee: Mr D G Walters

MATCH 77

9 December 1958, at Twickenham
Cambridge won by 1G 1PG 3T (17) to 1PG 1T (6)

Oxford		Cambridge	
J S M Scott	(Radley/Corpus Christi)	K J F Scotland	(Heriot's/Trinity)
J R C Young	(Bishop Vesey's GS/St Edmund Hall)	P R Mills	(Rutlish/Caius)
L D Watts	(Bristol GS/Wadham)	*G W Lewis	(Leys/Trinity Hall)
M S Phillips	(Arnold/Trinity)	H J Davies	(Cowbridge GS/Christ's)
T J Baxter	(Brisbane GS/Balliol)	M R Wade	(Wyggeston/Emmanuel)
A G R Sheil	(Southpot Sch Aus/Balliol)	G H Waddell	(Fettes/Pembroke)
A O'Connor	(Duffryn GS/St Edmund Hall)	S R Smith	(Eltham Coll/Emmanuel)
*L T Lombard	(Kingswood SA/St Edmund Hall)	D R J Bird	(St Paul's/St John's)
D M Davies	(Cardigan GS/St Edmund Hall)	M T Weston	(Marling/St Catharine's)
D Jesson	(W Hartlepool GS/St Edmund Hall)	J J Rainforth	(Oundle/Emmanuel)
J R Montgomery	(Michaelhouse/Lincoln)	D G Perry	(Clifton/Christ's)
F H ten Bos	(Fettes/St Edmund Hall)	V S J Harding	(Marylebone GS/Christ's)
L I Rimmer	(Birkenhead/Corpus Christi)	D A MacSweeney	(Rockwell/Christ's)
W I Plant	(RGS Worcester/St Edmund Hall)	K R F Bearne	(Rydal/Clare)
S H Wilcock	(Kirkham GS/St Peter's Hall)	D C Mills	(Clifton/Emmanuel)

Try: Young
Penalty Goal: Watts

Tries: Wade (2), Waddell, Mills
Conversion: Bearne
Penalty Goal: Scotland

Referee: Mr L M Boundy

MATCH 78

8 December 1959, at Twickenham
Oxford won by 3PG (9) to 1PG (3)

Oxford		Cambridge	
J G Willcox	(Ratclife/Worcester)	A R Lewis	(Neath GS/Christ's)
P M Dawkins	(West Point/Brasenose)	P R Mills	(Rutlish/Caius)
M S Phillips	(Arnold/Trinity)	M R Wade	(Wyggeston/Emmanuel)
D P Evans	(Tredegar GS/St Edmund Hall)	A Godson	(Wm Hulme's/Christ's)
J Glover	(Penzance GS/Corpus Christi)	F C Inglis	(Oundle/Caius)
R A W Sharp	(Blundell's/Balliol)	K J F Scotland	(Heriot's/Trinity)
D T Stevens	(Wellingborough GS/St Peter's Hall)	*S R Smith	(Eltham Coll/Emmanuel)
G C Murray	(Wrekin/University)	D R J Bird	(St Paul's/St John's)
D M Davies	(Cardigan GS/St Edmund Hall)	M T Weston	(Marling/St Catharine's)
D Jesson	(W Hartlepool GS/St Edmund Hall)	J J Rainforth	(Oundle/Emmanuel)
F H ten Bos	(Fettes/St Edmund Hall)	R L Makin	(Bedford/St John's)
J R S Higham	(Raynes Pk GS/Wadham)	V S J Harding	(Marylebone GS/Christ's)
F E R Butler	(Harrow/University)	D A MacSweeney	(Rockwell/Christ's)
S H Wilcock	(Kirkham GS/St Peter's Hall)	K R F Bearne	(Rydal/Clare)
T J Baxter	(Brisbane GS/Balliol)	J C Brash	(Fettes/Christ's)

Penalty Goals: Willcox (3)   *Penalty Goal*: Bearne

Referee: Mr R C Williams

MATCH 79

6 December 1960, at Twickenham
Cambridge won by 2G 1T (13) to 0

Oxford		Cambridge	
J G Willcox	(Ratcliffe/Worcester)	*K J F Scotland	(Heriot's/Trinity)
P M Dawkins	(West Point/Brasenose)	A Godson	(Wm Hulme's/Christ's)
J J McPartlin	(Wimbledon Coll/St Edmund Hall)	M R Wade	(Wyggeston/Emmanuel)
P J Burnet	(Edinburgh Academy/Lincoln)	M Lord	(Wm Hulme's/Christ's)
*J Glover	(Penzance GS/Corpus Christi)	W M Bussey	(Heath GS/Downing)
R A W Sharp	(Blundell's/Balliol)	G H Waddell	(Fettes/Pembroke)
M S Palmer	(Haverfordwest GS/Jesus)	T C Wintle	(Lydney GS/Christ's)
B L Spencer	(Raynes Pk GS/St Edmund Hall)	B A Dovey	(Lydney GS/Christ's)
D M Davies	(Cardigan GS/St Edmund Hall)	M T Weston	(Marling/St Catharine's)
N T Slater	(Birkenhead/Brasenose)	D F B Wrench	(Sandbach/Christ's)
F H ten Bos	(Fettes/St Edmund Hall)	V S J Harding	(Marylebone GS/Christ's)
L L Filby	(Sutton GS/St Edmund Hall)	B E Thomas	(Neath GS/Christ's)
F E R Butler	(Harrow/University)	R B Collier	(Marling/St Catharine's)
C M Payne	(Sherborne/Hertford)	R C B Michaelson	(Clifton/Christ's)
P J Bentley	(St George's Rhodesia/St Edmund Hall)	J C Brash	(Fettes/Christ's)

Tries: Godson, Lord (2)
Conversions: Scotland (2)

Referee: Mr D G Walters

227

MATCH 80

12 December 1961, at Twickenham
Cambridge won by 1DG 2T (9) to 1DG (3)

Oxford		Cambridge	
*J G Willcox	(Ratcliffe/Worcester)	I A Balding	(Millfield/Christ's)
P M Dawkins	(West Point/Brasenose)	S A Martin	(Birkenhead/Christ's)
J J McPartlin	(Wimbledon Coll/St Edmund Hall)	G P Frankcom	(KES Bath/Queens')
P M W Stafford	(Birkenhead/Corpus Christi)	*M R Wade	(Wyggeston/Emmanuel)
M A Ware	(Bec/St Edmund Hall)	W M Bussey	(Heath GS/Downing)
R A W Sharp	(Blundell's/Balliol)	G H Waddell	(Fettes/Pembroke)
T Cass	(QE GS Wakefield/St Edmund Hall)	T C Wintle	(Lydney GS/Christ's)
J A Collingwood	(St Mary's Liverpool/St Edmund Hall)	W A M Crow	(Merchiston/St Catharine's)
C S Wates	(Stowe/Brasenose)	C F W Higham	(Raynes Pk GS/St Catharine's)
J A H Curry	(KCS Wimbledon/St Edmund Hall)	N J Drake-Lee	(Stonyhurst/Downing)
J R L Adcock	(Radley/Trinity)	B E Thomas	(Neath GS/Christ's)
P K Stagg	(St Paul's/St Peter's Hall)	J E Owen	(Oundle/Emmanuel)
N Silk	(Lewes GS/Merton)	R B Collier	(Marling/St Catharine's)
G W Hines	(Christ's Hosp/Trinity)	R C B Michaelson	(Clifton/Christ's)
R G Bass	(Bedford/University)	J C Brash	(Fettes/Christ's)

Dropped Goal: Sharp

Tries: Higham, Frankcom
Dropped Goal: Waddell

Referee: Mr D G Walters

MATCH 81

11 December 1962, at Twickenham
Cambridge won by 1G 1PG 1DG 1T (14) to 0

Oxford		Cambridge	
J G Willcox	(Ratcliffe/Worcester)	C J Allan	(Truro/Downing)
M A Ware	(Bec/St Edmund Hall)	S A Martin	(Birkenhead/Christ's)
*J J McPartlin	(Wimbledon Coll/St Edmund Hall)	D W A Rosser	(Rochdale GS/Christ's)
P M W Stafford	(Birkenhead/Corpus Christi)	T G Arthur	(W Hartlepool GS/Christ's)
D M Sachs	(Princeton/Worcester)	W M Bussey	(Heath GS/Downing)
R H Lamb	(Merchiston/St Edmund Hall)	P D Briggs	(Pocklington/Christ's)
A J A Lewin	(Oundle/St Edmund Hall)	S J S Clarke	(Wellington Coll/Downing)
J A Collingwood	(St Mary's Liverpool/St Edmund Hall)	W A M Crow	(Merchiston/St Catharine's)
S B Richards	(Clifton/Exeter)	C F W Higham	(Raynes Pk GS/St Catharine's)
R M Wilcock	(Kirkham GS/St Edmund Hall)	N J Drake-Lee	(Stonyhurst/Downing)
P K Stagg	(St Paul's/St Peter's Hall)	B E Thomas	(Neath GS/Christ's)
I C Jones	(Stellenbosch Univ/Queen's)	P J Robinson	(Leys/St Catharine's)
G W Hines	(Christ's Hosp/Trinity)	J H H James	(Llandovery/Christ's)
B M Stoneman	(Durham Univ/Exeter)	*R C B Michaelson	(Clifton/Christ's)
N Silk	(Lewes GS/Merton)	J R H Greenwood	(Merchant Taylors' Crosby/Emmanuel)

Tries: Clarke, Martin
Conversion: Allan
Dropped Goal: Briggs
Penalty Goal Allan

Referee: Mr D G Walters

MATCH 82

10 December 1963, at Twickenham
Cambridge won by 2G 1PG 2T (19) to 1G 1DG 1PG (11)

Oxford		Cambridge	
S Wilson	(Pinner CGS / St Peter's Hall)	R M Walker	(KE Camp Hill / Christ's)
E L Rudd	(St Edward's Liverpool / Wadham)	S A Martin	(Birkenhead / Christ's)
D K Jones	(Gwendraeth GS / Merton)	D W A Rosser	(Rochdale GS / Christ's)
D J Whyte	(Bell-Baxter / St Edmund Hall)	G P Frankcom	(KES Bath / Queens')
A K Morgan	(Newport HS / Brasenose)	B J Hewett	(St John's Jo'burg / Trinity)
R H Lamb	(Merchiston / St Edmund Hall)	C M H Gibson	(Campbell Belfast / Queens')
A J A Lewin	(Oundle / St Edmund Hall)	S J S Clarke	(Wellington Coll / Downing)
E J H Gould	(St Edward's Oxford / St Edmund Hall)	N J Drake-Lee	(Stonyhurst / Downing)
A G D Whyte	(Robt Gordon's / St Edmund Hall)	B I Rees	(Neath GS / Christ's)
R B Britton	(King's Canterbury / Oriel)	A R Pender	(Cardiff HS / Queens')
F J R Craig	(Campbell Belfast / Balliol)	C S Dutson	(Grove Park Wrexham / St Catharine's)
I C Jones	(Stellenbosch Univ / Queen's)	J R W Harvey	(Marlborough / Christ's)
*N Silk	(Lewes GS / Merton)	J H H James	(Llandovery / Christ's)
E P Gush	(Grey Coll SA / St Edmund Hall)	L McMorris	(Fettes / Christ's)
B B King	(Umtali / Exeter)	*J R H Greenwood	(Merchant Taylors' Crosby / Emmanuel)

Try: Morgan
Conversion: Wilson
Penalty Goal: Wilson
Dropped Goal: Lamb

Tries: Martin, Greenwood, Gibson, James
Conversions: Harvey (2)
Penalty Goal: Harvey

Referee: Mr R P Burrell

MATCH 83

8 December 1964, at Twickenham
Oxford won by 2G 1PG 2T (19) to 1PG 1GM (6)

Oxford		Cambridge	
S Wilson	(Pinner CGS / St Peter's Hall)	M J Miliffe	(Wimbledon Coll / Caius)
E L Rudd	(St Edward's Liverpool / Wadham)	K J P Slater	(Temple Moor / Fitzwilliam)
R D Hearn	(Dublin Univ / St Edmund Hall)	*D W A Rosser	(Rochdale GS / Christ's)
K J Houston	(Belfast RA / St Edmund Hall)	G P Frankcom	(KES Bath / Queens')
A K Morgan	(Newport HS / Brasenose)	R S Fleming	(Wallasey GS / Emmanuel)
*R H Lamb	(Merchiston / St Edmund Hall)	C M H Gibson	(Campbell Belfast / Queens')
J M A Dorman	(Campbell Belfast / Corpus Christi)	A J C Hamp-Ferguson	(Stowe / Fitzwilliam)
E J H Gould	(St Edward's Oxford / St Edmund Hall)	G K M Webb	(Hilton Coll / Jesus)
E A Lloyd	(Hilton Coll / Corpus Christi)	B I Rees	(Neath GS / Christ's)
R B Britton	(King's Canterbury / Oriel)	J D Jenkins	(Caerphilly GS / Christ's)
F J R Craig	(Campbell Belfast / Balliol)	J R W Harvey	(Marlborough / Christ's)
I C Jones	(Stellenbosch Univ / Queen's)	C M Wiggins	(Peterhouse Rhodesia / Jesus)
C W Thorburn	(Glenalmond / Trinity)	J H H James	(Llandovery / Christ's)
W G Hadman	(Marlborough / St John's)	M Coley	(Bedford / Selwyn)
W S Wakelin	(New Plymouth HS / University)	R J Phillips	(Saltley GS / Downing)

Tries: Rudd (2), Wakelin, Houston
Conversions: Wilson (2)
Penalty Goal: Wilson

Penalty Goal: Harvey
Goal from Mark: Harvey

Referee: Mr D G Walters

MATCH 84

7 December 1965, at Twickenham
Drawn – each side scored 1G (5)

Oxford		Cambridge	
R Hiller	(Bec/St Edmund Hall)	D Gethin	(Neath GS/Selwyn)
M S Simmie	(Magdalen Oxford/St Edmund Hall)	R L K Jolliffe	(King's Peterborough/Jesus)
R C Broughton	(Heath GS/St Edmund Hall)	J D Gibbs	(Tonbridge/Trinity Hall)
J R Gabitass	(Plymouth Coll/St John's)	C P Carter	(Bradford GS/Christ's)
J B H Coker	(Fyling Hall/St Catherine's)	P A Kitchin	(Merchant Taylors'/Queens')
R F Read	(St John's Leatherhead/St Catherine's)	*C M H Gibson	(Campbell Belfast/Queens')
N C Starmer-Smith	(Magdalen Oxford/University)	A J C Hamp-Ferguson	(Stowe/Fitzwilliam)
E J H Gould	(St Edward's Oxford/St Edmund Hall)	G K M Webb	(Hilton Coll/Jesus)
E A Lloyd	(Hilton Coll/Corpus Christi)	B I Rees	(Neath GS/Christ's)
O C Waldron	(St Nessan's/Merton)	R D H Bryce	(Perth Acad/Emmanuel)
*F J R Craig	(Campbell Belfast/Balliol)	N O Martin	(Perse/St John's)
R J Brewer	(Milton HS/St Edmund Hall)	B J Morrison	(Fettes/Pembroke)
A L Bucknall	(Ampleforth/St Edmund Hall)	M J Green	(Solihull/Christ's)
W G Hadman	(Marlborough/St John's)	T R Drake	(Lewes CGS/Caius)
T P Bedford	(CBC Kimberley/St Edmund Hall)	M G Doyle	(Newbridge Coll/Christ's)

Try: Gabitass
Conversion: Gould

Try: Rees
Conversion: Gethin

Referee: Mr D G Walters

MATCH 85

6 December 1966, at Twickenham
Oxford won by 1G 1T (8) to 1DG 1T (6)

Oxford		Cambridge	
A C Barker	(Leighton Pk/St Edmund Hall)	D Gethin	(Neath GS/Selwyn)
M S Simmie	(Magdalen Oxford/St Edmund Hall)	C J Ryan	(St Edmunds Ware/Downing)
J R Croker	(Birkenhead/St Catherine's)	M A Smith	(Fettes/Trinity)
J R Gabitass	(Plymouth Coll/St John's)	N B Thomas	(St Boniface/St Edmund House)
C A Holroyd	(Wyggeston GS/Exeter)	J V Berman	(Newcastle HS/Fitzwilliam)
R H Phillips	(K Henry VII Abergavenny/Corpus Christi)	W H Raybould	(Cathay's HS/Emmanuel)
N C Starmer-Smith	(Magdalen Oxford/University)	N J Cosh	(Dulwich/Queens')
E J H Gould	(St Edward's Oxford/St Edmund Hall)	T M Corry	(Glenalmond/St Catharine's)
E A Lloyd	(Hilton Coll/Corpus Christi)	*B I Rees	(Neath GS/Christ's)
J S Baird	(Ch Coll NZ/Merton)	P S Onyett	(Oundle/St John's)
E K Moorcroft	(Queen's Coll SA/University)	N O Marton	(Perse/St John's)
S J B James	(Rossall/Merton)	R E Barker	(Canock GS/St John's)
A L Bucknall	(Ampleforth/St Edmund Hall)	M J Green	(Solihull/Christ's)
W G Hadman	(Marlborough/St John's)	C Duncan	(Nuneaton GS/Pembroke)
*T P Bedford	(CBC Kimberley/St Edmund Hall)	R G Sim	(Hutchesons'/Pembroke)

Tries: Holroyd, Bucknall
Conversion: Gould

Try: Rees
Dropped Goal: Raybould

Referee: Mr D G Walters

230

MATCH 86

12 December 1967, at Twickenham
Cambridge won by 1PG 1T (6) to 0

Oxford		Cambridge	
J Wilson	(Pinner CGS/Keble)	A J Anthony	(Bassaleg/Christ's)
P R E McFarland	(Ampleforth/St Edmund Hall)	M A Smith	(Fettes/Trinity)
J R Croker	(Birkenhead/St Catherine's)	C D Saville	(Whitgift/Selwyn)
A C Barker	(Leighton Pk/St Edmund Hall)	P R Price	(Blundell's/Selwyn)
D S Boyle	(Austin Friars/Hertford)	J S Spencer	(Sedbergh/Queens')
*R H Phillips	(K Henry VIII Abergavenny/Corpus Christi)	I Robertson	(Geo Watson's/Christ's)
N G C Wilson	(St Benedict's/St Catherine's)	M R Heslip	(Campbell Belfast/Christ's)
J S Baird	(Ch Coll NZ/Merton)	P S Onyett	(Oundle/St John's)
P Davey	(Ogmore GS/Lincoln)	D W Lyon	(Slough THS/St John's)
P A Painter	(Hastings HS NZ/St John's)	J D Monahan	(Kingswood/Trinity Hall)
R R Speed	(Millfield/St Edmund Hall)	A J S Folwell	(Towcester/Caius)
O C Waldron	(St Nessans/Merton)	N O Martin	(Perse/St John's)
M J Thorniley-Walker	(Ampleforth/St John's)	*M J Green	(Solihull/Christ's)
P J Dixon	(St Bees/St Edmund Hall)	R C Hannaford	(Crypt/Churchill)
T P Bedford	(CBC Kimberley/St Edmund Hall)	R G Sim	(Hutchesons'/Pembroke)

Try: Spencer
Penalty Goal: Saville

Referee: Mr K S John

MATCH 87

10 December 1968, at Twickenham
Cambridge won by 1DG 1PG 1T (9) to 2T (6)

Oxford		Cambridge	
P R Carroll	(Newington Coll/Mansfield)	A M Jorden	(Monmouth/Fitzwilliam)
R T Baker	(Bec/St Edmund Hall)	K Hughes	(Llanelli GS/St Catharine's)
D S Boyle	(Austin Friars/Hertford)	J S Spencer	(Sedbergh/Queens')
J L Cooke	(Whitgift/St Edmund Hall)	T G R Davies	(QEGS Carmarthen/Emmanuel)
J Wilson	(Pinner CGS/Keble)	C D Saville	(Whitgift/Selwyn)
*R H Phillips	(K Henry VIII Abergavenny/Corpus Christi)	I R Shackleton	(Bradford GS/Fitzwilliam)
C R Laidlaw	(Otago Univ/Merton)	J J Page	(Cambridgeshire HS/Queens')
R R Speed	(Millfield/St Edmund Hall)	R W Bowen	(Bromsgrove/Magdalene)
D M Barry	(Sherborne/Hertford)	*D W Lyon	(Slough THS/St John's)
P M Johnson	(Bec/Mansfield)	J D Monahan	(Kingswood/Trinity Hall)
A R Behn	(Skinners/Merton)	M R McKenzie	(Morpeth/St Catharine's)
M G Roberts	(Dublin Univ/St Edmund Hall)	A K Rodgers	(Shaftesbury GS/Trinity Hall)
P J Torry	(Dover Coll/New)	W A Jones	(Campbell Belfast/Queens')
P J Dixon	(St Bees/St Edmund Hall)	A J S Folwell	(Towcester GS/Caius)
R S Mulvey	(St Benedict's/Magdalen)	J R Tredwell	(Solihull/St Catharine's)

Tries: Dixon, Johnson

Try: Shackleton
Dropped Goal: Shackleton
Penalty Goal McKenzie

Referee: Mr D P d'Arcy

MATCH 88

9 December 1969, at Twickenham
Oxford won by 3PG (9) to 2PG (6)

Oxford		Cambridge	
P R Carroll	(Newington Coll / Mansfield)	A M Jorden	(Monmouth / Fitzwilliam)
E C Osborn	(Douai / St Edmund Hall)	K Hughes	(Llanelli GS / St Catharine's)
J L Cooke	(Whitgift / St Edmund Hall)	*J S Spencer	(Sedbergh / Queens')
D S Boyle	(Austin Friars / Hertford)	T G R Davies	(QEGS Carmarthen / Emmanuel)
R O P Jones	(Amman Valley GS / St Edmund Hall)	C D Saville	(Whitgift / Selwyn)
J R Williams	(Monmouth / Lincoln)	I R Shackleton	(Bradford GS / Fitzwilliam)
*C R Laidlaw	(Otago Univ / Merton)	J J Page	(Cambridgeshire HS / Queens')
R R Speed	(Millfield / St Edmund Hall)	R Brookstein	(KE VI Camp Hill / Selwyn)
D M Barry	(Sherborne / Hertford)	P D'A Keith-Roach	(Cheltenham / Pembroke)
R L Griffiths	(St Edward's Oxford / Jesus)	N P Hinton	(Tiffin / St Catharine's)
A R Behn	(Skinners' / Merton)	A K Rodgers	(Shaftesbury GS / Trinity Hall)
R Davies	(Cowbridge GS / St Edmund Hall)	R B French	(Edinburgh Academy / St Catharine's)
P J Torry	(Dover Coll / New)	W A Jones	(Campbell Belfast / Queens')
P J Dixon	(St Bees / St Edmund Hall)	G F Redmond	(Weston-s-Mare GS / Emmanuel)
D A Griffiths	(Univ of NSW / Merton)	R C Lister	(Ampleforth / Trinity)

Penalty Goals: Jones (3)   *Penalty Goals*: Jorden (2)

Referee: Mr M H Titcomb

MATCH 89

8 December 1970, at Twickenham
Oxford won by 1G 1DG 2T (14) to 1PG (3)

Oxford		Cambridge	
*P R Carroll	(Newington Coll / Mansfield)	H K Steele	(King's Auckland / Corpus Christi)
I T Dunbar	(Pontypridd GS / St Catherine's)	*T G R Davies	(QEGS Carmarthen / Emmanuel)
C P Kent	(Blundell's / Worcester)	P K Smith	(Aylesbury GS / Queens')
S James	(Penlan / Lincoln)	C D Saville	(Whitgift / Selwyn)
R O P Jones	(Amman Valley GS / St Edmund Hall)	R J D Linnecar	(Dulwich / Trinity)
D L Bell	(Geo Watson's / St Edmund Hall)	I R Shackleton	(Bradford GS / Fitzwilliam)
B M Carroll	(Newington Coll / Mansfield)	J J Page	(Cambridgeshire HS / Queens')
A I Douglas	(RGS Newcastle / University)	R C O Skinner	(Rugby / Fitzwilliam)
D M Barry	(Sherborne / Hertford)	P D'A Keith-Roach	(Cheltenham / Pembroke)
P M Johnson	(Bec / Mansfield)	N P Hinton	(Tiffin / St Catharine's)
N K J Witney	(Tonbridge / Corpus Christi)	A K Rodgers	(Shaftesbury GS / Trinity Hall)
P F C Gordon	(Ratcliffe / St Edmund Hall)	J R Watt	(Hitchin GS / Emmanuel)
C J Hawkesworth	(Campbell Belfast / St Edmund Hall)	W A Jones	(Campbell Belfast / Queens')
P J Dixon	(St Bees / St Edmund Hall)	G F Redmond	(Weston-s-Mare GS / Emmanuel)
D A Griffiths	(Univ of NSW / Merton)	J Shipsides	(Marple Hall GS / Christ's)

Tries: Bell, James, Barry   *Penalty Goal*: Steele
Conversion: Douglas
Dropped Goal: Bell

Referee: Air-Cdre G C Lamb

MATCH 90

7 December 1971, at Twickenham
Oxford won by 3PG 3T (21) to 1PG (3)

Oxford		Cambridge	
*R O P Jones	(Amman Valley GS/St Edmund Hall)	S P Berry	(Sedbergh/Selwyn)
I T Dunbar	(Pontypridd GS/St Catherine's)	G P Phillips	(Cray Valley/Queens')
P A Binham	(St Brendan's/Hertford)	J M Howard	(Birkenhead/Trinity)
T M Seymour	(Natal Univ/Oriel)	C R Williams	(Bridgend GS/Clare)
S H Beamish	(Belfast RA/St Edmund Hall)	T A G Beazley	(Radley/Emmanuel)
M G Heal	(St Brendan's/St Edmund Hall)	N W Drummond	(Merchiston/Fitzwilliam)
B M Carroll	(Newington Coll/Mansfield)	A P Webster	(Harrow/Selwyn)
A I Douglas	(RGS Newcastle/University)	R C O Skinner	(Rugby/Fitzwilliam)
A Jenkins	(Peer's/St Edmund Hall)	P d'A Keith-Roach	(Cheltenham/Pembroke)
D F Badenoch	(Marlborough/Lincoln)	R J Edwards	(Blundell's/Selwyn)
N K J Witney	(Tonbridge/Corpus Christi)	R M Wilkinson	(St Albans/Emmanuel)
T B Neville	(Yale Univ/New)	M A Biggar	(Sedbergh/Queens')
S James	(Penlan/Lincoln)	E F Edwards	(Newbridge GS/St John's)
C J Hawkesworth	(Campbell Belfast/St Edmund Hall)	*G F Redmond	(Weston-s-Mare/Emmanuel)
T J Donovan	(Belmont Abbey/St Edmund Hall)	J R W Clayton	(KE VI Camp Hill/Downing)

Tries: Carroll, Seymour, Jones
Penalty Goal: Douglas (3)

Penalty Goal: Howard

Referee: Mr R Lewis

MATCH 91

12 December 1972, at Twickenham
Cambridge won by 1G 1PG 1DG 1T (16) to 2PG (6)

Oxford		Cambridge	
B D Mead	(Dunstable GS/St Edmund Hall)	I S Williamson	(Sidcup/Chislehurst GS/Fitzwilliam)
J M Ward	(Newcastle-u-Lyme HS/Mansfield)	G P Phillips	(Cray Valley THS/Queens')
C P Kent	(Blundell's/Worcester)	*J M Howard	(Birkenhead/Trinity)
R J Lee	(Sydney CEGS/Worcester)	C R Williams	(Bridgend GS/Clare)
E J F Littlechild	(Arnold/St Edmund Hall)	R S Page	(Haberdashers' Aske's/Emmanuel)
*D R R Jones	(Neath GS/Keble)	M F Rosser	(Campbell Belfast/Queens')
P R Sawtell	(Bromsgrove/Regent's Pk)	A W Jessop	(Wellingborough GS/Fitzwilliam)
R D Love	(Sewanee/Keble)	G Rees	(Neath GS/Selwyn)
W P Maddock	(Campbell Belfast/Pembroke)	J M Smith	(Neath GS/Selwyn)
D C Kay	(St Edward's Liverpool/University)	R J Edwards	(Blundell's/Selwyn)
T B Neville	(Yale Univ/New)	D R Thomas	(Llandeilo GS/Christ's)
S J T Davies	(St Illtyd's/Balliol)	R M Wilkinson	(St Albans/Emmanuel)
J M Hutchinson	(King's Canterbury/Worcester)	S Warlow	(Llanelli GS/St Catharine's)
C J Hawkesworth	(Campbell Belfast/St Edmunds Hall)	J P Dickins	(Oundle/Corpus Christi)
R A E Davey	(RBAI/St Edmund Hall)	W A Jones	(Campbell Belfast/Queens')

Penalty Goals: Ward (2)

Tries: Phillips, Dickins
Conversion: Howard
Penalty Goal: Howard
Dropped Goal: Rosser

Referee: Mr R F Johnson

MATCH 92

11 December 1973, at Twickenham
Cambridge won by 1DG 1PG 2T (14) to 1G 2PG (12)

Oxford		Cambridge	
B D Mead	(Dunstable GS / St Edmund Hall)	M E Hodgson	(Radley / Selwyn)
I T Dunbar	(Pontypridd GS / St Catherine's)	D B Williams	(St Thos Aquinas GS / Christ's)
C P Kent	(Blundell's / Worcester)	A J Wordsworth	(Whitgift / Selwyn)
T M Seymour	(Michaelhouse / Oriel)	C R Williams	(Bridgend GS / Clare)
E J D Clarke	(Harrow / University)	R S Page	(Haberdashers' Aske's / Emmanuel)
T R Glover	(RGS Lancaster / Lincoln)	M F Rosser	(Campbell Belfast / Queens')
S M Lewis	(Abertillery GS / Keble)	R M Harding	(Millfield / St John's)
*D C Kay	(St Edward's Liverpool / University)	A H Monro	(Rugby / Pembroke)
C J Ashby	(Sir Thomas Rich's / St Edmund Hall)	J W Campbell	(Dalriada GS / St John's)
A P Newman	(Cardiff HS / St Edmund Hall)	*G Rees	(Neath GS / Selwyn)
P St L Kyrke-Smith	(Ellesmere / Worcester)	D R Thomas	(Llandeilo GS / Christ's)
S J T Davies	(St Illtyd's / Balliol)	R M Wilkinson	(St Albans / Emmanuel)
J M Hutchinson	(King's Canterbury / Worcester)	N J French	(Haberdashers' Aske's / St Catharine's)
R N McClure	(KE VI Norwich / Corpus Christi)	J P Dickins	(Oundle / Corpus Christi)
J W Lee	(Christchurch HS / Christ Church)	S R G Pratt	(Fettes / Christ's)

Try: Lewis
Conversion: Lewis
Penalty Goals: Lewis (2)

Tries: Rosser (2)
Penalty Goal: Rosser
Dropped Goal: Wordsworth

Referee: Mr K H Clark

MATCH 93

10 December 1974, at Twickenham
Cambridge won by 1G 2PG 1T (16) to 5PG (15)

Oxford		Cambridge	
J S Waterman	(Isleworth GS / St Catherine's)	A J Hignell	(Denstone / Fitzwilliam)
P R Asquith	(Clifton / Balliol)	J L Moyes	(Bournemouth / Emmanuel)
*C P Kent	(Blundell's / Worcester)	M W O'Callaghan	(Christchurch HS / Emmanuel)
T R Glover	(RGS Lancaster / Lincoln)	P J Warfield	(Haileybury / St John's)
R M Burse	(Centre Coll Kentucky / St John's)	G E Wood	(Uppingham / Downing)
P N Quinnen	(St Benedict's / Wadham)	J N F Breakey	(Fettes / Christ's)
D W Mackenzie	(Wyggeston / St Edmund Hall)	R M Harding	(Millfield / St John's)
P G Woodhead	(Bradford GS / Lincoln)	T M R Lintott	(Blundell's / Christ's)
P S Rees	(Cardiff HS / Magdalen)	J W Campbell	(Dalriada GS / St John's)
J W Lee	(Christchurch HS / Christ Church)	S K Young	(Raynes Pk GS / Pembroke)
P St L Kyrke-Smith	(Ellesmere / Worcester)	D R Thomas	(Llandeilo GS / Christ's)
R A Davis	(King's Sydney / Pembroke)	S R R Edlmann	(Tonbridge / Trinity Hall)
D S M MacDonald	(Diocesan Coll / University)	*S Warlow	(Llanelli GS / St Catharine's)
J A Taylor	(RGS Lancaster / St Edmund Hall)	S R G Pratt	(Fettes / Christ's)
C Shaw	(Orangefield Belfast / Ruskin)	J J Hartley	(Arnold / Fitzwilliam)

Penalty Goals: Quinnen (5)

Tries: Warfield, Hignell
Conversion: Hignell
Penalty Goals: Hignell (2)

Referee: Mr K A Pattinson

9 December 1975, at Twickenham
Cambridge won by 2G 1DG 5PG 1T (34) to 3PG 1DG (12)

Oxford		Cambridge	
P N Quinnen	(St Benedict's/Wadham)	A J Hignell	(Denstone/Fitzwilliam)
D C Willis	(Haberdashers' Aske's/Worcester)	M W O'Callaghan	(Christchurch HS/Emmanuel)
T A Bryan	(Hampton/St Edmund Hall)	J L Moyes	(Bournemouth/Emmanuel)
C P Kent	(Blundell's/Worcester)	A R Grant	(Glasgow HS/Fitzwilliam)
B S Clements	(Kimberley BS/St Catherine's)	G E Wood	(Uppingham/Downing)
A W Ellis	(Neath GS/Keble)	A J Wordsworth	(Whitgift/Selwyn)
M Hockley	(Sherborne/Trinity)	A D Lewis	(Caerphilly GTS/St John's)
E C Horne	(Emanuel/Jesus)	P V Boulding	(Cambridgeshire HS/Downing)
P S Rees	(Cardiff HS/Magdalen)	G G Beringer	(Campbell Belfast/St Catharine's)
P K Tongue	(KE Aston/St Edmund Hall)	D B Allen	(Solihull/Downing)
R A Davis	(King's Sydney/Pembroke)	P R Ellis	(Redruth GS/Christ's)
D S M MacDonald	(Diocesan Coll/University)	S L Brown	(KE VI Nuneaton/St Catharine's)
P E King	(Sydney CEGS/Worcester)	*A A Stewart	(St George's Vancouver/St Catharine's)
D A MacDonald	(Diocesan Coll/University)	S R R Edlmann	(Tonbridge/Trinity Hall)
*C Shaw	(Orangefield Belfast/St Edmund Hall)	N A Malik	(Dunsmore/Trinity Hall)
P St L Kyrke-Smith replaced Shaw	(Ellesmere/Worcester)	J N F Breakey replaced Wordsworth	(Fettes/Christ's)

Penalty Goals: Quinnen (3)
Dropped Goal: Ellis

Tries: Edlmann, Grant, Lewis
Conversions: Hignell (2)
Penalty Goals: Hignell (5)
Dropped Goal: Lewis

Referee: Mr A Welsby

7 December 1976, at Twickenham
Cambridge won by 1G 3PG (15) to 0

Oxford		Cambridge	
W R Cooke	(Lord Williams' Thame/St Edmund Hall)	A J Hignell	(Denstone/Fitzwilliam)
R M C Hoolahan	(Reigate GS/St Edmund Hall)	M W O'Callaghan	(Christchurch HS/Emmanuel)
F J Rahmatallah	(St Paul's/Keble)	A R Grant	(Glasgow HS/Fitzwilliam)
T A Bryan	(Hampton/St Edmund Hall)	J F Thornton	(Dulwich/Magdalene)
D C Willis	(Haberdashers' Aske's/Worcester)	G E Wood	(Uppingham/Downing)
S J Fisher	(Rossall/University)	G G Lewis	(Caerphilly GTS/St John's)
R K Hood	(Bromsgrove/Mansfield)	A D Lewis	(Caerphilly GTS/St John's)
E C Horne	(Emanuel/Jesus)	P V Boulding	(Cambridgeshire HS/Downing)
C M Sexton	(St Edward's Oxford/Keble)	G G Beringer	(Campbell Belfast/St Catharine's)
T P Enevoldson	(RGS Newcastle/Brasenose)	J M Vivian	(Rugby/St John's)
K A Watt	(St Andrew's Grahamstown/St Catherine's)	P J L Nixon	(Repton/Selwyn)
R G Robinson	(Oundle/Lincoln)	S L Brown	(KE VI Nuneaton/St Catharine's)
G L White	(Diocesan Coll/University)	*A A Stewart	(St George's Vancouver/St Catharine's)
*D A MacDonald	(Diocesan Coll/University)	E T Butler	(Monmouth/Fitzwilliam)
D S M MacDonald	(Diocesan Coll/University)	G A Edmonds	(Gordonstoun/St Catharine's)

Try: Brown
Conversion: Hignell
Penalty Goals: Hignell (3)

Referee: Mr N R Sanson

MATCH 96

6 December 1977, at Twickenham
Oxford won by 4PG 1T (16) to 2PG 1T (10)

Oxford		Cambridge	
K M Hopkins	(Maesteg CS / St Edmund Hall)	*A J Hignell	(Denstone / Fitzwilliam)
R M C Hoolahan	(Reigate GS / St Edmund Hall)	M W O'Callaghan	(Christchurch HS / Emmanuel)
A F Watkinson	(Belmont Abbey / St Edmund Hall)	M K Fosh	(Harrow / Magdalene)
*T A Bryan	(Hampton / St Edmund Hall)	J S Davies	(Ch Coll Brecon / St John's)
D C Willis	(Haberdashers' Aske's / Worcester)	I A Greig	(Queen's Queenstown SA / Downing)
W G Davies	(Gwendraeth GS / St Catherine's)	J N F Breakey	(Fettes / Christ's)
S J Faktor	(Latymer Upper / University)	J C Robbie	(Dublin HS / Christ's)
E C Horne	(Emanuel / Jesus)	R J Brooman	(Merchant Taylors' / Trinity)
B Light	(Lewis S Pengam / St Edmund Hall)	K F Geoghegan	(Gonzaga Dublin / King's)
T P Enevoldson	(RGS Newcastle / Brasenose)	P A V Shaw	(QEGS Wakefield / Downing)
R G Robinson	(Oundle / Lincoln)	N R M Heath	(Solihull / Downing)
K J Budge	(Rossall / University)	J N Ford	(Millfield / Emmanuel)
G L White	(Diocesan Coll / University)	S F Glanvill	(Exeter / Pembroke)
M J P Moir	(Ampleforth / Lincoln)	E T Butler	(Monmouth / Fitzwilliam)
M D Mitchell	(Westerford HS Cape Town / St Catherine's)	R J Stead	(Radley / Selwyn)
		H J Stevenson	(Haberdashers' Aske's / St Catharine's)
		replaced Shaw	
		G Crothers	(Belfast RA / Hughes Hall)
		replaced O'Callaghan	

Try: Moir
Penalty Goals: Watkinson (4)

Try: Greig
Penalty Goals: Hignell, Robbie

Referee: Mr C Norling

MATCH 97

12 December 1978, at Twickenham
Cambridge won by 2G 3PG 1T (25) to 1PG 1T (7)

Oxford		Cambridge	
T M Davis	(Hale School W Aust / Balliol)	I R Metcalfe	(KE Birmingham / St Catharine's)
E A K Quist-Arcton	(Taunton / St Benet's Hall)	I A Greig	(Queen's Queenstown / Downing)
R M C Hoolahan	(Reigate GS / St Edmund Hall)	M K Fosh	(Harrow / Magdalene)
R B Clark	(Brinkburn CS / Christ Church)	M F Parr	(St Joseph's Blackpool / Trinity Hall)
D R Woodrow	(QEGS Wakefield / Regent's Pk)	R H Tyler	(Cheltenham GS / Fitzwilliam)
*A F Watkinson	(Belmont Abbey / St Edmund Hall)	J F Thornton	(Dulwich / Magdalene)
P V Brett	(Sevenoaks / St Edmund Hall)	*J C Robbie	(Dublin HS / Christ's)
T W Jones	(Mill Hill / Wadham)	R J Brooman	(Merchant Taylors' / Trinity)
P S Rees	(Cardiff HS / Magdalen)	J J H Grant	(Haileybury / St Catharine's)
T P Enevoldson	(RGS Newcastle / Brasenose)	S E Killick	(Dulwich / Queens')
K J Budge	(Rossall / University)	N R M Heath	(Solihull / Downing)
C J Dew	(Cowbridge GS / St Edmund Hall)	J N Ford	(Millfield / Emmanuel)
C J Finch	(Marling / Queen's)	C O'Callaghan	(St Joseph's Port Talbot / St John's)
J N Edmonds	(Truro / Oriel)	E T Butler	(Monmouth / Fitzwilliam)
R A Hughes	(Warwick / Wadham)	B D F Clarke	(Solihull / St John's)

Try: Quist-Arcton
Penalty Goal: Watkinson

Tries: Tyler, Greig, Robbie
Conversions: Robbie (2)
Penalty Goals: Robbie (3)

Referee: Mr C Norling

MATCH 98

11 December 1979, at Twickenham
Oxford won by 2PG 1DG (9) to 1PG (3)

Oxford		Cambridge	
T M Davis	(Hale School W Aust/Balliol)	I R Metcalfe	(KE Birmingham/St Catharine's)
E A K Quist-Arcton	(Taunton/St Benet's Hall)	J F Thornton	(Dulwich/Magdalene)
S J Halliday	(Downside/St Benet's Hall)	A M Laycock	(St Michael's Leeds/Emmanuel)
A C Thomas	(Colston's/Keble)	A M J McGahey	(King's Taunton/Fitzwilliam)
D R Woodrow	(QEGS Wakefield/Regent's Pk)	R H Tyler	(Cheltenham GS/Fitzwilliam)
R B Clark	(Brinkburn CS/Christ Church)	W M H Rose	(Loughborough GS/Magdalene)
D J Morgan	(Bablake/Keble)	*I G Peck	(Bedford/Madalene)
T W Jones	(Mill Hill/Wadham)	H J Stevenson	(Haberdashers' Aske's/St Catharine's)
S M Hofmeyr	(Diocesan Coll/University)	W D Gilliland	(Methodist Belfast/Trinity)
*T P Enevoldson	(RGS Newcastle/Brasenose)	N A Stothard	(Hymers Coll Hull/Selwyn)
K J Budge	(Rossall/University)	P J Ackford	(Plymouth Coll/Magdalene)
N T Roberts	(Glenalmond/Jesus)	J N Ford	(Millfield/Emmanuel)
W E A Morrison	(Felsted/Oriel)	P S Chalmers	(Fettes/St Catharine's)
N V H Mallett	(St Andrew's SA/University)	A J Macklin	(Felsted/St John's)
C N Bray	(Leeds GS/Keble)	S F Glanvill	(Exeter/Pembroke)

Penalty Goals: Morgan, Mallett
Dropped Goal: Clark

Penalty Goal: Metcalfe

Referee: Mr A M Hosie

MATCH 99

9 December 1980, at Twickenham
Cambridge won by 3PG 1T (13) to 3PG (9)

Oxford		Cambridge	
T M Davis	(Hale School W Aust/Balliol)	*W M H Rose	(Loughborough GS/Magdalene)
A J Bibby	(St George's Vancouver/St Catherine's)	S P Moriarty	(Wallington HS/Magdalene)
S J Halliday	(Downside/St Benet's Hall)	R J Boyd-Moss	(Bedford/Madgalene)
D C A Barr	(Bradford GS/Corpus Christi)	A M J McGahey	(King's Taunton/Fitzwilliam)
D R Woodrow	(QEGS Wakefield/Regent's Pk)	R H Tyler	(Cheltenham GS/Fitzwilliam)
P Jenkins	(Maesteg CS/St Catherine's)	G H Davies	(KE VI Stourbridge/Selwyn)
R S Luddington	(KCS Wimbledon/St Edmund Hall)	J C Cullen	(Christ's Hosp/Downing)
J G M Webster	(Uppingham/Oriel)	C J Kingston	(Durham/Madalene)
W S Ross	(Brisbane GS/St Catherine's)	M A Wainwright	(Arnold/Queens')
*T P Enevoldson	(RGS Newcastle/Brasenose)	S M Gill	(RGS Lancaster/Fitzwilliam)
M F Gargan	(St Peter's York/St Edmund Hall)	D R Walker	(RGS Lancaster/Downing)
N T Roberts	(Glenalmond/Jesus)	C W Biddell	(Christ's Hosp/Magdalene)
W E A Morrison	(Felsted/Oriel)	T J Allchurch	(Abbey HS/Downing)
A W Brooks	(Plymouth Coll/Hertford)	A J Macklin	(Felsted/St John's)
W D R Habergham	(Batley GS/Keble)	S F Glanvill	(Exeter/Pembroke)
P Baker	(Bettws CS Newport/St Edmund Hall		
replaced Jenkins			

Penalty Goals: Halliday (2), Webster

Try: Tyler
Penalty Goals: Rose (3)

Referee: Mr D I H Burnett

MATCH 100

8 December 1981, at Twickenham
Cambridge won by 3PG (9) to 2PG (6)

Oxford		Cambridge	
C J Millerchip	(K Henry VIII Coventry/Lincoln)	W M H Rose	(Loughborough GS/Magdalene)
A J Bibby	(St George's Vancouver/St Catherine's)	S J Cooke	(Stonyhurst/Magdalene)
S J Halliday	(Downside/St Benet's Hall)	R J Boyd-Moss	(Bedford/Magdalene)
P J Crowe	(Scots Coll Sydney/University)	A M J McGahey	(King's Taunton/Fitzwilliam)
D M Wyatt	(RGS Colchester/St Catherine's)	T S O'Brien	(Bradford GS/Jesus)
S Barnes	(Bassaleg/St Edmund Hall)	*G H Davies	(KE VI Stourbridge/Selwyn)
R S Luddington	(KCS Wimbledon/St Edmund Hall)	J C Cullen	(Christ's Hosp/Downing)
J G M Webster	(Uppingham/Oriel)	C J Kingston	(Durham/Magdalene)
A H Hobart	(The Minister Southwell/Exeter)	J N Johnson	(Bedford/Downing)
N J Herrod	(K Henry VIII Coventry/St John's)	S M Gill	(RGS Lancaster/Fitzwilliam)
C T Hugo-Hamman	(SA Coll School/Jesus)	D R Walker	(RGS Lancaster/Downing)
*N T Roberts	(Glenalmond/Jesus)	C W Biddell	(Christ's Hosp/Magdalene)
J P Searle	(King's Tynemouth/Hertford)	T J Allchurch	(Abbey HS/Downing)
A W Brooks	(Plymouth Coll/Hertford)	P M Lillington	(Fettes/Magdalene)
A Q Peck	(Truro/Exeter)	N J Bennett	(Richard Hale/Fitzwilliam)

Penalty Goals: Barnes (2)   *Penalty Goals*: Rose (3)

Referee: Mr C Norling

MATCH 101

7 December 1982, at Twickenham
Cambridge won by 3PG 1DG 2T (20) to 1G 1PG 1T (13)

Oxford		Cambridge	
H P MacNeill	(Dublin Univ/St Edmund Hall)	A K R Hampel	(Marlborough/Downing)
C J Millerchip	(K Henry VIII Coventry/Lincoln)	S T Smith	(K Henry VI Lichfield/Magdalene)
D J Coleman	(St Edward's Liverpool/University)	T S O'Brien	(Bradford GS/Jesus)
*P J Crowe	(Scots Coll Sydney/University)	R J Boyd-Moss	(Bedford/Magdalene)
C B Ewart	(St Edward's Oxford/St Edmund Hall)	M D Bailey	(Ipswich/Corpus Christi)
S Barnes	(Bassaleg/St Edmund Hall)	C R Andrew	(Barnard Castle/St John's)
R S Luddington	(KCS Wimbledon/St Edmund Hall)	J C Cullen	(Christ's Hosp/Downing)
N J Herrod	(K Henry VIII Coventry/St John's)	*C J Kingston	(Durham/Magdalene)
J P Webster	(Bradford GS/Queen's)	R A Murray	(Friary Grange/Trinity)
A Beare	(Haberdashers' Aske's/St Edmund Hall)	R C Bailey	(RGS Lancaster/Fitzwilliam)
C T Hugo-Hamman	(S A Coll School/Jesus)	S J W Attfield	(Windsor/St John's)
M F Gargan	(St Peter's York/St Edmund Hall)	P M Lillington	(Fettes/Magdalene)
J P Searle	(King's Tynemouth/Hertford)	D G Taylor	(Reed's/Magdalene)
A W Brooks	(Plymouth Coll/Hertford)	A J Macklin	(Felsted/St John's)
W D R Habergham	(Batley GS/Keble)	P J Horner	(Campbell Belfast/St Catharine's)

Tries: Luddington, Gargan   *Tries*: Smith, Bailey
Conversion: MacNeill   *Penalty Goals*: Andrew (3)
Penalty Goal: Barnes   *Dropped Goal*: Andrew

Referee: Mr D I H Burnett

MATCH 102

6 December 1983, at Twickenham
Cambridge won by 4PG 2T (20) to 3PG (9)

Oxford		Cambridge	
*H P MacNeill	(Dublin Univ/St Edmund Hall)	A W Martin	(Cardiff HS/St Edmund's House)
A C Findlay	(Marlborough/St Edmund Hall)	S T Smith	(K Henry VI Lichfield/Magdalene)
T S O'Brien	(Bradford GS/University)	T Paterson-Brown	(Glenalmond/Magdalene)
D J Coleman	(St Edward's Liverpool/University)	K G Simms	(West Park/Emmanuel)
P J Crowe	(Scots Coll Sydney/University)	*M D Bailey	(Ipswich/Corpus Christi)
S Barnes	(Bassaleg/St Edmund Hall)	C R Andrew	(Barnard Castle/St John's)
S B Pearson	(Uppingham/Trinity)	S N J Roberts	(Manchester GS/Christ's)
D J Mills	(Maritzburg Coll/St Catherine's)	R C Bailey	(RGS Lancaster/Fitzwilliam)
J P Webster	(Bradford GS/Queen's)	F J Timmons	(Wimbledon Coll/Magdalene)
N J Herrod	(K Henry VIII Coventry/St John's)	J D Bush	(Batley GS/Pembroke)
J B Thomson	(Collyers GS/Keble)	P David	(RGS Guildford/Trinity Hall)
J R H Rosier	(Haileybury/Keble)	C F Ewbank	(Felsted/St John's)
A S J McQuaid	(Bradford GS/Keble)	I R Morrison	(Glenalmond/Pembroke)
M F Gargan	(St Peter's York/St Edmund Hall)	J F Ellison	(St Peter's York/Corpus Christi)
R de R Morgan	(Christ Coll Brecon/Worcester)	A G Harper	(Sydney GS/Downing)

Penalty Goals: Barnes (3)

Tries: Bailey, Martin
Penalty Goals: Andrew (4)

Referee: Mr J A F Trigg

MATCH 103

11 December 1984, at Twickenham
Cambridge won by 4G 2T (32) to 2PG (6)

Oxford		Cambridge	
H P MacNeill	(Dublin Univ/St Edmund Hall)	A G Hastings	(Geo Watson's/Magdalene)
S J R Vessey	(Magdalen Oxford/Merton)	A W Martin	(Cardiff HS/St Edmund's House)
*T S O'Brien	(Bradford GS/University)	F J Clough	(St John Rigby/Magdalene)
J M Risman	(Wellington/St Edmund Hall)	K G Simms	(West Park/Emmanuel)
L R L Phillips	(Harrow/St John's)	*M D Bailey	(Ipswich/Corpus Christi)
C D Evans	(Y Pant/Jesus)	C R Andrew	(Barnard Castle/St John's)
S B Pearson	(Uppingham/Trinity)	R H Q B Moon	(Q Mary's GS Walsall/Magdalene)
D J Mills	(Cape Town Univ/St Catherine's)	R C Heginbotham	(Bedford/St John's)
J E Greenhalgh	(Sedbergh/Pembroke)	P Combe	(Marlborough/Magdalene)
A L Joyce	(Colston's/Keble)	P R Williamson	(Canford/Jesus)
N W MacDonald	(Cape Town Univ/University)	S J W Attfield	(Windsor/St John's)
A R Welsh	(Oundle/St Anne's)	S T O'Leary	(Plymouth Coll/Fitzwilliam)
T G R Marvin	(Radley/St Catherine's)	I R Morrison	(Glenalmond/Pembroke)
P M Simonet	(St Edward's Liverpool/Oriel)	J F Ellison	(St Peter's York/Corpus Christi)
D K Reed	(Pocklington/St Edmund Hall)	P A Green	(Kent College/Trinity Hall)

Penalty Goals: MacNeill (2)

Tries: Simms, Moon, Andrew, Hastings, Martin, Clough
Conversions: Andrew (4)

Referee: Mr L Prideaux

MATCH 104

10 December 1985, at Twickenham
Oxford won by 1PG 1T (7) to 2PG (6)

Oxford		Cambridge	
A P Kennedy	(Wallace H S / Keble)	*A G Hastings	(Geo Watson's / Magdalene)
S J R Vessey	(Magdalen C S Oxford / Merton)	A T Harriman	(Radley / Magdalene)
J M Risman	(Wellington / St Edmund Hall)	F J Clough	(St John Rigby / Magdalene)
R A Rydon	(Sherborne / Pembroke)	K G Simms	(West Park / Emmanuel)
S B Pearson	(Uppingham / Trinity)	K T Wyles	(Wymondham / Churchill)
A M Johnson	(Radley / St Catherine's)	M D Bailey	(Ipswich / Magdalene)
S N J Roberts	(Manchester GS / Exeter)	J M P C Turner	(Sherborne / Magdalene)
J M Dingemans	(Radley / Mansfield)	N J Herrod	(K Henry VIII Coventry / Clare Hall)
R I Glynn	(Leeds GS / St Edmund Hall)	P H Combe	(Marlborough / Magdalene)
T G Willis	(Wellington / St Edmund Hall)	T J L Borthwick	(Tonbridge / Magdalene)
*N W MacDonald	(Cape Town Univ / University)	W M C Stileman	(Wellington / Selwyn)
C Crane	(West Mon GS / St Edmund Hall)	S T O'Leary	(Plymouth Coll / Fitzwilliam)
T G R Marvin	(Radley / St Catherine's)	S R Kelly	(Richard Huish / Corpus Christi)
C P MacDonald	(Diocesan Coll / University)	T A Withyman	(Spalding GS / Emmanuel)
S J M Griffin	(Ch Coll Brecon / University)	P A Green	(Kent Coll / Trinity Hall)
N S M Pritchard replaced Glynn	(Durham Univ / St Edmund Hall)	D J Pierce replaced Harriman	(RGS Newcastle / St John's)

Try: C P MacDonald
Penalty Goal: Kennedy

Penalty Goals: Hastings (2)

Referee: Mr R C Quittenton

MATCH 105

9 December 1986, at Twickenham
Oxford won by 3PG 2DG (15) to 1PG 1DG 1T (10)

Oxford		Cambridge	
J M Risman	(Wellington / St Edmund Hall)	M D C Thomas	(Gowerton / Magdalene)
S J R Vessey	(Magdelen C S Oxford / Green)	T W D Isaac	(Welbeck Coll / Churchill)
R A Rydon	(Sherborne / Pembroke)	K T Wyles	(Wymondham / Trinity Hall)
B J Mullin	(Blackrock / University)	*F J Clough	(Sir John Rigby / Magdalene)
A L Duthie	(Phillip, Canberra / Balliol)	C Oti	(Millfield / St Edmund's)
A M Johnson	(Radley / St Catherine's)	T M Lord	(Bedford Modern / Christ's)
S N J Roberts	(Manchester GS / Exeter)	A Cushing	(Magdalen Coll Brackley / Magdalene)
T G Willis	(Wellington / St Edmund Hall)	N J Herrod	(K Henry VIII Coventry / Clare)
J Chislett	(Plymouth / Keble)	B W Gilchrist	(Sevenoaks / Magdalene)
S M Ferguson	(R B A I / St Edmund Hall)	N Hunt	(Hutton GS / Selwyn)
C M Crane	(West Monmouth GS / St Edmund Hall)	A R Hobbs	(Worth / Magdalene)
C P MacDonald	(Diocesan Coll / University)	N P Topping	(RGS High Wycombe / St John's)
W J Calcraft	(Scots Coll Sydney / Brasenose)	S R Kelly	(Richard Huis / Corpus Christi)
N S McBain	(Ampleforth / St Anne's)	T A Withyman	(Spalding GS / Emmanuel)
*S J M Griffin	(Ch Coll Brecon / University)	R I Wainwright	(Glenalmond / Magdalene)

Penalty Goals: Risman (3)
Dropped Goals: Johnson (2)

Try: Oti
Penalty Goal: Thomas
Dropped Goal: Wyles

Referee: Mr F A Howard

8 December 1987, at Twickenham
Cambridge won by 1DG 3T (15) to 2PG 1T (10)

Oxford		Cambridge	
R H Egerton	(Sydney Univ / University)	P L Beard	(Berkhamsted / St John's)
S J R Vessey	(Magdalen CS Oxford / Green)	M D C Thomas	(Gowerton / Magdalene)
B J Mullin	(Blackrock / University)	M R Hall	(Brynteg CS / Wolfson)
A L Duthie	(Phillip, Canberra / Balliol)	F J Clough	(Sir John Rigby / Magdalene)
A G D Furnival	(Millfield / Christ Church)	C Oti	(Millfield / St Edmund's)
A M Johnson	(Radley / St Catherine's)	A J Sutton	(Llanishen HS / Magdalene)
D E Kirk	(Otago Univ / Worcester)	M E Hancock	(Heversham GS / Hughes Hall)
V E Ubogu	(W Buckland / St Anne's)	N J Herrod	(K Henry VIII Coventry / Clare)
J Chislett	(Plymouth / Keble)	B W Gilchrist	(Sevenoaks / Magdalene)
N C Peacock	(Nunthorpe GS / St Edmund Hall)	J Freeman	(Warwick / St John's)
C M Crane	(West Monmouth GS / St Edmund Hall)	A R Hobbs	(Worth / Magdalene)
W Campbell	(Queensland Univ / St Catherine's)	N P Topping	(RGS High Wycombe / St John's)
*W J Calcraft	(Scots Coll Sydney / Brasenose)	*S R Kelly	(Richard Huish / Corpus Christi)
N S McBain	(Ampleforth / St Anne's)	C B Vyvyan	(Downside / Wolfson)
A J Rolfe	(Eton / St Edmund Hall)	R I Wainwright	(Glenalmond / Magdalene)
		M A Risman	(Wellington / Emanuel)
		replaced Oti	

Try: Kirk
Penalty Goals: Johnson (2)

Tries: Oti (2), Thomas
Dropped Goal: Hancock

Referee: Mr R C Quittenton

SCORING RECORDS

Biggest winning points margin

32	Oxford in 1909-10
30	Cambridge in 1925-26

Most points in a match

By a team

35	Oxford in 1909-10
34	Cambridge in 1975-76
33	Cambridge in 1925-26
32	Cambridge in 1984-85
30	Cambridge in 1926-27

By a player

19	A J Hignell	Cambridge	1975-76
17	J C Robbie	Cambridge	1978-79
15	R W Poulton	Oxford	1909-10
15	P N Quinnen	Oxford	1974-75
12	H Martin	Oxford	1909-10
12	S M Lewis	Oxford	1973-74
12	A J Hignell	Cambridge	1974-75
12	C R Andrew	Cambridge	1982-83
12	C R Andrew	Cambridge	1983-84
12	C R Andrew	Cambridge	1984-85
11	J P Horrocks-Taylor	Cambridge	1956-57
11	A J Hignell	Cambridge	1976-77

Most tries in a match

By a team

9	Oxford in 1909-10
9	Cambridge in 1925-26
8	Cambridge in 1926-27
7	Oxford in 1883-84
6	Cambridge in 1899-1900
6	Cambridge in 1934-35
6	Cambridge in 1984-85

By a player

5	R W Poulton	Oxford	1909-10
4	H Martin	Oxford	1909-10
3	G C Wade	Oxford	1883-84
3	H Martin	Oxford	1907-08
3	W P Geen	Oxford	1910-11
3	B L Jacot	Oxford	1920-21
3	R H Hamilton-Wickes	Cambridge	1922-23
3	Sir T G Devitt	Cambridge	1925-26
3	R W Smeddle	Cambridge	1928-29
3	K C Fyfe	Cambridge	1934-35

Most conversions in a match

By a team

4	Oxford in 1909-10
4	Oxford in 1910-11
4	Cambridge in 1984-85

By a player

4	F H Turner	Oxford	1910-11
4	C R Andrew	Cambridge	1984-85
3	C W Berry	Oxford	1883-84
3	C W Berry	Oxford	1884-85
3	E Fearenside	Oxford	1903-04
3	H F P Hearson	Cambridge	1904-05
3	L M MacLeod	Cambridge	1905-06

Most dropped goals in a match

By a team

2	Oxford in 1986-87

By a player

2	A M Johnson	Oxford	1986-87

Most penalty goals in a match

By a team

5	Oxford in 1974-75
5	Cambridge in 1975-76
4	Oxford in 1977-78
4	Cambridge in 1983-84

By a player

5	P N Quinnen	Oxford	1974-75
5	A J Hignell	Cambridge	1975-76
4	A J Watkinson	Oxford	1977-78
4	C R Andrew	Cambridge	1983-84

Most goals from mark in a match

By a team

1	Cambridge in 1964-65

By a player

1	J R W Harvey	Cambridge	1964-65

The following tables of Varsity Match players appear courtesy of *Rothmans Rugby Yearbook*.

VARSITY MATCH PLAYERS

Each year indicates a separate appearance, and refers to the first half of the season. Thus 1879 refers to the match played in the 1879-80 season

OXFORD

Abbott, J S	1954-55	Boobbyer, B	1949-50-51	Carroll, B M	1970-71
Abell, G E B	1923-24-25-26	Booker, J L	1880	Carroll, P R	1968-69-70
Adamson, J A	1928-29-31	Booth, J L	1956	Carter, C R	1885
Adcock, J R L	1961	Bos, F H ten	1958-59-60	Cartwright, V H	1901-02-03-04
Aitken, G G	1922-24	Boswell, J D	1885-86-87	Cass, T	1961
Aldridge, J E	1888	Botfield, A S G	1871	Castens, H H	1886-87
Alexander, H	1897-98	Botting, I J	1949-50	Cattell, R H B	1893
Alexander, P C	1930	Bourdillon, H	1873-74-75	Cave, H W	1881
Allaway, R C P	1953-54-55	Bourns, C	1903	Cawkwell, G L	1946-47
Allen, C P	1881-82-83	Bowers, J B	1932-34	Chadwick, A J	1898-99
Allen, T	1909	Boyce, A W	1952-53	Chambers, J C	1921
Allen, W C	1910	Boyd, A de H	1924	Champain, F H B	1897-98-99
Allison, M G	1955	Boyd, E F	1912	Champneys, F W	1874-75-76
Almond, R G P	1937	Boyle, D S	1967-68-69	Charles, A E S	1932
Ashby, C J	1973	Brace, D O	1955-56	Cheesman, W I	1910-11
Asher, A G G	1881-82-83-84	Bradby, G F	1882-85	Cheyne, H	1903-04
Asquith, P R	1974	Bradford, C C	1887	Chislett, J	1986-87
Atkinson, C C	1876	Branfoot, E P	1878-79	Cholmondeley, F G	1871-73
		Bray, C N	1979	Christopherson, P	1886-87-88
Back, A	1878	Bremridge, H	1876-77	Clark, R B	1978-79
Badenoch, D F	1971	Brett, J A	1935-36-37	Clarke, E J D	1973
Baden-Powell, F S	1873	Brett, P V	1978	Clarke, I A	1913
Baggaley, J C	1953-54	Brewer, R J	1965	Clauss, P R	1889-90-91
Bain, D McL	1910-11-12-13	Brewer, T J	1951	Clements, B S	1975
Bainbrigge, J H	1874-76-77	Bridge, D J W	1946-47-48	Cleveland, C R	1885-86
Baird, J S	1966-67	Brierley, H	1871	Cochran, P C	1889-91
Baiss, R S H	1894-95	Britton, R B	1963-64	Cohen, B A	1884
Baker, C D	1891-93	Bromet, W E	1889	Coker, J B H	1965
Baker, D G S	1951-52	Brooks, A W	1980-81-82	Cole, B W	1945
Baker, E M	1893-94-95-96	Brooks, M J	1873	Coleman, D J	1982-83
Baker, P	1980 (R)	Brooks, W	1872	Coles, D G G	1937-38
Baker, R T	1968	Broster, L R	1912	Coles, P	1884-85-86
Balfour, E R	1893-94-95	Broughton, R C	1965	Coles, S C	1954-56-57
Bannerman, J MacD	1927-28	Brown, L G	1910-11-12	Collingwood, J A	1961-62
Barker, A C	1966-67	Brunskill, R F	1873-74	Colville, A H	1892-93
Barnes, S	1981-82-83	Bryan, T A	1975-76-77	Conway-Rees, J	1891-92-93
Barr, D C A	1980	Bryer, L W	1953	Cooke, J L	1968-69
Barry, C E	1897-98-99	Buchanan, F G	1909-10	Cooke, P	1936-37
Barry, D M	1968-69-70	Bucknall, A L	1965-66	Cooke, W R	1976
Barwick, W M	1880-81	Budge, K J	1977-78-79	Cookson, G H F	1891-92
Bass, R G	1961	Budworth, R T D	1887-88-89	Cooper, A H	1951
Batchelor, T B	1906	Bullard, G L	1950-51	Cooper, M McG	1934-35-36
Bateson, H D	1874-75-77	Bullock, H	1910-11	Cooper, R A	1937
Baxter, T J	1958-59	Bulpett, C W L	1871	Cooper, R M	1946
Beamish, S H	1971	Burnet, P J	1960	Cornish, W H	1876
Beare, A	1982	Burrow, K C	1933	Couper, T	1899-1900
Bedford, T P	1965-66-67	Burse, R M	1974	Court, E D	1882-83
Behn, A R	1968-69	Bush, A	1934	Cousins, F C	1885-86
Bell, D L	1970	Bussell, J G	1903-04	Coutts, I D F	1951
Benson, E T	1928	Butcher, W M	1954	Coventry, R G T	1889-90-91
Bentley, P J	1960	Butler, F E R	1959-60	Cowen, T J	1938
Berkley, W V	1924-25-26	Button, E L	1936	Cowlishaw, F I	1890-91
Berry, C W	1883-84	Byers, R M	1926	Cox, G V	1878
Bettington, R H B	1920-22			Cozens-Hardy, B	1904-05-06
Bevan, J H	1946	Caccia H A	1926	Crabbie, J E	1898-99-1900-01
Bibby, A J	1980-81	Cadell, P R	1890	Craig, F J R	1963-64-65
Binham, P A	1971	Cairns, A G	1899-1900-01	Crane, C M	1985-86-87
Birrell, H B	1953	Calcraft, W J	1986-87	Cranmer, P	1933-34
Black, B H	1929	Campbell, E	1919-20-21	Crawfurd, J W F A	1900
Blair, A S	1884	Campbell, W	1987	Creese, N A H	1951
Blencowe, L C	1907-08	Cannell, L B	1948-49-50	Cridlan, A G	1928-29-30
Bloxham, C T	1934-35-36-37	Cardale, C F	1929-30	Croker, J R	1966-67
Blyth, P H	1885-86	Carey, G M	1891-92-94	Crole, G B	1913-19
Bolton, W H	1873-74-75	Carey, W J	1894-95-96-97	Cronje, S N	1907-08
Bonham-Carter, E	1890-91	Carlyon, H B	1871	Crosse, C W	1874

Name	Years	Name	Years	Name	Years
Crowe, P J	1981-82-83	Farquharson, J C L	1903	Hammond, C E L	1899-1900
Crump, L M	1896	Fearenside, E	1903	Hands, K C M	1912
Cuff, T W	1945	Fellows-Smith, J P	1953-54	Hands, P A M	1910
Cunningham, G	1907-08-09	Ferguson, S M	1986	Hands, R H M	1908-09
Currie, J D	1954-55-56-57	Fergusson, E A J	1952-53	Harcourt, A B	1945-46
Curry, J A H	1961	Field, H	1873	Harding, R F	1935
Curtis, A B	1949	Filby, L L	1960	Harper, C H	1897-98
		Fildes, D G	1922-25	Harrison, C F	1873-74-75
Dalby, C	1923	Finch, C J	1978	Hartley, J C	1894-95-96
Davey, P	1967	Findlay, A C	1983	Harvey, R C M	1886
Davey, R A E	1972	Fisher, C D C	1902	Harvard, W T	1919
David, A M	1921-22	Fisher, S J	1976	Hawkesworth, C J	1970-71-72
Davies, D B	1905-06-07	Fleming, C J N	1887-88-89-90	Heal, M G	1971
Davies, D E	1951	Flemmer, W K	1906	Hearn, R D	1964
Davies, D M	1958-59-60	Fletcher, K R	1871	Heath, A H	1875-77-78-79
Davies, J A B	1920	Fletcher, W R B	1871-73-74	Hefer, W J	1949-50
Davies, L L J	1927	Forman, J	1875-76	Henderson, J H	1952
Davies, R	1969	Forsayth, H H	1920-21	Henderson, N F	1886
Davies, R H	1955-56-57	Forster, F M McL	1937	Henley, W E	1929-30-31
Davies, S J T	1972-73	Fowler, H	1877-78	Heppenstall, A F	1926-27
Davies, W G	1977	Francis, C K	1871	Herring, D G	1909
Davis, R A	1974-75	Francis, D G	1919	Herrod, N J	1981-82-83
Davis, T M E	1978-79-80	Franklin, H W F	1923	Higham, J R S	1959
Dawkins, P M	1959-60-61	Fraser, E C	1872-73-74-75	Hillard, R J	1923-24
Deacon, E A	1871-72	Freakes, H D	1936-37-38	Hiller, R	1965
De Winton, R F C	1888-89-90	Furnival, A G D	1987	Hines, G W	1961-62
Dew, C J	1978			Hirst, E T	1877-78-79
Diamond, A J	1957	Gabitass, J R	1965-66	Hoadley, A A	1905-06
Dickson, M R	1903	Gaisford, R B	1876	Hoare, A H M	1956-57
Dickson, W M	1912	Galbraith, J H	1947	Hobart, A H	1981
Diggle, P R	1908-09	Game, W H	1872-73-74	Hockley, M	1975
Dingemans, J M	1985	Gardner, C J	1905-06	Hodges, H A	1905-06-07-08
Dingle, A J	1911	Gardner, J W	1871	Hodgson, F W	1881
Disney, P C W	1935	Gargan, M F	1980-82-83	Hofmeyr, K de J	1927
Dixon, P J	1967-68-69-70	Gedge, H T S	1893	Hofmeyr, M B	1948-49-50
Dobson, D D	1899-1900-01	Geen, W P	1910-11-12	Hofmeyr, S J	1928-29-30
Donald, D G	1911-12-13	Gent, G N	1949	Hofmeyr, S M	1979
Donaldson, C L	1895	German, G J	1922	Hollis, G	1938
Donaldson, D W	1893	Gibson, A G	1894-95	Holroyd, C A	1966
Donaldson, W P	1892-93-94	Gibson, C H	1927	Honey, R	1909-10
Donnelly, M P	1946	Gill, R D	1947-48	Hood, R K	1976
Donovan, T J	1971	Gilmour, A	1911	Hoolahan, R M C	1976-77-78
Douglas, A I	1970-71	Gilray, C M	1908-09	Hopkins, K M	1977
Dorman, J M A	1964	Gilthorpe, C G	1946-47	Hordern, P C	1928
Dowson, A O	1896	Glover, J	1959-60	Horne, E C	1975-76-77
Druitt, W A H	1929-30-31	Glover, T R	1973-74	Hoskin, W W	1904-05-06-07
Dryburgh, D J W	1926	Glubb, J M	1887	Houston, K J	1964
Drysdale, D	1925	Glynn, R I	1985	Hovde, F L	1931
Dunbar, I T	1970-71-73	Gooding, W F	1872-73	Howard, A	1907
Duncan, D D	1919-20	Goold, A N	1927	Howard, P D	1929-30
Dunn, L B	1897	Gordon, P F C	1970	Howe-Browne, N R F G	1905-06
Duthie, A L	1986-87	Gotley, A L H	1909	Hoyer-Millar, G C	1952
		Gould, E J H	1963-64-65-66	Hughes, H M	1935-36
Eberle, G S J F	1901-02	Grant, A D	1922	Hughes, R A	1978
Edgell, E M R	1871-73	Grant, A H	1892	Hugo-Hamman, C T	1981-82
Edmiston, J H F	1926-27	Green, R	1948-49-50	Hume, J W G	1927-28
Edmonds, J N	1978	Greenhalgh, J E	1984	Humfrey, L C	1892-93
Egerton, R H	1987	Gregson, R E S	1903	Humphrey, M W	1923
Ellis, A W	1975	Grellet, R C	1899-1900-01-02	Hunt, R W	1890
Elwes, A C	1892-93	Grenfell, W T	1888	Hunter, R S	1888-89
Emms, D A	1949-50	Grieve, C F	1934-35-36	Hutchinson, J M	1972-73
Enevoldson, T P	1976-77-78-79-80	Griffin, S J M	1985-86	Hutchison, R O	1902
Evans, A H	1877-78	Griffith, C J L	1950-51-52		
Evans, C D	1984	Griffiths, D A	1969-70	Ilett, N L	1947
Evans, C H	1919-20	Griffiths, R L	1969	Inglis, R E	1883-84
Evans, D P	1959	Grischotti, W	1899	Irwin, H	1880
Evans, D W	1887-88	Gubb, T W	1926-27-28-29	Isherwood, F W	1871
Evanson, A M	1880-81	Guy, J C	1934		
Evers, C P	1897-98	Gush, E P	1963	Jackson, K L T	1932-33
Evers, R W	1909			Jackson, W M	1938
Ewart, C B	1982	Habergham, W D R	1980-82	Jacob, G O	1878-79
Ewing, M H O	1886	Hadman, W G	1964-65-66	Jacob, H P	1923-24-25
		Hall, J D	1885-86	Jacot, B L	1920
Faktor, S J	1977	Halliday, S J	1979-80-81	James, A I	1934
Fallon, T J	1953-55	Hamilton, C W	1872	James, J	1875-76-77

James, S	1970-71	Light, B	1977
James, S J B	1966	Lindsay, G C	1882-83-84-85
Jenkin, J M	1952	Littlechild, E J F	1972
Jenkins, A	1971	Littlewood, R B	1893
Jenkins, O	1913-19	Lloyd, E A	1964-65-66
Jenkins, P	1980	Lloyd, J E	1872-74
Jenkins, V G J	1930-31-32	Lloyd, R	1908
Jesson, D	1957-58-59	Lombard, L T	1956-57-58
Johnson, A M	1985-86-87	Longdon, J S	1889
Johnson, P M	1968-70	Lorraine, H D B	1932-33-34
Johnson, T F	1875	Loudoun-Shand, E G	1913-19
Johnstone, P G	1952-53-54	Love, R D	1972
Jones, D R R	1972	Low, R C S	1933
Jones, D K	1963	Luce, F M	1899-1900
Jones, G S A	1896	Luddington, R S	1980-81-82
Jones, I C	1962-63-64	Lusty, W	1927
Jones, K W J	1931-32	Luyt, R E	1938
Jones, R O P	1969-70-71	Lyle, A M P	1902-04-05
Jones, T O	1898		
Jones, T W	1978-79	McBain, N S	1986-87
Jones, V W	1954	McCanlis, M A	1926-27
Joyce, A L	1984	McClure, R N	1973
Jupp, H B	1873	MacDonald, C P	1985-86
		MacDonald, D A	1975-76
Kay, A R	1889-90-91	MacDonald, D S M	1974-75-76
Kay, D C	1972-73	MacDonald, G E	1922
Kelly, H M	1932	MacDonald, N L	1926
Kendall-Carpenter, J MacG K	1948-49-50	MacDonald, N W	1984-85
Kennedy, A P	1985	MacEwen, G L	1895
Kennedy, N	1901	McFarland, P R E	1967
Kennedy, W D	1904	MacGibbon, R R	1930-31
Kent, C P	1972-73-74-75	McGlashan, J R C	1945
Kent, P C	1970	McGrath, N F	1934-35-36
Kershaw, F	1898-99-1900-01	MacGregor, A	1871
Key, K J	1885-86	Mackenzie, A O M	1880-81
Kindersley, R S	1882-83	Mackenzie, D W	1974
King, B B H	1963	Mackenzie, F J C	1882-83
King, P E	1975	Mackintosh, C E W C	1925
King, T W	1929	MacLachlan, L P	1953
Kininmonth, P W	1947-48	MacLachlan, N	1879-80
Kirk, D E	1987	Macmillan, M	1876
Kitson, J A	1895	McNeill, A	1884
Kittermaster, H J	1922-24	MacNeill, H P	1982-83-84
Kitto, R C M	1884-85-86-87	McPartlin, J J	1960-61-62
Knight, R L	1879	Macpherson G P S	1922-23-24
Knott, F H	1910-11-12-13	Macpherson, N M S	1928
Koe, A P	1886	McQuaid, A S J	1983
Kyrke, G V	1902-03	McShane, J M S	1933-35
Kyrke-Smith, P St L	1973-74-75 (R)	Maddock, W P	1972
		Mallalieu, J P W	1927
Lagden, R O	1909-10-11	Mallett, N V H	1979
Laidlaw, C R	1968-69	Marshall, H P	1921
Lamb, R H	1962-63-64	Marshall, R M	1936-37-38
Lamport, N K	1930-31-32	Martin, H	1907-08-09
Landale, D F	1925-26	Marvin, T G R	1984-85
Lane, R O B	1887-88-89	Mather, E G S	1933
Langley, P J	1949	Maxwell-Hyslop, J E	1920-21-22
Latham, H E	1907	Mayhew, P K	1937
Latter, A	1892	Mead, B D	1972-73
Law, A F	1875	Meadows, H J	1948
Lawrence, W S	1954-56	Merivale, G M	1874
Lawrie, A A	1903-05	Merriam, L P B	1913
Lawton, T	1921-22-23	Michell, A T	1871-72-73-74
Lee, F H	1874-75-76-77	Millerchip, C J	1981-82
Lee, J W	1973-74	Mills, D J	1983-84
Lee, R J	1972	Milton, N W	1905-06-07
Legge, D	1897	Minns, P C	1930-31-32
Lennox-Cook, J M	1945	Mitchell, M D	1977
Leslie, C F H	1880-81	Moberly, W O	1871-72-73
Leslie, R E	1954	Moir, M J P	1977
Leslie-Jones, F A	1894-95-96	Molohan, M J B	1928
Lewin, A J A	1962-63	Monteath, J G	1912
Lewis, A K	1888	Montgomery, J R	1958
Lewis, D J	1950	Moorcroft, E K	1966
Lewis, S M	1973	Moore, E J	1882-83

Moore, H B	1912-13
Moore, H R	1956
Moore, P B C	1945-46
Moresby-White, J M	1913-19
Morgan, A K	1963-64
Morgan, D J	1979
Morgan, F	1888
Morgan, R de R	1983
Morris, E G	1904
Morrison, W E A	1979-80
Mortimer, L	1892
Moubray, J J	1876-77-78
Muller, H	1938
Mullin, B J	1986-87
Mullins, R C	1894
Mulvey, R S	1968
Munro, P	1903-04-05
Murray, G C	1959
Nash, E H	1874-75
Nelson, T A	1897-98
Nesbitt, J V	1904-05
Neser, V H	1919-20
Neville, T B	1971-72
Newman, A P	1973
Newman, S C	1946-47
Newton, H F	1895-96-97
Newton, P A	1879-80
Newton-Thompson, J O	1945-46
Nicholas, P L	1897-98-99
Nicholson, E S	1931-32-33-34
North, E G H	1888-89-90
Novis, A L	1927
Nunn, J A	1925-26
Obolensky, A	1935-37
O'Brien, T S	1983-84
O'Connor, A	1958
Odgers, W B	1901-02
Orpen, L J J	1898
Osborn, E C	1969
Osborne, S H	1900-01-02
Osler, S G	1931
Owen-Smith, H G O	1932-33
Page, H V	1884-85
Painter, P A	1967
Palmer, M S	1960
Parker, L	1905
Parker, T	1888
Parkin, W H	1890
Paterson, A M	1889-90
Patterson, A R	1879-80-81
Patterson, L R	1886-87
Payne, C M	1960
Peacock, M B	1880
Peacock, M F	1932-33
Peacock, N C	1987
Peake, H W	1871
Pearce, J K	1945
Pearson, S B	1983-84-85
Pearson, T S	1871
Peat, W H	1898
Peck, A Q	1981
Pennington, H H	1937-38
Percival, L J	1889-91
Percy, H R G	1936-38
Pether, S	1938
Phillips, C	1876-77-78-79
Phillips, E L	1933
Phillips, L R L	1984
Phillips, M S	1956-57-58-59
Phillips, P C	1938
Phillips, R H	1966-67-68
Pienaar, J H	1933-34-35

Pitman, I J	1921	Sachs, D M	1962
Plant, W I	1958	Sampson, D H	1945
Pleydell-Bouverie, Hon B	1923	Sampson, H F	1910-11
Plumbridge, R A	1954-55-56	Sanctuary, C F S	1879-80
Podmore, G	1872	Sandford, J R P	1902-03
Pollard, D	1952	Saunders, C J	1951
Poole, F O	1891-92-93-94	Sawtell, P R	1972
Poulton, R W	1909-10-11	Sayer, J	1871
Prescott, A E C	1928	Sayer, J B	1887
Prescott, R E	1932	Scholefield, B G	1920-21
Preston, B W	1925	Scott, J S M	1957-58
Price, H L	1920-21	Searle, J P	1981-82
Price, V R	1919-20-21	Seccombe, L S	1925
Pritchard, N S M	1985 (R)	Selby, E	1891
Prodger, J A	1955	Sexton, C M	1976
		Seymour, T M	1971-73
Quinnen, P N	1974-75	Shacksnovis, A	1922-23
Quist-Arcton, E A K	1978-79	Sharp, H S	1910-11
		Sharp, R A W	1959·60-61
Rahmatallah, F J	1976	Sharp, R G	1919
Ramsay, A W	1952-53	Shaw, C	1974-75
Ramsden, J E	1945	Shearman, M	1878-79
Raphael, J E	1901-02-03-04	Sheffield, R W	1873-74
Rashleigh, W	1887-88	Sheil, A G R	1958
Ravenscroft, J	1877-78	Shillito, G V	1930
Raymond, R L	1924	Sidgwick, A	1872
Rayner-Wood, A C	1895-96	Siepmann, C A	1921
Read, R F	1965	Silk, N	1961-62-63
Reed, D K	1984	Sim, A C	1876
Reeler, I L	1955-56	Simmie, M S	1965-66
Rees, H	1930	Simonet, P M	1984
Rees, H J V	1913	Simpson, E P	1887
Rees, P S	1974-75-78	Simpson, H B	1920
Rees-Jones, G R	1933-34-35	Skipper, D J	1952
Reid, C J	1896	Slater, N T	1960
Reid, G A	1935-36	Sloan, T	1908
Reid, N	1912-13	Sloane, A D	1902
Renwick, W N	1936-37	Small, H D	1949-50
Rice-Evans, W	1890	Smith, A R	1894-95-96-97
Richards, C A L	1932	Smith, I S	1923
Richards, S B	1962	Smith, J A	1892-93
Richardson, J V	1925	Smith, M J K	1954-55
Richardson, W R	1881	Southee, E A	1913
Rigby, J P	1955-56	Speed, R R	1967-68-69
Rimmer, L I	1958	Spence, K M	1951-52
Risman, J M	1984-85-86	Spencer, B L	1960
Rittson-Thomas, G C	1949-50	Spragg, F F	1926
Robbins, P G D	1954-55-56-57	Springman, P	1877-78
Roberts, G D	1907-08	Squire, W H S	1882-83-84
Roberts, M G	1968	Stagg, P K	1961-62
Roberts, N T	1979-80-81	Stafford, P M W	1961-62
Roberts, S N J	1985-86	Starmer-Smith, N C	1965-66
Roberts, W	1928-29-30-31	Steel, J J	1953
Robertson, A M	1903	Steinthal, F E	1906
Robertson, J W	1921	Stevens, D T	1959
Robertson, M A	1894-96	Stewart, A	1947-48
Robinson, D A B	1952-53	Stewart, W B	1892
Robinson, R G	1976-77	Steyn, S S L	1911-12
Robson, M	1929	Still, E R	1871-73
Rogers, W L Y	1898-1900	Stobie, A M	1945
Rolfe, A J	1987	Stobie, W D K	1947
Roos, G D	1936	Stone, T	1897
Rosier, J R H	1983	Stoneman, B M	1962
Ross, W S	1980	Stoop, A D	1902-03-04
Rotherham, A	1882-83-84	Strand-Jones, J	1899-1900-01
Roughead, W N	1924-25-26	Stratton, J W	1897
Rousseau, W P	1929	Strong, E L	1881-83
Row, A W L	1921	Strong, W I N	1924-25
Rowley, J V D'A	1929	Stuart-Watson, J L	1935
Rucker, R W	1874-76	Summerskill, W H J	1945
Rudd, E L	1963-64	Surtees, E A	1885
Russell, H	1872-73-74-75	Sutherland, I W	1938
Russell, J H	1929	Sutherland, J G B	1885
Russell-Roberts, F D	1931	Sutton, M A	1945-46
Rydon, R A	1985-86	Swan, M W	1957

Swanston, J F A	1897-98-99-1900
Swanzy, A J	1901-02
Swarbrick, D W	1946-47-48
Swayne, D H	1930-31
Sweatman, E A	1927
Taberer, H M	1892
Tahanay, M P	1945
Tanner, T L	1931
Tarr, F N	1907-08-09
Tatham, W M	1881-82-83
Taylor, E G	1926-27-28
Taylor, J A	1974
Terry, H F	1900-01
Theron, T P	1923
Thomas, A C	1979
Thomas, T R	1938
Thomas, W E	1911-12
Thomas, W L	1893-94
Thomson, B E	1951-52
Thomson, C	1896
Thomson, F W	1912-13
Thomson, J B	1983
Thomson, W J	1895-96
Thorburn, C W	1964
Thorniley-Walker, M J	1967
Tongue, P K	1975
Torry, P J	1968-69
Travers, B H	1946-47
Tristram, H B	1882-83-84
Troup, D S	1928
Tudor, H A	1878-79-80-81
Turcan, H H	1928
Turner, A B	1884
Turner, F H	1908-09-10
Ubogu, V E	1987
Unwin, G T	1894-95-96
Valentine, A C	1923-24-25
Van Der Riet, E F	1920-21
Van Ryneveld, A J	1946-47-48
Van Ryneveld, C B	1947-48-49
Vassall, H	1879-80-81-82
Vassall, H H	1906-07-08
Vecqueray, A H	1877-78
Vecqueray, G C	1873
Vessey, S J R	1984-85-86-87
Vidal, R W S	1872
Vincent, A N	1948-49
Wade, C G	1882-83-84
Waide, S L	1932
Wake, H B L	1922
Wakefield, W H	1891-92
Wakelin, W S	1964
Waldock, F A	1919
Waldock, H F	1919-20
Waldron, O C	1965-67
Walford, M M	1935-36-37
Walker, A	1880
Walker, J C	1955
Walker, J G	1879-80-81
Walker, M	1950-51
Wall, T W	1875-76-77
Wallace, A C	1922-23-24-25
Walton, E J	1900-01
Ward, J M	1972
Ware, M A	1961-62
Warr, A L	1933-34
Waterman, J S	1974
Wates, C S	1961
Watkins, L	1879
Watkinson, A F	1977-78
Watson, P W	1954-55

Watt, K A	1976	Williams, C D	1945	Winn, R R	1953
Watts, I H	1937-38	Williams, J R	1969	Witney, N K J	1970-71
Watts, L D	1957-58	Williamson, A C	1913	Wix, R S	1904-05-06-07
Webster, J G M	1980-81	Williamson, R H	1906-07-08	Wood, A E	1904
Webster, J P	1982-83	Willis, D C	1975-/6-77	Wood, D E	1952-53
Welsh, A R	1984	Willis, T G	1985-86	Wood, G F	1919
Wesche, V V G	1924	Wilson, C T M	1948	Woodhead, P G	1974
Weston B A G	1957	Wilson, D B	1874	Woodrow, D K	1978-79-80
Weston, J W	1871	Wilson, G A	1946-48	Wooldridge, C S	1882
White, G L	1976-77	Wilson, J	1967-68	Wordsworth, C R	1922-23-24
White, N T	1905-06	Wilson, J H G	1888-89-90	Wordsworth, C W	1902
Whyte, A G D	1963	Wilson, N G C	1967	Wordsworth, J R	1885
Whyte, D J	1963	Wilson, R W	1956	Wray, M O	1933-34
Wilcock, R M	1962	Wilson, S	1963-64	Wyatt, D M	1981
Wilcock, S H	1957-58-59	Wilson, S E	1890	Wydell, H A	1951
Willcox, J G	1959-60-61-62	Wilson, W G	1887	Wynter, E C C	1947
Wilkinson, J V S	1904	Wimperis, E J	1951		
Wilkinson, W E	1891	Winn, C E	1950	Young, J R C	1957-58

CAMBRIDGE

Aarvold, C D	1925-26-27-28	Beer, I D S	1952-53-54	Bull, H A	1874-75
Ackford, P J	1979	Bell, R W	1897-98-99	Bunting, W L	1894-95
Adams, G C A	1929	Bell, S P	1894-95-96	Burt-Marshall, J	1905
Adams, H F S	1884-85	Bennett, G M	1897-98	Burton, B C	1882-83
Agnew, C M	1875-76	Bennett, N J	1981	Bush, J D	1983
Agnew, G W	1871-72-73	Benthall, E C	1912	Bussey, W M	1960-61-62
Agnew, W L	1876-77-78	Beringer, F R	1951-52	Butler, E T	1976-77-78
Albright, G S	1877	Beringer, G G	1975-76		
Alderson, F H R	1887-88	Berman, J V	1966	Campbell, D A	1936
Alexander, E P	1884-85-86	Berry, S P	1971	Campbell, H H	1946
Alexander, J W	1905-06	Bevan, G A J	1951	Campbell, J A	1897-98-99
Allan, C J	1962	Bevan, J A	1877-80	Campbell, J D	1927
Allan, J L F	1956	Bevan, W	1887	Campbell, J W	1973-74
Allen, A D	1925-26-27	Biddell, C W	1980-81	Campbell, R C C	1907
Allen, D B	1975	Biggar, M A	1971	Candler, P L	1934
Allen, J	1875-76	Bird, D R J	1958-59	Cangley, B T G	1946
Allchurch, T J	1980-81	Birdwood, C R B	1932	Carey, G V	1907-08
Anderson, W T	1931-32	Bishop, C C	1925	Carpmael, W P	1885
Andrew, C R	1982-83-84	Black, M A	1897-98	Carris, H E	1929
Anthony, A J	1967	Blair, P C B	1910-11-12-13	Carter, C P	1965
Archer, G M D	1950-51	Blake, W H	1875	Cave, J W	1887-88
Arthur, T G	1962	Boggon, R P	1956	Cave, W T C	1902-03-04
Ashcroft, A H	1908-09	Bole, E	1945-46-47	Chadwick, W O	1936-37-38
Ashford, C L	1929	Bonham-Carter, J	1873	Chalmers, P S	1979
Askew, J G	1929-30-31	Bordass, J H	1923-24	Chambers, E L	1904
Asquith, J P K	1953	Borthwick, T J L	1985	Chapman, C E	1881-84
Aston, R L	1889-90	Boughton-Leigh, C E W	1878	Chapman, E S	1879-80
Atkinson, M L	1908-09	Boulding, P V	1975-76	Chapman, G M	1907-08-09
Attfield, S J W	1982-84	Bowcott, H M	1927-28	Chapman, J M	1873
		Bowcott, J E	1933	Chilcott, E W	1883
Back, F F	1871-72	Bowen, R W	1968	Child, H H	1875-76
Bailey, G H	1931	Bowhill, J W	1888-89	Clarke, B D F	1978
Bailey, M D	1982-83-84-85	Bowman, J H	1933-34	Clarke, S J S	1962-63
Bailey, R C	1982-83	Boyd, C W	1909	Clayton, H R	1876-77-78
Balding, I A	1961	Boyd-Moss, R J	1980-81-82	Clayton, J R W	1971
Balfour, A	1896-97	Brandram, R A	1896	Clements, J W	1953-54-55
Bance, J F	1945	Brash, J C	1959-60-61	Clifford, P H	1876-77-78
Barker, R E	1966	Brathwaite, G A	1934	Clough, F J	1984-85-86-87
Barlow, C S	1923-24-25-26	Breakey, J N F	1974-75(R)-77	Coates, C H	1877-78-79
Barlow, R M M	1925	Bree-Frink, F C	1888-89-90	Coates, V H M	1907
Barrow, C	1950	Briggs, P D	1962	Cobby, W	1900
Barter, A F	1954-55-56	Bromet, E	1887-88	Cock, T A	1899
Bartlett, R M	1951	Brook, P W P	1928-29-30-31	Cocks, F W	1935
Bateman-Champain, P J C	1937	Brookstein, R	1969	Coghlan, G B	1926-27-28
Batten, J M	1871-72-73-74	Brooman, R J	1977-78	Cohen, A S	1922
Batty, P A	1919-20	Browell, H H	1877-78	Colbourne, G L	1883
Baxter, R	1871-72-73	Brown, A C	1920-21	Coley, M	1964
Baxter, W H B	1912-13	Brown, S L	1975-76	Collett, G F	1898
Bealey, R J	1874	Browning, O C	1934	Collier, R B	1960-61
Beard, P L	1987	Bruce Lockhart, J H	1910	Collin, T	1871
Bearne, K R F	1957-58-59	Bruce Lockhart, L	1945-46	Collins, W O H	1931
Beazley, T A G	1971	Bruce Lockhart, R B	1937-38	Collis, W R F	1919-20
Bedell-Sivright, D R	1899-1900-01-02	Brutton, E B	1883-85-86	Collison, L H	1930
Bedell-Sivright, J V	1900-01-02-03	Bryce, R D H	1965	Combe, P H	1984-85

Considine, W C D	1919	Edmonds, G A	1976	Greenwood, J E	1910-11-12-13-19
Conway, G S	1919-20-21	Edwards, E F	1971	Greenwood, J R H	1962-63
Cook, D D B	1920-21	Edwards, R J	1971-72	Greg, A H	1893
Cook, S	1920-21	Elliott, A E	1891	Greig, I A	1977-78
Cooke, S J	1981	Ellis, P R	1975	Griffith, J M	1933
Cooper, H S	1881	Ellison, J F	1983-84	Griffith, R	1894-95
Cooper, P T	1927-28	Embleton, J J E	1928-29-30	Griffiths, H B	1953
Cope, W	1891	Evans A E	1906-07	Gurdon, C	1877
Corry, T M	1966	Evans, D P	1922	Gurdon, E T	1874-75-76
Cosh, N J	1966	Evans, E D	1903-04	Guthrie, G B	1883
Covell, G A B	1949	Evans, M R M	1955	Gwilliam, J A	1947-48
Cove-Smith, R	1919-20-21	Evans, W R	1955		
Cox, F L	1879	Ewbank, C F	1983	Hacking, A	1898-99
Craig, H J	1891			Hall, M R	1987
Craigmile, H W C	1920	Fairbanks, W	1873-74	Hamilton, G A C	1925-26
Crichton-Miller, D	1928	Fairgrieve, J	1945	Hamilton, H A	1871-73
Crothers, G	1977 (R)	Falcon, W	1894-95	Hamilton-Smythe, A F	1926
Crow, W A M	1961-62	Fasson, F H	1897-98-99	Hamilton-Wickes, R H	1920-21-22-23
Cullen, J C	1980-81-82	Fforde, A B	1891	Hammond, J	1881
Cumberlege, B S	1910-11-12-13	Fiddian, J V	1908-09	Hampel, A K R	1982
Cumberlege, R F	1897	Field, E	1892-93-94	Hamp-Ferguson, A J C	1964-65
Cumming, D C	1922-23-24	Finch, R T	1876-77-78-79	Hancock, M E	1987
Currie, W C	1905	Fitch, C E	1889	Hannaford, C	1967
Cushing A	1986	Fleming, R S	1964	Harding, R M	1973-74
		Fletcher, N C	1897-98-99	Harding, V S J	1958-59-60
Dalgleish, K J	1951-52-53	Fogg-Elliott, J W	1887	Harding, W R	1924-25-26-27
Dalton, E R	1872-73-74	Folker, E L A	1937	Harper, A G R	1983
Dalton, W L T	1875-76	Folwell, A J S	1967-68	Harriman, A T	1985
Daniell, J	1898-99-1900	Forbes, A S	1873	Harris, B G	1904-05-06
Darby, A J L	1896-97-98	Ford, J N	1977-78-79	Harrison, R B	1951
Darch, W J	1875	Fordham, J G	1898	Hartley, B C	1900
David, P W	1983	Forman, A	1904-05	Hartley, J J	1974
Davies, G	1948-49-50	Forrest, J G S	1936-37-38	Harvey, M J	1957
Davies, G H	1980-81	Fosh, M K	1977-78	Harvey, J R W	1963-64
Davies, H J	1958	Fowler, T G	1911-12	Hastings, A G	1984-85
Davies, J C	1949	Fox, S	1945	Hearfield, J	1901
Davies, J S	1977	Francis, T E S	1922-23-24-25	Hearson, H F P	1904-06
Davies, P M	1952-53-54	Frankcom, G P	1961-63-64	Heath, F M N	1936-37
Davies, T G R	1968-69-70	Fraser, R M	1908-09-10	Heath, N R M	1977-78
Davies, W G	1946-47	Freeman, J	1987	Heginbotham, R C	1984
Deakin, J E	1871	French, N J	1973	Henderson, A P	1945-46-47
Delafield, G E	1932	French, R B	1969	Herbert, A J	1954-55-56
De Nobriga, A P	1948	Fuller, H G	1878-79-80-81-82-83	Herrod, N J	1985-86-87
De Villiers, D I	1913	Fyfe, K C	1932-33-34-35	Heslip, M R	1967
Devitt, Sir T G	1923-24-25			Hetherington, J G G	1955
Dewhurst, J H	1885-86	Gardiner, F A	1921-22-23	Hewett, B J	1963
Dick, R C S	1933	Gatford, H J H	1946	Heywood, F M	1928
Dickins, J P	1972-73	Geddes, K I	1938	Higham, C F W	1961-62
Dickson, J W	1881	Geoghegan, K F	1977	Hignell, A J	1974-75-76-77
Dinwiddy, H P	1934-35	Gethin, D	1965-66	Hill, D B	1892
Dixon, A M	1928	Gibbins, R B	1905-06	Hind, A E	1900
Dixon, C	1894	Gibbons, J F	1882	Hinton, N P	1969-70
Dods, M	1938	Gibbs, J D	1965	Hobbs, A R	1986-87
Doherty, H D	1950	Giblin, L F	1894-95-96	Hockey, J R	1957
Doherty, W D	1913	Gibson, C M H	1963-64-65	Hodges, E C	1903-04-05
Don Wauchope, A R	1880-81	Gibson, E	1925-26	Hodgson, J T	1955
Dorward, A F	1947-48-49	Gibson, T A	1901-02	Hodgson, M E	1973
Douglas, E A	1882-83-84	Gilchrist, B W	1986-87	Holloway, B H	1907-09
Douglas, R N	1891	Gill, S M	1980-81	Holmes, W B	1947-48
Douty, P S	1924	Gilliland, W D	1979	Hooper, C A	1890
Dovey, B A	1960	Glanvill, S F	1977-79-80	Hopkins, A A	1874
Downes, K D	1936-37-38	Gloag, I S	1949-50-52	Hopkins, W D B	1929
Downey, W J	1954-55-56-57	Gloag, L G	1948	Hopper, L B	1897
Doyle, M G	1965	Godby, T A	1906-07	Hornby, J J	1873-74-76
Drake-Lee, N J	1961-62-63	Godson, A	1959-60	Horner, P J	1982
Drake, T R	1965	Golightly, C H	1879	Horrocks-Taylor, J P	1956-57
Druce, W G	1893-94	Goodhue, F W J	1885-86	Horsfall, J	1903-04
Drummond, N W	1971	Gover, J J	1879	Horsley, S	1901-02-03
Drysdale, T	1900-01	Gowans, J J	1892-93	Howard, J M	1971-72
Dudgeon, R F	1871	Grant, A R	1975-76	Howell, R G B	1924
Duncan, C	1966	Grant, J J H	1978	Hughes, K	1968-69
Duncan, M M	1885-86-87	Green, M J	1965-66-67	Hull, F M	1871-72-73
Dutson, C S	1963	Green, P A	1984-85	Hunt, N	1986
		Greenlees, J R C	1898-99-1900-01	Hunter, J M	1946
Edlmann, S R R	1974-75	Greenwood, G M	1929-30		

Name	Year(s)
Illingworth, P H	1889-90
Inglis, F C	1959
Inglis, W M	1935-36
Irving, K G	1935
Isaac, T W D	1986
Jackson, A L	1889
Jackson, T L	1892
Jacob, F	1895-96
Jacob, P G	1894-95-96
Jagger, D	1954
James, A M	1948-49
James, J H H	1962-63-64
James, S R	1876-77-78
Jameson, A	1874
Jeffcock, C E	1877
Jeffery, G L	1884-85
Jenkins, J D	1964
Jenkins, J M	1949-51
Jenkins, W G	1948
Jessop, A W	1972
Johnson, J N	1981
Johnston, D	1897
Johnston, W G S	1932-33-34
Johnstone, H B L	1931
Jollife, R L K	1965
Jones, B M	1949
Jones, C W	1933-34-35
Jones, D G H	1951-52
Jones, E A A	1895
Jones, F H	1898-99-1900
Jones, J S	1908-09
Jones, R B	1931-32-33
Jones, S E	1878
Jones, T R K	1921
Jones, W W A	1968-69-70-72
Jones, W I	1923-24-25
Jorden, A M	1968-69
Juckes, R	1913
Juckes, T R	1938
Keeton, G H	1899-1900
Keith-Roach, P d'A	1969-70-71
Kelly, S R	1985-86-87
Kemp, T A	1936
Kennedy, C M	1877-78
Kennedy, R S	1907-09
Kershaw, M E	1955
Killick, S E	1978
Kimberley, H M	1945-46-47-48
King, R H	1950
Kingston, C J	1980-81-82
Kirby, T K M	1945
Kitchin, P A	1965
Kitching, A E	1910-11
Koop, G G	1905
Laborde, C D	1933-34-35-36
Laing, H	1893
Lambert, I C	1871
Langton, E C	1888-89
Lawry, S J	1894-95
Laxon, H	1903-04
Laycock, A M	1979
Leadbetter, V H	1951-52
Leake, W R M	1885-86-87
Leather, W H	1931-32
Leather, W J	1931-32-33-34
Lee, H	1904
Lees, J	1883
Le Fanu, V C	1884-85-86
Le Fleming, J	1884-85-86
Leishman, F J	1938
Lely, W G	1906-07-08
Leonard, R J N	1957
Lewis, A D	1975-76
Lewis, A R	1874-75
Lewis, A R	1959
Lewis, B R	1909-10-11
Lewis, G A	1872-73-75
Lewis, G G	1976
Lewis, G W	1956-57-58
Lewis, J M C	1913-19
Lewis, W H	1926-27
Lewthwaite, W	1872-73
Lillington, P M	1981-82
Lindsay, P A R	1937-38
Linnecar, R J D	1970
Lintott, T M R	1974
Lister, R C	1969
Lloyd-Davies, R H	1947
Lord, J R C	1933-34-35
Lord, M	1960
Lord, T M	1986
Loveday, B R	1956-57
Low, J D	1935-36-37
Lowden, G S	1945
Lowe, C N	1911-12-13
Lowry, R H W	1923
Loxdale, J W	1874
Lucas, P M	1882
Luscombe, R P	1871-72-73-74
Lushington, A J	1872
Luxmoore, A F C C	1896-97
Lyon, C E	1871
Lyon, D W	1967-68
McAfee, L A	1910
McClung, T	1954
McCosh, E	1910
McCosh, R	1905-06-07
McMorris, L	1963
MacDonald, A	1871
MacDonald, J A	1936-37
MacDonnell, J C	1889
MacEwen, D L	1887
MacEwen, R K G	1953-54
McGahey, A M J	1979-80-81
McGown, T M W	1896
MacGregor, G	1889-90
McIlwaine, G A	1926-27-28
Mackenzie, W G B	1922
McKenzie, M R	1968
Mackie, O G	1895-96-97
Macklin, A J	1979-80-82
Maclay, J P	1920
MacLeod, K G	1905-06-07-08
MacLeod, L M	1903-04-05
Macleod, W M	1880-82
MacMyn, D J	1921-22-23-24
McNeill, A H	1902-03
McRoberts, T S	1946-47-48
MacSweeney, D A	1957-58-59
Mainprice, H	1902-03-04-05
Makin, R L	1959
Malik, N A	1975
Mann, F T	1910
Marburg, C L H	1909-10
Margerison, R	1871-72-73
Marques, R W D	1954-55-56-57
Marr, D M	1929-30-31-32
Marr, T C K	1945
Marsden, E W	1950
Marriott, C J B	1881-82-83
Marshall, T R	1950
Martin, A W	1983-84
Martin, N O	1965-66-67
Martin, S A	1961-62-63
Massey, D G	1952
Massey, M J O	1951-52-53
Maxwell, D M W	1922
Mayfield, E	1891
Maynard, A F	1912-13
Mayne, W N	1888
Mellor, J E	1906
Melluish, R K	1922
Metcalfe, I R	1978-79
Methuen, A	1886-87-88
Michaelson, R C B	1960-61-62
Michell, W G	1873-75-76
Middlemas, P	1912
Miliffe, M J	1964
Millard, D E S	1956
Miller, J L H	1920
Mills, D C	1958
Mills, H H	1947-48
Mills, P R	1958-59
Milne, C J B	1882-83-84
Mitchell, F	1893-94-95
Mitchell, W G	1886
Monahan, J D	1967-68
Monro, A H	1973
Monteith, H G	1903-04-05
Montgomery, R	1891
Moon, R H Q B	1984
Moore, A W	1874
Moore, P J de A	1947-48
Morel, T E	1920-22
Morgan, H P	1952-53
Morgan, W G	1926-27-28-29
Moriarty, S P	1980
Morpeth, S	1925
Morrison, B J	1965
Morrison, I R	1983-84
Morrison, P H	1887-88-89-90
Morse, E St J	1871
Mortimer, W	1895-96
Morton H J S	1908
Moyes, J L	1974-75
Mulligan, A A	1955-56-57
Murray, R A	1982
Murray, R O	1933-34
Napier, Hon M F	1871
Neild, W C	1911-12
Neilson, H	1884
Neilson, W	1891-92-93
Nelson, W E	1892
Newbold, C J	1902-03
Newman, C H	1882
Newton-Thompson, C L	1937-38
Nicholl, C B	1890-91-92-93
Nixon, P J L	1976
O'Brien, T S	1981-82
O'Callaghan, C	1978
O'Callaghan, M W	1974-75-76-77
O'Leary, S T	1984-85
Odgers, F W	1901
Ogilvy, F J L	1887
Onyett, P S	1966-67
Orr, J C S	1891
Orr-Ewing, D	1919
Oswald, G B R	1945
Oti, C	1986-87
Oulton, E V	1901
Ovens, A B	1910-11
Owen, A V	1945
Owen, J E	1961
Page, J J	1968-69-70
Page, R S	1972-73
Palmer, H R	1899
Parker, G W	1932-33-34-35
Parr, M F	1978

Name	Year	Name	Year	Name	Year
Parry, T R	1936-37-38	Robinson, P J	1962	Steel, D Q	1877
Parsons, J	1938	Rocyn-Jones, D N	1923	Steele, H K	1970
Pater, S	1880-81	Roden, W H	1936-37	Steele, J T	1879-80
Paterson, L R	1886-87	Rodgers, A K	1968-69-70	Steele-Bodger, M R	1945-46
Paterson-Brown, T	1983	Roffey, D B	1874-75	Stevenson, H J	1977(R)-79
Patterson, H W T	1890	Rose, H	1872	Stevenson, L E	1884-85
Patterson, W M	1956	Rose, W M H	1979-80-81	Steward, R	1875-76
Pattisson, R M	1881-82	Rosser, D W A	1962-63-64	Stewart, A A	1975-76
Payne, J H	1879	Rosser, M F	1972-73	Stewart, J R	1935
Payne, O V	1900	Ross-Skinner, W M	1924	Stileman, W M C	1985
Pearce, D	1873-74	Rotherham, A	1890-91	Stokes, R R	1921
Pearson, T C	1952-53	Rottenburg, H	1898	Stone, R J	1901
Peck, I G	1979	Rowell, W I	1890	Storey, E	1878-79-80
Pender, A R	1963	Ryan, C J	1966	Storey, L H T	1909
Penny, W M	1906	Ryan, P H	1952-53	Storey, T W P	1889-90-91-92
Perry, D G	1958	Ryder, D C D	1921-23	Stothard, N A	1979
Perry, S V	1946-47			Style, H B	1921
Phillips, G P	1971-72	Salmon, W B	1883	Surtees, A A	1886
Phillips, J H L	1930-32	Sagar, J W	1899-1900	Sutherland, J F	1908
Phillips, R J	1964	Sample, C H	1882-83-84	Sutton, A J	1987
Pienaar, L L	1911	Sample, H W	1884	Swanson, J C	1938
Pierce, D J	1985 (R)	Sanderson, A B	1901	Swayne, F G	1884-85-86
Pilkington, L E	1893-94	Saunders-Jacobs, S M	1929	Symington, A W	1911-12-13
Pilkington, W N	1896-97	Saville, C D	1967-68-69-70	Synge, J S	1927
Pinkham, C	1910	Sawyer, B T C	1910		
Pitt, T G	1905-06	Saxon, K R J	1919-21	Tait, J G	1880-82
Plews, W J	1884	Scholfield, J A	1909-10	Talbot, S C	1900
Pope, E B	1932	Schwarz, R O	1893	Tallent, J A	1929-30-31
Powell, P	1900	Scotland, K J F	1958-59-60	Tanner, C C	1930
Pratt, S R G	1973-74	Scott, A W	1945-48	Tarsh, D N	1955
Price, P R	1967	Scott, C T	1899	Taylor, A S	1879-80-81
Pringle, A S	1897-98	Scott, J M	1927	Taylor, D G	1982
Pringle, J S	1902	Scott, M T	1885-86-87	Taylor, H B J	1894-96
Prosser-Harries, A	1957	Scott, R R F	1957	Taylor, W J	1926
Pumphrey, C E	1902	Scott, W B	1923-24	Templer, J L	1881-82
Purves, W D C L	1907-08-09	Scott, W M	1888	Thomas, B E	1960-61-62
Pyman, F C	1907-08	Scoular, J G	1905-06	Thomas, D R	1972-73-74
		Seddon, E R H	1921	Thomas, H W	1912
Rae, A J	1901	Shackleton, I R	1968-69-70	Thomas, J	1945
Raffle, N C G	1954-55	Shaw, P A V	1977	Thomas, M D C	1986-87
Raikes, W A	1872-74	Shepherd, J K	1950	Thomas, N B	1966
Raine, J B	1947	Sherrard, P	1938	Thomas, R C C	1949
Rainforth, J J	1958-59	Shipsides, J	1970	Thomas, T J	1895-96
Ramsay, A R	1930	Shirer, J A	1885	Thomas, W H	1886-87
Ransome, H F	1882-83-84	Silk, D R W	1953-54	Thompson, M J M	1950
Rawlence, J R	1935-36	Sim, R G	1966-67	Thompson, R	1890
Raybould, W H	1966	Simms, K G	1983-84-85	Thompson, R V	1948-49
Redmond, G F	1969-70-71	Simpson, C P	1890	Thorman, W H	1890
Reed, E D E	1937	Simpson, F W	1930-31	Thorne, C	1911
Rees, A M	1933-34	Sisson, J P	1871	Thornton, J F	1976-78-79
Rees, B I	1963-64-65-66	Skinner, R C O	1970-71	Threlfall, R	1881-83
Rees, G	1972-73	Slater, K J P	1964	Timmons, F J	1983
Rees, J I	1931-32	Smallwood, A M	1919	Todd, A F	1893-94-95
Reeve, P B	1950-51	Smeddle, R W	1928-29-30-31	Todd, T	1888
Reid, J L P	1932	Smith, A F	1873-74	Topping, N P	1986-87
Rendall, H D	1892-93	Smith, A R	1954-55-56-57	Touzel, C J C	1874-75-76
Reynolds, E P	1909	Smith, H K P	1920	Tredwell, J R	1968
Rice, E	1880-81	Smith, H Y L	1878-79-80-81	Trethewy, A	1888
Richards, T B	1955	Smith, J	1889	Trubshaw, A R	1919
Richardson, W P	1883	Smith, J J E	1926	Tucker, W E	1892-93-94
Rigby, J C A	1982	Smith, J M	1972	Tucker, W E	1922-23-24-25
Riley, H	1871-72-73	Smith, J V	1948-49-50	Tudsbery, F C T	1907-08
Risman, M A	1987 (R)	Smith, K P	1919	Turnbull, B R	1924-25
Ritchie, W T	1903-04	Smith, M A	1966-67	Turner, J A	1956
Robbie, J C	1977-78	Smith, P K	1970	Turner, J M P C	1985
Roberts, A F	1901-02	Smith, S R	1958-59	Turner, M F	1946
Roberts, A J R	1901-02	Smith, S T	1982-83	Tyler, R H	1978-79-80
Roberts, J	1952-53-54	Sobey, W H	1925-26		
Roberts, J	1927-28	Spencer, J S	1967-68-69	Umbers, R H	1954
Roberts, S N J	1983	Spicer, N	1901-02	Ure, C McG	1911
Robertson, D D	1892	Spray, K A N	1946-47		
Robertson, I	1967	Sprot, A	1871	Valentine, G E	1930
Robinson, A	1886-87	Staunton, H	1891	Van Schalkwijk, J	1906
Robinson, B F	1891-92-93	Stead, R J	1977	Vaughan, G P	1949
Robinson, J J	1892	Steeds, J H	1938	Vaux, J G	1957

Vincent, C A	1913	Webb, G K M	1964-65	Wilson, C P	1877-78-79-80
Vivian, J M	1976	Webster, A P	1971	Wilton, C W	1936
Vyvyan, C B	1987	Wells, C M	1891-92	Winthrop, W Y	1871
		Wells, T U	1951	Wintle, T C	1960-61
Wace, H	1873-74	Wetson, M T	1958-59-60	Withyman, T A	1985-86
Wade, M R	1958-59-60-61	Wheeler, P J F	1951-52-53	Wood, G E	1974-75-76
Waddell, G H	1958-60-61	White, J B	1922	Wood, G E C	1919
Wainwright, J F	1956	White, W N	1947	Woodall, B J C	1951
Wainwright, M A	1980	Whiteway, S E A	1893	Woodroffe, O P	1952
Wainwright, R I	1986-87	Wiggins, C E M	1928	Woods, S M J	1888-89-90
Wakefield, W W	1921-22	Wiggins, C M	1964	Wooler, W	1933-34-35
Walker, A W	1929-30	Wilkinson, R M	1971-72-73	Wordsworth, A J	1973-75
Walker, D R	1980-81	Will, J G	1911-12-13	Wotherspoon, W	1888-89
Walker, E E	1899-1900	Williams, A G	1926-27	Wrench, D F B	1960
Walker, R M	1963	Williams, C C U	1950	Wright, C C G	1907-08
Walkey, J R	1902	Williams, C H	1930	Wrigley, P T	1877-78-79-80
Wallace, W M	1912-13	Williams, C R	1971-72-73	Wyles, K T	1985-86
Waller, G S	1932	Williams, D B	1973	Wynne, E H	1887
Wallis, H T	1895-96	Williams, E J H	1946		
Ward, R O C	1903	Williams, H A	1876	Yetts, R M	1879-80-81
Ware, C H	1882	Williams, J M	1949	Young, A B S	1919-20
Warfield, P J	1974	Williams, L T	1874-75	Young, A T	1922-23-24
Warlow, S	1972-74	Williams, N E	1950	Young, J S	1935
Waters, F H	1927-28-29	Williams, P T	1888-89	Young, J V	1906
Waters, J B	1902-03-04	Williamson, I S	1972	Young, P D	1949
Watherston, J G	1931	Williamson, P R	1984	Young, S K	1974
Watson, C F K	1919-20	Willis, H	1949-50-51	Young, W B	1935-36-37
Watt, J R	1970	Wilson, A H	1911-12-13		

VARSITY MATCH REFEREES

From 1881, when referees first officiated at the match. Prior to this date, the match was controlled by a pair of umpires elected by the Universities. Each year indicates a separate appearance, and refers to the first half of the season. Thus 1881 refers to the match played in the 1881-82 season.

Allan, M A	1933-34	Freethy, A E	1923-25-27-29-31-32	Murdoch, W C W	1952
Ashmore, H L	1891-92-93-95-96	Gadney, C H	1935-36-37-38-45-47	Norling, C	1977-78-81
Bean, A S	1948-49	Gillespie, J I	1905	Pattinson, K A	1974
Bolton, W N	1882	Harnett, G H	1897-98-99-1900-01-02	Potter-Irwin, F C	1909-11-13-19
Boundy, L M	1958	Hill, G R	1883-84-86-87-88-89-90	Prideaux, L	1984
Burnett, D I H	1980-82	Hosie, A M	1979	Quittenton, R C	1985-87
Burrell, R P	1963	Howard, F A	1986	Sanson, N R	1976
Clark, K H	1973	Jeffares, R W	1930	Sturrock, J C	1921
Cooper, Dr P F	1951-53	John, K S	1956-67	Taylor, H H	1881
Crawford, S H	1920	Johnson, R F	1972	Titcombe, M H	1969
Currey, F I	1885	Jones, T	1950	Trigg, J A F	1983
Dallas, J D	1910-12	Lamb, Air Cdre G C	1970	Vile, T H	1922-24-26-28
D'Arcy, D P	1968	Lambert, N H	1946	Walters, D G	1957-60-61-62-64-65-66
David, I	1954-55	Lawrence, Capt H D	1894	Williams, R C	1959
Evans, G	1907	Lewis, R	1971	Williams, T	1903
Findlay, J C	1904-08	Marsh, F W	1906	Welsby, A	1975

Details concerning University rugby matches have appeared in numerous collections of records and histories. In compiling the records these sources have been invaluable:

Football: The Rugby Union Game	(1892; 1894)	Editions edited by Rev F Marshall
	(1925)	Edition edited by L R Tosswill
Rugby Union Football	(1912)	Compiled by L M Holden
Oxford versus Cambridge	(1931)	Compiled by H M Abrahams and J Bruce-Kerr
Rugby Football Today	(1931)	E H D Sewell
Oxford v Cambridge: The story of the University Rugby Match	(1951)	H Marshall and J P Jordan
Centenary History of Oxford University R F C	(1969)	R McWhirter and Sir Andrew Noble Bt., K C M G

Furthermore, the *Rugby Football Annuals* (1913-40); the *Playfair Annuals* (1948-73); and *Rothmans Rugby Yearbooks* (1972 to date) have proved useful for checking scorers and referees against those reported in the leading newspapers. *The Times*, *The Daily Telegraph*, *The Daily Mail* and *The Sportsman* have been the chief newspapers consulted for checking details and match reports, while the match programmes have also been useful for verifying the playing positions of players.

Index